Lexicon of the Mouth

Lexicon of the Mouth

Poetics and Politics of Voice and the Oral Imaginary

Brandon LaBelle

BLOOMSBURY

NEW YORK · LONDON · NEW DELHI · SYDNEY

Bloomsbury Academic
An imprint of Bloomsbury Publishing Inc

1385 Broadway	50 Bedford Square
New York	London
NY 10018	WC1B 3DP
USA	UK

www.bloomsbury.com

Bloomsbury is a registered trade mark of Bloomsbury Publishing Plc

First published 2014

Library of Congress Cataloging-in-Publication Data
LaBelle, Brandon.
Lexicon of the mouth : poetics and politics of voice and
the oral imaginary / Brandon LaBelle.
pages cm.
Includes bibliographical references and index.
ISBN 978-1-62356-188-8 (pbk.) – ISBN 978-1-62356-026-3 (hardback)
1. Grammar, Comparative and general–Voice. 2. Oral communication.
3. Speech acts (Linguistics) 4. Lexicology. I. Title.
P281L13 2014
401'.452–dc23
2014000992

ISBN: HB: 978-1-6235-6026-3
PB: 978-1-6235-6188-8
ePDF: 978-1-6235-6162-8
ePub: 978-1-6235-6773-6

Typeset by Newgen Knowledge Works (P) Ltd., Chennai, India
Printed and bound in the United States of America

For S, um, ee, not I, rose, cjljml, & A

CONTENTS

PREFACE: ASSOCIATIVE

My interest over the years has been to think about the acoustical as a specific paradigm, a type of knowledge structure from which understandings of social life, bodily identities, and cultural practices can be considered and brought into dialogue. As part of this work I've also been keen to write as a listening subject, and by extension, to utilize the auditive as a methodology for inquiry. This is based on considering sound as an intensely dynamic analytical and poetical platform defined by notions of the migratory, the connective, the associative, and the emergent; in short, that the operations of the acoustical, by immersing us in a continual flux of animate (and rather invisible and immaterial) force comes to afford dramatic opportunities for relational contact, and a subsequent form of acoustical thinking, one imbued with imagination. If sound can be appreciated as that which agitates the boundaries of things, as a force of continual departure and propagation, to unsettle a stable form of "origin," it may supply us with a medium for an expanded practice of creative and critical thinking—of occupying that "in-between" sound comes to reveal. I understand this *expandedness*, this relationality, as one that remains susceptible to and curious about what (or who) may lie outside or external to any discursive model or social system. In this regard, the acoustical produces a dynamic epistemology, one aligned with complex modalities of cohabitation and the intersubjective, of being involved.

While the connectedness of sound promotes a continual encounter with the other—that which is hovering to the side of any given object or body—it also supplies us with a rich medium for intimate sharing. From my perspective, this functions as an extremely provocative combination: that the agitating and contaminating behavior of any sound is at one and the same time a means for rupture *and* attachment, interference *and* nurturing assurance, and resistance *and* solidarity. Hence my work has sought to follow through with such a combination, surveying the expressivity of sonic cultures and aural perceptions, a study that is equally a proposition for an acoustical position of *caring for the extremes*.

I approach listening then as the basis for a knowledge production that is equally a position of *radical empathy*: the unfixed qualities of sound have indicated a methodology of critical and creative thought, as well as how *to be a body*, one that explicitly tunes itself to the migratory and the associative, or what Édouard Glissant calls "the poetics of relation."[1] This is a position based on harnessing the dynamics of hybridity and multiplicity, seeking out new forms of knowing and of being known, as well as resisting certain hegemonic orders, and one that fully aligns with the emergent potentiality at the center of audition.

Subsequently, I've come to recognize how sound is deeply connected to experiences of closeness, social bonding, and reassurance, as well as disruption, interruption, and threat. How easily these acoustic polarities brush against each other, which to my understanding comes to suggest that audition is precisely an opportunity for vulnerability, of the body and the senses, as well as for prompting greater porosity between knowledge boundaries and social borders.

This has led to a series of perspectives, or lines of inquiry and imagining: Might the itinerant behavior of sound, with its suggestive propagations and flushed exchanges, afford opportunities for bending the disciplinary orders of the proper and the powerful? For the construction of a micro-politics precisely never singular? A spatiality of association that may spirit a sense for *being public*?

Such inquiries remain central to my work, and most certainly have been the basis for my previous publications: *Background Noise: Perspectives on Sound Art* (2006) and *Acoustic Territories: Sound Culture and Everyday Life* (2010). These works are marked by an inquiry into sound as a complex material equally tied to expressions of identity formation and social experience, the first from the view of artistic and sonic practices, and the second in terms of urban culture and public life. Each publication, while being specific, shares in a more general way the project of proposing the acoustical as a paradigmatic platform from which questions of perception and embodiment, spatiality and territoriality are pursued. With the current work, *Lexicon of the Mouth*, it is my aim to consider more directly the issue of the voice and related modalities of oral behavior and imagination. Subsequently, these three works can be read as a trilogy, which moves from sound art to sonic culture, and finally, toward questions of the spoken and the unspeakable, or what I might call "cultures of the paralinguistic." In this regard, I've been working to contribute to the fields of sound studies and the sound arts a deep view onto the specificities of aural experience, sonic culture, and acoustic politics, while broadening the map of the acoustical and what it may suggest in terms of knowledge production and social relations. Ultimately, I've been led to a dedication to sound as the result of a certain fixation on making connections between bodies and things, culture and social experience, and diverse fields of thought, as well as for a type of "utopian idea": the way in which sound supports the emergent—how it draws forward a continual agitation onto the order of things—is for me a platform for a creative life.

In short, the listening that I'm after is one of deep affordance, enabling through both its dedications and its distractions a potentiality for what may come, and for what we may do or say. I'd suggest that to listen is to adopt a position of *not knowing*; it is to stand *in wait* for the event, for the voice that may come; it is a preparation for common recognition. Listening as a space of encounter made from primary agitations, those that encircle and enfold the senses, to animate the in-between. In this regard, listening is an unsettling of boundaries—what draws me forward, away from what I know. I would propose that to *give* one's ear is to invest in the making of a future public; it is to give the body over, for a distribution of agency. As David Michael Levin proposes, the attention one may bring forward in that instant of listening, in *lending* an ear, is defined as a "listening to the other"—the making of a mutual space.[2] Yet this listening, as I've been interested to argue, is tensed by not only empathy and care, but also nervousness and hesitation, with longing and capture, by the invitations as well as the demands of the other—a combination that is highly suggestive for a culture of radical ethics and inclusion.

Is not sound already a type of restlessness? Can we not understand sound as the shaking of an object, the squirming of a body, as a point of friction between this and that, you and I, and which stirs the in-between with its sudden, generative energy? Something that tries to escape, as a continual departure, but also which seeks to find connection, and to be heard? Sound as an unsteady economy of the between, of the shared, and the common.

In this regard, sound teaches me how *not* to be myself; how to trespass certain lines, supplement particular languages, and relate to another body. In short, it leads the way for how to depart, but also, how to arrive, elsewhere. It literally enfolds and unfolds me, as a *you*. A listening that gains in momentum precisely by integrating the productions inherent to auditory experience, expressed in the migration of voices, the shifting of the body, the animation of knowledge, as well as the deepening of attention; in short, the production of radical sharing. Hence the languages and pedagogies used to analyze and describe such auditory provocations and productions must also tune themselves to a rather "undisciplined" discourse, one located *in public*. "Listening draws upon those depths where 'truth' does not lend itself to representation by means of institutionalized languages."[3] I want to underscore this as a fundamental perspective: sound as a force of expressivity that is always already dialogic and associative, that is, in-between and in search; an *emerging* body, which is equally an emergent sociality. A crowd.

In this regard, *Lexicon of the Mouth* is envisioned as a map rendering the interconnectedness between voice and the oral imagination, and the subsequent expressions that spirit so many conversations. Such a map aims to give suggestion for an experimental orality, one fully in support of a *poetics of relation*.

INTRODUCTION: MOVEMENT

Is not the voice always already intervening, as a sounded body that searches for its place, one that projects forward to incite response? An intervention with great resonance, and one lodged within the power dynamics of particular structures—linguistic, familial, pedagogic, governmental, etc. A voice that is subsequently often overheard, underrepresented, and interrupted.

Around these vocal conditions the mouth operates, *performs*, as that architecture or vessel or stage—*the mouth has many descriptions . . .*—that gives form to voice, and that is informed by the push and pull of an oral drive. Yet the voice is but one type of production generated by the mouth; parallel to voicing, it also continually fills with breath and food, to respire and ingest; it lingers over the taste of another (the central axis of a primary memory), to also move with sudden hiccups or stutters, kisses, and murmurs, and to mediate innumerable exchanges. The mouth, in other words, is an extremely active cavity whose movements lead us from the depths of the body to the surface of the skin, from the materiality of things to the pressures of linguistic grammars—from breath to matter, and to the spoken and the sounded. Subsequently, I would highlight the mouth as an essential means by which the body is always already put into relation.

The mouth is thus wrapped up in the voice, and the voice in the mouth, so much so that to theorize the performativity of the spoken is to confront the tongue, the teeth, the lips, and the throat; it is to feel the mouth as a fleshy, wet lining around each syllable, as well as a texturing orifice that marks the voice with specificity, not only in terms of accent or dialect, but also by the depth of expression so central to the body.

As Mladen Dolar states, the voice is projected from the body to circulate *out there*—"a bodily missile which has detached itself from its source, emancipated itself, yet remains corporeal."[1] The expressiveness of this projection can be seen and heard as an amplification of not only words, but also the exchange between an inside and an outside, one that intersects there in the mouth to force all sorts of productions. In doing so, the mouth also draws into tension the relation between language, as an abstract socializing system, and our embodied, sensual experiences. It is a meeting point, a contact zone where language performs as a powerful agent, yet one that also spirits so many oral imaginings and poetics, where surfaces and depths continually interweave in feverish exchange.

The mouth functions to figure and sustain the body as a subject, a subject within a network of relations.

If voice is the very thing that forces itself outward, to carve out a space for the self amid all the intensities of surroundings, the mouth can be highlighted as the cavity that resonates with all such negotiations and brings them back *into* the body, to gather and to inflect future expression. Subsequently, the mouth is precisely what puts into question the separation of interior and exterior, as distinct and stable; as a primary conduit that brings into contact the material world with the depths of the body, the mouth continually unsettles the limits of embodiment. It performs as an extremely vital link—the essential link—to the world and those around us, to echo and vibrate with a multitude of forces that pass through its chamber, from the edible to the inedible, the symbolic to the semiotic, the proper to the improper. Even before we come to voice, the mouth has already initiated a confrontation with the forces surrounding and penetrating us, leaving their deep impressions firmly upon the tongue and hence our psychological life.

Accordingly, it is my view that the mouth requires greater attention within discourses on the performativity of the body and the politics of voice. It may figure alongside considerations of the gendered or racial body, as a performative chamber fully wed to identity and its social conditioning; it inserts within the linguistic field an extremely rich and problematic force—a poetics—by drawing language up against a multitude of somatic expenditures and dreamy expressions; and it places us into profound contact with the materiality of things and bodies, extending the experiences of taste and touch, and the limits of the flesh. The mouth affords entry onto the complicated weave of language and power, inscription and iteration, by locating speech as part of a greater assemblage where breath and spit, food and vomit, desire and angst, for instance, all stage their particular events to ultimately surround, interrupt, flavor, and support forms of agency and communion. In short, the mouth is so radically connected to both language and the body, desire and the other, as to provide an extremely pertinent education on what it means to be—*and to create oneself as*—a subject.

The aim of this work is to ultimately figure the mouth as an agile and animating creature, an assemblage of parts whose productions and expressions are heterogeneous, spiriting multiple personalities and multiple drives. This work is thus structured specifically to articulate this expanded territory of oral performativity and to insist upon its multiplicity. It is constructed as a lexicon so as to capture *and* let loose its central theme: the expressivity of the oral cavity.

Voice

The voice is that primary event that circulates to wrap us in its sonorities, silences and rhythms, and intonations. It operates as an essential force that animates the other to bring him or her closer to me, while also prompting my own: it is this voice that calls me into speech; I respond, return—to turn toward or away—and repeat, in that primary citation defined by Judith Butler, not only in terms of language and the coerciveness of power, but importantly, in the wish to be desired.[2] I turn to the other, with a voice shaped by *this other one*: I speak in order to locate myself near you.

The mouth can be understood as the physical site of such vocal productions, longings, and powerful interactions. While the voice may come at me, and *into* me, as a projected sound, it is the other's mouth to which my body turns—I rest upon this mouth; and while the voice may also come *out* of me, it is the mouth that shapes these outpourings, which I must move and that provides a reverberant space where exchanges of deep intimacy may take shape, through words as well as by a range of oral gestures—how often a kiss overcomes the estrangement voice can produce! The voice may extend the range of the body precisely by returning us to the mouth. In this regard, is it truly possible to separate the two, the voice and the mouth?

It is my view that the mouth is unavoidable. It figures as that point of vital animation upon the body, *for* the body, and which I focus on when spoken to: I watch the lips, awaiting their nuanced movements, their sudden exuberance, to reveal so much about this one who speaks. The mouth is so clearly *around* voice—it is the voice's physical envelope that can in turn say so much; it is entirely invested in the production and sustainability of a subject—it is required.

As the space of (not only) voice's reverberations, the mouth may be said to be *ringed* by language; it lingers in the mouth, as so much grammar and vocabulary, with so much hope and fear, pressure as well as possibility. Yet the mouth is also a dwelling wherein longing finds resonance: it searches in and around language for what is missing (as Julia Kristeva poses, what is missing is the mother . . .)[3] and for what can be done to fill those gaps with energy or matter: with laughter and humming, licking and kissing, which might assuage such fundamental absence.

In addition, the mouth is the central entry point *into* the body, and that interior space brought forward by the voice. As Walter Ong emphasizes, it is through the voice that "interiors commune with interiors"; speech *sounds out* our interiority to deliver it to another, and deeper, into the interior private space of their hearing. Yet it is the mouth that operates as interiority's material lining.[4] These surfaces of the mouth fully surround our vocality, and should be followed beyond what we can see. Rather, the mouth starts there on the face and folds into the oral cavity, to tunnel down the throat. A series of surfaces equally muscular and viscous, resounding and relational. From flexed expressions and liquid operations to vibrational and reverberant productions, and finally, to the movements of social contact, the interior announced by Ong is not buried within the self, but rather flows as a membrane across and through the body; the interior is embedded in words not only according to the soul, but also the physical linings and muscles, the depths and surfaces that function in speech, to force it out.

The mouth thus performs an absolutely dynamic conditioning to how the voice operates, how it sounds and gestures, exposes and hides, figures and disfigures. The voice is such an effective and sensual material precisely because it comes from the mouth; it rises from the chest, up into the throat to shudder the vocal cords, to appear (for surely, it appears!) in and then from out of the mouth, rippling behind the facial muscles, the nasal passage, and along the jaw. We experience the voice by feeling it *in our body*.

These physical features of voice are drawn out here not to insist upon the body as an essential site for voice—not as nostalgia for a totalizing and secure presence. Rather, they are located within this work to highlight how recognition—to be a subject—is unmistakably tied to *having a say*, which is also fully predicated on having a mouth. It is my argument that to understand the full range of the voice, as an event (and discourse) entangling itself around bodies, desires, politics, identities, and nations, it is important to recognize the mouth in all its performative verve, effective influence, and complicated drama.

In this regard, I also pose the mouth as *never always* about voice. While much of this work seeks to remind the voice of its oral chamber, I equally aim to query the mouth in and of itself, as an extremely complex bodily *thing*. (What might I call this—this thing: an organ? A site? A machine? . . .) The mouth is a certain forcefulness—a sensitive muscularity, a soft and impressionable arena open to innumerable experiences, and wielding profound influence.

Subsequently, I would put into question what Dolar further identifies as the inherent "acousmatic" nature of the voice, as a sounded event that is both mine and not mine, and that never fully synchronizes with the one who speaks. "The source of the voice can never be seen, it stems from an undisclosed and structurally concealed interior, it cannot possibly match what we can see. [. . .] Every emission of the voice is by its very essence *ventriloquism*."[5] Accordingly, the voice is defined as a "paradoxical enigma." While it may come from my body, it never quite belongs to me; in short, it brings me into the world according to a fundamental separation from myself. This leads Dolar to map the voice as an *object* whose essential condition is determined by a fundamental gap between what we see and what we hear, between this voice and this body. "Now the voice as the object, that paradoxical creature that we are after, is also a break"[6]—a break from the very fulfillment of presence it seems to also endorse.

In contrast, might the voice be thought of more as a tension—a tensed link, a flexed respiration, and equally, a struggle to *constitute* the body, rather than a disembodied sound? Not so much an object, but rather a primary production of a body? A body trying to be a subject? As Fred Moten poses, the voice is precisely what resists forces of objectification, which relegates bodies to a space of abstraction, forces that in fact erase the body by separating an understanding of desire from the material of the voice—a system that, in short, refuses to connect the voice to a subject that speaks. For Moten, in contrast, the voice is an "irruption of phonic substance that cuts and augments meaning," an irruption in other words that is always already a *someone* intervening onto the structures of the social.[7]

To return to Dolar's proposition—of the voice as "a bodily missile which has detached itself from its source, emancipated itself, yet remains corporeal"[8]—it is this "yet" which I grab hold of here, and which has driven this work. The vocal link *back* to the corporeal is precisely a ground for agency; it is the process by which the voice is understood as an articulation of personhood, however unstable, to tense the relation between the forces of objectification and the demand for subjectivity. It is the linguistics that I'm after, one defined by the irrupting orifice, phonic substance, and the assembly of oral movements that challenge separation, commodification, and the forces that may define *my voice* as an object.

As I present, it is my view that the mouth acts to mobilize an extended animate field, one that "moves with the interruptive–connective force of polyrhythmic organization"[9]—to link precisely the interrupting drive and imagination of this body with the connective social reach of this voice.

It is my interest to emphasize the voice as something expelled from the mouth, but which *never* leaves me behind—this is both the promise of voice and its ultimate problematic. The voice does not move away from my body, but rather it carries it forward—the voice *stretches* me; it drags me along, as a body bound to its politics and poetics, its accents and dialectics, its grammars, as well as its handicaps.[10]

Subject

Is not the voice then precisely a sound so full of body, a body under pressure and in search? A body textured by the force of emotion, sexuality, longing, intellect, and language, and that vocally labors to negotiate and explore the exchanges intrinsic to being a subject? In this regard, the "disembodied voice," the "voice object," and the primary ventriloquism of voicing often espoused is never the whole story: it is my view that the voice is also a *full body*, always already a *voice subject*, rich with intentions and meanings; sexed and gendered, classed and raced, accented, situated, and inflected by the intensities of numerous markings and their performance (inscriptions, erasures, recitals, . . .). I would argue that the voice is always identified (though not always identifiable); it is flexed by the body, by the subject in all its complicated vitality. Someone (or *something*) speaks to me, and it is not the voice I hear, but rather the body, the subject; not a disembodied intensity, a speech without body, but as *someone* that enters, intrudes, demands, or requests, and that also seeks. A voice, as I understand it, that does not aspire to be an object.

The voice, in this way, *promises* a subject; it excites or haunts a listener to recognize in the voice a "someone." An *implicit* body on the way toward an explicit drama: the anticipation or expectation every voice instigates, that of a figure soon to appear—someone I may hope for, or that I might also dread, or one that I may not even understand. This has certainly been the case when examining the operations of the whisper: the unvoiced nature of whispering operates so well within narratives of haunting because it is a voice that promises the imminent arrival of someone (or something). The voice, in this regard, *announces* the subject, however illusory or unseen, fragmented or fictional.

In other words, the voice is such a meaningful sound: even when my voice trips me up, falls short, or loses direction, such slippages also *mean*, if not all the more. From this view, I learn from the voice who I am precisely as it carries me, as it sounds me, as I feel it as part of my face, in my throat and mouth, and up my nose; the voice does not leave me, as something that is external to myself; rather, voice is my sounded self, which is equally a *faciality*, a *bodily figuring*, an *expression full of depth*—it is an animate production, a gesture, and subsequently, a form of behavior.

To accentuate this further, the voice might be imaged as a cord, one that may extend outward, unfurled, or cast like a line, but which retains an extremely vital link back to the one who speaks, to the face and further, to the depths. Subsequently, it invites or requests that we feel the presence of a body. Such dynamics may also force us to tremble under the weight of an ideological system whose "voice" wields such power by always projecting the possibility of a real body that may suddenly step forward. I may be hailed by a voice, but I am arrested by a body and its grip: its mouth that may clamp down onto this flesh or "bite my head off." The voice is thus linked to an alimentary *grain*—the body in the voice as Barthes suggests[11]— on the verge of fuller materialization.

Sounds operate to often impart force to matter, to excite, and to animate, and in this way can also be heard as a type of *voicing*. Is not every object a potential body with a voice? A thing whose sudden vibration calls it forth into the realm of life, to become a subject? To bring forward a certain agency onto the scene? Are not the figures of puppets, dolls, and all such machines underscoring the voice as in need of a mouth? As predicated on a reference to the buccal? Even the smallest of objects, or rudimentary of renderings, are enough to perform as a mouth, and therefore, as the projection of a voice.

The voice draws my attention to the radio object for instance, the speaker in the corner, from which a voice arises; or from the puppet, the machine, or the digital device that speaks to me—even such seemingly inanimate objects or banal materials function as a body. I turn toward *It* as the object from which the voice appears and which comes to lend animation to its surfaces and its thingness. Is this not the power of ventriloquy and radiophony, to draw us toward a thing which suddenly speaks? That thing: *the mouth*.

Mouthing

In researching the voice, I was led to the mouth. I couldn't get around it; it always interrupted my discursive gaze, demanding attention, as well as critical consideration. I wanted the voice, in all its complexity: it was my desire, my aim. Yet I recognized that in speaking of voice, I found the mouth—I fell into it; and in following this direction, by going in, I came to recognize how voicing is most often what I may call "mouthing." *To mouth* is that instance of oral gesturing, whether in the drama of the yawn or in the sinister potential of the whisper; an action, in other words, that circulates in and around voicing, encapsulating it—*mouthing the words* should thus be taken literally, for the mouth wraps the voice, and all such wording, in its wet and impressionable envelope, its paralanguages. The mouth is a vessel piloting numerous utterances and potent silences, so much stuff, as to condition and influence acts of *coming out* as well as *going in*; of entries and exits, and the ways in which we cross boundaries or reinforce their presence; the mouth is first and foremost a device for modulating the limits of the body. In this regard, the mouth delivers an epistemology founded on processes and experiences of ingestion and incorporation, emanation and expulsion, attachment and loss: a series of knowledge paths defined by this orifice and its generative and volatile movements.

It captures and figures the somatic, the alimentary, the resonant, and the viscous as always already surrounding language, "cutting and augmenting meaning," flinging it all over the place. I might turn here to Samuel Beckett's short play *Not I*, a monologue delivered by a mouth only.[12] This mouth breaks the darkness with its agitations, restlessness, and ranting, an outpouring that veers across memories, delirium, and breathlessness—*an irrupting orifice*. This mouth cannot stop and bites down onto language in search of transformation.

Is not the body sustained through our ability to chew properly? To speak up, repeat, and recite? To swallow, respire, and speak forth? Is not the acquisition of speech based on the ability to *fit* the words in one's mouth? To push the lips this way and that, shaping breath into particular forms? To handle all sorts of materials and issues, desires and commands, by way of the oral? We may be called into language, on a symbolic level, but it is through the movements of the mouth that we negotiate entry (as well as exit).

The linguist John Laver points to this aspect in his study of phonetics, explicitly mapping the relation of the movements of the mouth—the positioning of the tongue, modulations of loudness and pitch, respiration, etc.—with the development of personality traits. For Laver, the interweaving of anatomy and muscular skills with speech patterns opens up toward an important understanding of the voice as embedded within a greater process of *configuring* the body.[13] Words, in this regard, wield a physical, as well as socializing, effect onto the *constitution* of the body.[14] This finds extension in William Labov's important work in sociolinguistics.[15] For Labov, the articulations of the voice are thoroughly interlocked with their movements through social life, and are always conditioned by our family history, and by our place within particular environments. Language and voice are thus bound to the fact of our social experiences, which come to fundamentally shape our mouths, to contour the "mother tongue" with the particularities of dialect, and to impress upon the body a map of potential routes in and around vocal pressures: for bending, flexing, silencing, or exaggerating our vocal alliances. From such perspectives, linguistics is deeply fixed to the corporeal, to form a highly charged assemblage of words *and* the matters of the body.

In addition to readings in linguistics, as well as psychoanalytic studies, I've also considered examples from an array of cultural fields, such as art, television, literature, and music, which have provided material for expounding the ways in which the mouth performs to generate a variety of contacts and conversations that often bypass or extend the semantic. Yet it has also been my observation that often within cultural theory the mouth is obscured by the question of the voice. This has led me to wonder if the mouth has been lost in discourses on voice, disappearing under the looming notions of vocality and the general "reign" of a linguistic (and textual) imperative (to which I am also surely bound . . .). Even work that seeks to deepen our sense for voice as phonic material, that challenge the dominating logic of the semantic, seem also to pose voice as a given, a somewhat "natural" thing always already there, rather than as lodged in someone's throat, upon someone's tongue—in other words, as an oral tension.[16] While such discursive perspectives are extremely rich and valuable, and continue to lend to my own thinking, I increasingly feel the mouth has been forgotten, as the physical cavity inside of which voicing takes place. Even within the significant work done on "the Body"—and the interrogation of the subject under the dynamics of ideology, ordering inscriptions, and the performativity of power—here I am at a loss to find the tongue and the lips, and especially, the oral cavity as an extremely dynamic site where "body" is regularly negotiating relations to language, social structures, and the field of representations.[17]

It is toward the mouth then that I am drawn, and that I attempt to draw out here; to interlace the voice with the mouth, and to fill the mouth with a range of issues; and in doing so, to discover in what ways mouthing surrounds the voice, to operate as a central influence. In this respect, I understand voice and mouth as forming a *strained* relation, full of poetics and politics, where the voice negotiates as well as gives way to the psychoemotional depths—the spit, spasms, and shimmers—of an oral drive. It is my view that what surrounds the voice proper—the paralinguistic, the sociolinguistic, the glossolalic, etc.—contributes a vitalizing base to the spoken by extending, problematizing, and saturating its communicative aim.

Theater

As a central orifice, the mouth conducts numerous things and materials in and out of the body—defending and sustaining, sexing and socializing. Such diversity positions the mouth as a conduit by which we learn specifically a relation to the world, as well as develop psychological and emotional bonds. In this regard, the psychoanalytic work of Donald Meltzer provides an important reference. Meltzer understood the mouth as a "stage" upon which a number of essential performances are enacted. His notion of the "Theater of the Mouth" proposes the mouth as the pivotal site for negotiating a relation between the inside and the outside of the body (leading to the making of boundaries); for establishing the emotional dynamics of attachment and care, love and loss; and for experiencing the oral as a channel for communication and its consequences. "In his view, the mouth is the first theater in which meaning is generated through the child's interpretation of the shape, texture, and taste of food; of the feel of mouthed objects; and of the sensory properties of words."[18]

Accordingly, I've sought to map these fundamental events through the form of a cultural study so as to highlight the processes by which such meanings and interpretations are brought forward, to condition not only experiences of childhood, but also the general field of subjectivity. In this regard, the mouth is posited as an extremely profound cavity—what René Spitz termed "the primal cavity"[19]—within which language is given shape, specifically drawing it through our body. Subsequently, the mouth is explored as a challenge to the power dynamics of language, and the ways in which the rational and the reasonable come to shape our verbal expressivity. The theater of the mouth is one that plays out the very drama of *subjectification*; it is fundamentally a site of conflict, and from which we may learn the skills for negotiating—through acts of singing, burping, and laughing, for instance—the script that precedes us and that captures the force of our oral drives, our oral imaginary, in its directing logic. Grabbing words in its wet cavity, biting down onto the consonantal, sounding out the resonance of the vowel, it is by way of the mouth that we might supplement the foundational narrative of proper speech with an oral poetics.

Fever

To consider these operations of the mouth, I've attempted to move from a certain phenomenology of its physical dimensions and toward more social and political arenas. This integrates understandings of the formation of subjectivity, as well as the field of the imaginary. In doing so, my attention has never settled upon one particular theoretical terminology, or discursive model. Instead, I've been keen to follow the mouth as a vehicle for complicating any form of singularity; the mouth, in other words, is always mashing things together, and accordingly, my analysis has aimed for this diversity, moving from depths to surfaces, bodily matters to soft wording, and from somatic to social concerns. In this sense, there is a profound way in which the mouth stages a form of production that demands a rather feverish analysis—a thinking process tuned to the actions and attributes of this *primal cavity*.

Cavity

The mouth as a collection of surfaces—of lips and teeth, tongue and cheek, and from the roof down to the throat—is equally an open space, an *oral cavity*. It is a small cavern wherein resonances proliferate, where matter is held and ingested, and where the desires that lead us toward another materialize in movements of oral pleasure—*the gap wherein one is entered, to give space for the other*. It is this gap that affords a literal grip onto the world. While the buccal surfaces channel a plethora of tastes and textures, the oral cavity *gives* room—for breaths and couplings, words and their shaping.

A continual fluctuation thus defines the mouth, between opening and closing, reverberations that expand within the cavity and then collapse, contracted and folded across its surfaces. A rhythm of somatic orientation, production, contact . . . *choreography*. Accordingly, the voice may be understood to draw upon the mouth as an *instrument*, a resonant cavity, while from a physiological perspective the mouth is more an *operation*, a series of surfaces. The assemblage of the voice and the mouth thus dramatically brings together the texture of oral surfaces with the vocal reverberations of the cavity, the thrust of operations with the composition of instruments, to generate lyrical as well as lustful productions. The weave of surfaces and cavities, operations and instrumentation, conditioning this assemblage of the mouth and the voice, opens out onto acts of representation and expression, from the ways in which we figure ourselves, as a vocal subject, to how such figuring is also an expressive punctuation. In this regard, speech is housed within a greater collection of oral behaviors, forcing a continual play and politics of meaning. Moten's emphasis on the "cutting and augmenting" of meaning enacted by *this body that speaks* (and that may also cry . . . or whisper) gives suggestion for a radical poetics, one that fully draws upon the surfaces and cavities of the oral—rhythms and improvisations that force themselves onto the territories of meaning.

It is just such a musicality that fills these pages. My approach has been to both capture the voice as a linguistic operation—as a method for demanding representational presence, for *speaking up*—and to draw forth the mouth as that expressive chamber surrounding and conditioning such representation.

Subsequently, I'm interested to hang onto the tension of the mouth, as a site of negotiation and mediation, contact and drives. This is elaborated in *Lexicon of the Mouth* through the study of what I call "mouth movements." These can be defined as "modalities of mouthing," or methodologies of bodily figuring, each of which contours, interrupts, conspires with, or elaborates subjectivity. In surveying the movements that shape the mouth—movements that are also choreographies, improvisations, rhythms—it has become clear that what counts as "communicative acts" are much greater than speech proper. Rather, I understand the movements of the mouth as extremely vital productions by which the spoken is deeply extended, as well as brought into question. Mouthing is always occupying the very limits of the spoken; in doing so, it both reveals the borders of the linguistic while enlivening understandings of what counts as language.

Modalities such as laughing, stuttering, whispering, singing, and burping, among others, are examined so as to track the mouth as it encounters the voice, as well as extends the body toward other materialities and socialities, imaginings and productions. I've been interested to give a cultural study of the expressions that radically inflect, if not make possible speech, and that also generate a range of bodily epistemologies—in the fold of the lips, within the breath of the sounded, or upon the surface of the tongue.

It is my intention to argue for the mouth as that very cavity inside of which such expressions find their resonance; a site of negotiation first and foremost, and from which other negotiations follow: between the imperative to speak and the functionality (or not) of the body to perform; a meeting point between depths and surfaces, interiors and exteriors, and through which each overlaps, where eating and kissing, vomiting and breathing, singing and speaking interrupt *and* support each other, especially in relation to the law of the proper.

The mouth might be said to produce such proliferation. It is a means for modulating the structures that surround us.

In bringing forward such questioning, I am interested in hearing the voice as a performative event that calls forth an essential animating and corporeal dynamic, while at the very same time remaining vulnerable to the intrusions of another: of silence and noise, and the interventions of the foreign; of rupture and loss, as well as love and sexuality; and the powers of discourse. That is, my argument is that the voice is never so simple, nor does it maintain any strict form of stable presence (especially in relation to "the body"). In contrast, the voice is precisely that which remains in a dynamic state, tensed between presence and absence, phonic and textual substance, and driven by the pressures and pleasures of being a body. The mouth not only shapes voice, but also fills it in; it is a cavity by which to capture additional voices, to put them on the tongue, supplying us with the potentiality to reshape, impersonate, sample, and reconstruct who we can be.

Oral Imaginary

Throughout *Lexicon of the Mouth* I focus on examining a range of vocal and oral modalities, as a way to consider the relation of identity and the politics of speech. While it is through the force of discourses that the voice may gain traction, what of the excesses and energies, the sloppy and the inchoate wordings that hover in and around discourses? The paralinguistic flourishes that ghost wording? The subsequent drives that may fuel the mouth to speak other? The poetics of an experimental orality? I'm interested to consider how such poetics gains its primary drive through the lessons of the mouth, the chamber of contact and expression, rhythm and dreaming; its sheer elasticity and vitality, and its position between language and the body, the proper and the improper, law and lawlessness, locate the mouth as a cavity by which the poetical may gain intensity. It puts into dynamic contact the ideality of thought (that inner voice . . .) with the materiality of language; as a site of expressivity, it leads the way for an appropriation of the articulations of voice and their meanings.

I have chosen to focus on these movements surrounding and contouring the spoken so as to register such poetics as an expanded (and imaginary) material—beyond the strictly linguistic to that of worldly experience—to ultimately enrich our understanding of all the signifying modalities by which the body comes to perform. It is my view that the mouth supplies us with an opportunity, a literal site by which to witness this poetical production, *a hinging of bodily rhythmicality with the force of vocal expression.* Here I'm interested to prolong this meeting, to finally propose speech and voice as productions manifested not only in words, but also equally in the breath of the whisper, the break of the stutter, the sigh of relief: all these mouth movements and oral gestures from which we may learn of the processes that enable subjects to negotiate, enjoy, and create their individuality.

In this regard, I would propose a politics of the performative that engages the dynamics of iteration and iterability as a question of the mouth; a discourse of the paralinguistic and the buccal, which might also spirit a *parapolitics*. That is, in support of an expanded voice not only for finding a representational space, as a point of entry, and reasonable debate, but also a voice full of imaginary drive, and those animate and poetical expressions that turn our bodies toward other species, other material forms, or immaterial apparitions, as well as each other.

1

Bite, Chew, Eat

The mouth displays an incredible range of movements that readily pass from the most aggressive to the most gentle, from the most exuberant to the most subtle, from puckered or pouted lips to the gnashing and gnawing of teeth. These oral actions deliver the *expressiveness* of the body, which is so articulate precisely by weaving together the nuances of our emotional life with the suppleness and gregariousness of the mouth—a "body language" rife with affective agitations. The mouth, in this regard, contributes to our individuated embodiment, and the potential to extend, or reach outward, movements that also connect us to experiences of attachment and loss, love and distress. Each modality of oral expression I'm tracing here—of the voiced and the unvoiced, the sounded and the gestured—twists and turns the mouth to register the extreme breadth of our vitality.

The mouth as a "chief aperture"[1] that *gathers in* while *pushing out*, to link and chart all sorts of relations, presents a range of means for literally carving out a space for individual presence. With biting and chewing, this reaches an extreme edge. The bite literally *cuts* into the material world; it grabs what is around, like a voracious hand, to pull it back and into the body, in moments not only of hunger or want, but also as a primary negotiation between self and surrounding. The bite is precisely a modality of mouthing that obtains material *for* the body, though as I'll develop, this extends well beyond a relation to food only. In addition, the primary act of biting participates within a greater and more significant process of individuation and by which our essential relationships are defined. This finds softer expression in chewing—we might snap at the world in the thrust of the bite, but we savor its rich textures by chewing. Biting and chewing thus perform as fundamental operations by which we sustain ourselves as flesh and blood, with eating as the central operation, but also through which we test, enjoy, or combat the materiality around us.

Monster

By taking hold of the world, biting expresses in a raw and palpable way the unquestionable *animality* central to being a physical body. Biting occupies a complex zone defined by our *bodiliness*, giving way to behaviors at the core, but absolutely held at a distance, of humankind. Echoing Georges Bataille's discussion of the "big toe," as that appendage of the body reminding of our more animal nature, biting may reinsert through sudden exaggeration our deepest instinct within the behaviors of social life.[2] Restrained through a variety of social etiquettes, and those rigors of taboo, the bite is refined or delimited according to good manners and the proper as well as the organizational structures of productive society.

John Berger, in his essay "The Eaters and the Eaten," examines how social status and the economic perform to govern when and how much we may put into our mouths. Through a comparison between the "eating habits and rituals" of the bourgeois and the peasant, Berger highlights the dramatic ways in which eating (and food) operates culturally, to ultimately condition a relation to "consumption." The act of eating, in other words, underscores the individual body as being held within particular social and economic brackets. For the peasant, this appears with the midday meal—as Berger says, the meal that is placed "in the day's stomach" and surrounded by work. In contrast, the central meal for the bourgeois is placed at the end of the day, close to "the head" and to "that of dreams."[3] For the peasant, "food is familiar like his own body. Its action on his body is continuous" with that of labor, while for the bourgeois "food is not directly exchangeable with his own work."[4] Rather, the bourgeois *overeats*, while the peasant eats in continuity with his own abilities to produce.

Eating, as that prominent act of "consumption," is regulated by the conditions of social standing, plenty and scarcity, and labor and leisure. What interests me is how these dynamics effectively *shape* the individual body, tapering it to particular contexts, economies, and geographies. Moving closer, we might register this upon the mouth itself, and the behaviors of biting and chewing: as that extremely vital oral action, biting is tuned to the presence or absence of food, and its location within the daily rituals and rhythms of life. These regulatory structures come to place emphasis on biting as a gesture of participation within a productive modality: I bite as part of the operations of *the market*, which immediately extends to affirming my place within the social order.

Relations to the social order find expression on and through the body, in the habits of mastication, and it is with the meal that these relations are defined as an order of the edible and the eaten. A political economy thus surrounds the mouth to radically shape how we use it. In this way, biting is directed toward eating, and the structures of production and consumption, but it may also endanger the balance of a social order by turning toward other matters. As Mary Douglas examines in her compelling account of taboo, every bodily orifice "symbolizes" the balancing between an interior and an exterior, and effectively regulates in a larger way the "social body." Ultimately, this expresses itself according to what can go in and what must be kept out, when and where we bite and chew, as well as how much we eat, and certainly *what* we bite into.[5]

The potentially transgressive nature of the bite can be glimpsed in the sport of boxing, and especially with the example of Mike Tyson. On June 28, 1997, during a fight against Evander Holyfield, Tyson infamously took a bite out of his opponent's right ear. Although boxing already occupies a zone to the edge of social behavior, literally calling forth the dramas of blood sport and the animality at the center of the human body, Tyson's bite went even further. Leading to the cancellation of the fight, and the suspension of the boxer's license, the act of tearing off another's flesh with one's own teeth stages a beastly confrontation. "You could never think there would be anything more outrageous that would occur until this . . . Fights were breaking out throughout the stands and fans were throwing things toward the ring. It was really bad. It was a scary time . . . We made Tyson into a monster . . ."[6]

The Tyson–Holyfield "bite fight" throws us into the mouth as unquestionably tied to the monstrous, a body impelled by violence. Biting firmly locates the mouth as a fulcrum by which law and taboo are held in the balance—a balance equally found in the management of what goes in and out of the body, what we ingest, and what we spit out. Accordingly, the mouth performs as the central organ around which so many regulations and contagions circulate.

Bat

The tensions surrounding the biting mouth carry within them additional erotic energies. From a gentle tug at the skin, that of the "love bite," which leaves its mark, to the more forceful bites that may even draw blood, biting has its place within acts of lovemaking. The erotic is precisely an operative space for entertaining animal behavior, of a body stripped bare or in masquerade, and by which gender and the sexed individual may play at heterogeneity.[7] Here, biting appears within the gestural vocabulary of such enactments, further highlighting the mouth as an organ of radical expression. From the catlike hiss to the full bite, flirtations with animality may supply us with means for bending the often-rigid vocabularies of subjectivity and sexuality.

This "animal eroticism" finds particular articulation in the tale of Count Dracula. Bram Stoker's narrative of the vampire captures the bite as a mesmerizing and magical puncture. Luring his (mostly female) victims through his haunting stare, Dracula's bite ultimately draws blood, casting his victims into a nether realm, a liminal zone between life and death. The tale of Dracula locates the bite as an *uncivil* gesture which fully usurps the social order, if not the order of the human, one haunted by the ambiguous energies of the undead. Following Dracula, biting appears as the very act that disrupts the order of human society, inserting instead one defined by blood, fangs, and above all, by the bat and its nocturnal qualities.

Dracula performs according to the logic of the bat—a *hauntological* order operating according to the nocturnal movements of blood passing from one to another. The bat symbolizes a supplemental order functioning alongside that of the human, to ultimately ghost the mouth with an unspeakable hunger—the fang quite dramatically reinforces the oral element within this haunted imaginary. In feeding off the blood of humans—a central taboo to normative oral productions—the vampiric bite comes to haunt the orality of the social, sharpening the teeth according to greater mythologies of the animalistic and the undead, the supernatural and the occult. The vampire ultimately gives expression to a primary oral ambiguity, which is equally a sexual ambiguity, a bodily uncertainty, tapping into a greater fever of unconscious grammars, hidden drives, forgotten myths: is not Dracula a figure whose nocturnal habits and occult strategies give radical expression for literally tasting what should not be tasted?

Relations

Returning to the human order, we might read the bite as an action of the mouth shaped by the central conditions of being a physical body—it is the forceful expression of want, need, and the existential condition of *hunger*. The bite, in other words, is never to be trusted, for it easily succumbs to an inherent drive, that of *drawing blood*, or of taking too much. Here we might linger over the intersection of the erotic and hunger, the oscillation between desire and craving, and how the intensities of physical need echo with that of sexual longing. Dracula is a type of seducer, giving shape to this dark sexuality—that is, the articulation of lustful appetites, a hunger *for the other*. Hunger is thus marked by these dual trajectories that accordingly are not so far apart and that may crisscross to form an unsteady zone of passions to which the mouth is extremely central. This finds articulation not only in lustful bites, but also in oral fantasies, for instance, the fear of being impregnated through eating. Such an oral fantasy and phobia immediately draws parallels between eating and sexual penetration, emphasizing the mouth as an orifice whose dramatic function of *taking things in* imprints itself onto our psychological life. As Melanie Klein notes, fear of impregnation through eating often leads to disgust for certain foods, and a general paranoia fixated on the oral.[8]

Klein's work on the topic of object relations, in particular, provides a deeper view onto this interweave of eating and desire, hunger and longing. For Klein, our psychoemotional life is fully charged by the relations we have as infants, and in particular, experiences of warmth and affection, of love, and importantly, its withdrawal or absence. These experiences are fundamentally produced and represented by parents, as well as by extended family relations, who are subsequently incorporated as "objects"—features or conditions whose repetition through infancy come to solidify and rest within our psychological view. Objects are thus internalized and reappear as subconscious references that interfere with as well as support the dynamics of future relationships.

Object relations highlight the degree to which our experiences with other people as well as things are continually negotiated or modulated through expressions or acts of introjection and expulsion, between what we take in and what we force away—in short, through the establishment of boundaries. Our sense for attachments, for example, is shaped by distinguishing between "good and bad objects," which are also often the same object, the same relationship, but under different conditions or states.

Following our primary relationship to the mother, and the experiences of breast-feeding—which also relate to experiences of affection, such as cuddling and caressing, as well as types of oral expression, that of kissing, nose-touching, smiling, etc.—it is clear that the mouth performs a vital channel for developing connections between people and things and, importantly, for often "holding onto" the loved object. The mouth is a type of cradle, an active container for capturing and prolonging the love relationship, and all such intimacies. *To keep it in the mouth.* Experiences of love are deeply connected to an oral drive, an oral wish, and the range of oral behaviors that dramatically reveal the ways in which the world passes across our lips.

Relating to the world, as well as to others, is radically shaped by these oral experiences, whether in the form of verbal language or in acts of tasting, chewing, and ingesting: a constellation of oral gestures by which self and other are brought into relation. Although to incorporate the loved object into oneself—that primary oral drive—also runs the risk of devouring, endangering, or even destroying it. One might bite too hard, or even tear it apart.

Marks

As an instance of punctured skin, Vito Acconci's *Trademarks* (1970) opens, or rather closes the bite onto the body, where the teeth take aim at one's own flesh. The performance, as Acconci suggests, aims for his body, to take stock of oneself through the skin: "Turning in on myself, turning on myself (my action drives me into a circle): a way to connect, reconnect, my body . . ."[9]

Tracing over his bodily contours, wherever the mouth may reach, from shoulders to knees, Acconci's biting leaves its mark. In doing so, *Trademarks* surveys the skin as the limit of the self, the exterior sheathe, or envelope of individuality which literally defines physical form. He tries to get back into the body, into himself, by way of the mouth (Figure 1.1).

Such gestures, as Kathy O'Dell suggests, act to stage the skin as an extended surface of self-containment, self-protection, as well as where so many exterior elements force their inscription.[10] Following the work of Didier Anzieu, and his theory of the "skin ego," O'Dell poignantly highlights how skin *holds* us in, to keep us safe, while also conditioning relations to our surroundings; skin is susceptible to worldly intensities, and their interrupting presence, as what might at times press too hard, back onto the skin—to puncture, imprint, or breech. Acconci takes aim at his skin: to turn against himself, test his own exterior, and register this body that he is. (As a final aspect of the work, Acconci applied ink to his bite marks, producing prints onto various surfaces, including another person's body.)

While animals often lick themselves, turning the mouth back onto their bodies, and gnawing flesh, such gestures appear radically out of place within human behavior. We've long given up licking each other in acts of communal grooming, or even in moments of playfulness; biting each other, or oneself,

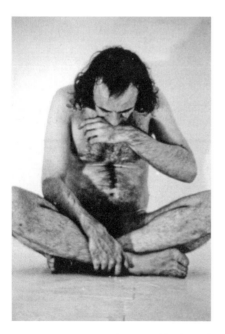 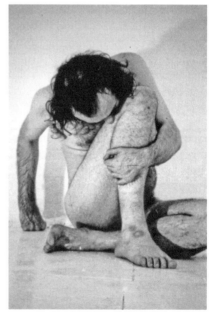

FIGURE 1.1 *Vito Acconci,* Trademarks, *1970 (photographed activity, ink prints). Photos: Bill Beckley, courtesy Vito Acconci/Acconci Studio.*

undercuts the borders of our particular social and bodily orders. The bite performs upon this line: the material it grabs hold of, and which the body needs, is always a fraction away from an entire range of other stuff that once bitten would violate particular boundaries.

Trademarks brings such dynamics to the fore by staging a self grappling with its physicality, by turning on itself, and in doing so, returning us to the oral drive so fundamental to our earliest experiences of affection. The bite, as I've been exploring here, as a gesture of the mouth cutting into the material world, once turned back toward one's own flesh sharpens our perspective: that the mouth is precisely the chamber balancing us between life and death, the civilized and the uncivil, need and obsession, social functionality and unconscious drives—between human contact and fantasies of the undead. Might we understand the fantasy of the undead precisely as the incarnation of the repressed bite, of that primal instant of or demand for affection? In this regard, the mouth is not necessarily a portal to the soul; rather, it leads us directly into the *appetites* of the body—the desiring nexus of any subjectivity.

In marking his body with the bite, Acconci drives the mouth and all its signifying force away from the social order; in tasting himself, he short circuits the mechanisms of proper behavior. Yet, he also returns us to those primary and essential desires, for profound human contact to which the mouth is both designed for as well as repressed from. We read Acconci's skin, each tooth mark a sign of the bite trying to capture what is so close and yet often so distant.

Cannibal

Acts of self-tasting and self-eating find additional expression in Oswald de Andrade's concept of "anthropophagy" espoused in his *Cannibal Manifesto*.[11] Writing in the 1920s in Brazil, cannibalism for Andrade specifically articulates the possibility for negotiating the historical legacy and presence of European colonialism, which for Brazilian society is fully embedded *in the body*. The colonial empire is already in the flesh, and the blood, within the very status of national identity, and any "return" to precolonial times is impossible. Thus to cannibalize the other, the empire—that is, to take on the power structure that forces itself upon the "native"—is to *incorporate* what is already present, all too present. *Eating the other*, in this regard, may disrupt the legacy of a particular European logic: the logic of the civilized, and the Western operations of the imperial conqueror as well as that of the revolutionary. Each for Andrade—the conqueror and the revolutionary— refers us to a Western structure. In contrast, the cannibal is a figure of Indian practices, particularly of the indigenous Tupi, to which Andrade refers in the manifesto. ("Tupi or not Tupi that is the question."[12])

The concept of anthropophagy developed by the Brazilian in the 1920s sought to usurp the power dynamics that kept Portuguese and Brazilian cultures in opposition. In fact, to speak of opposition, and dualities, was to confront an inherent contradiction. For the Brazilian is already a mix, a combination, a hybrid body. Andrade's cannibalism aims precisely at turning the bite onto a body already disrupting the imagined borders of one's skin separate from another's, of one people standing in opposition to another.

Additionally, I understand Andrade's manifesto as spiriting other modes of being political, for finding alternative positions of opposition. *Eating the other* sabotages the greater powers by radically incorporating *pieces*, by taking bites out of the colonial body. Ingesting colonial power therefore is, in turn, to eat oneself. To deepen the very reach of the colonial occupation, as found in one's own body, the cannibalistic gesture is an attempt to rupture the master–slave relation in favor of a new subject.

The cannibal, within this order of colonialism, sets the scene for unsettling the power structure of the empire by way of the bite, and is found also within the example of the Hauka movement originating in Niger and Ghana. Appearing as a ritual of incorporation and possession, with black Africans mimicking white colonial officers, Hauka delivers a complicated performativity. Captured in a film by Jean Rouch in 1955, *Les maîtres fous*, a group of men possessed by the spirit of white power adopt the military movements of British soldiers, donning officer uniforms, saluting each other, and even replicating a hierarchy of command. As Michael Taussig suggests, their mimetic "appropriation" of the European colonizers performs to destabilize the logic of imperial power.[13]

As an instance of cannibalistic performance, Hauka incorporates into the flesh the order of the whites, to play back in parodic form so as to unsettle the lines that keep such order in place. Here "mimicry" can be read through the lens of Andrade's anthropophagy, underscoring it as Homi Bhabha further suggests, as a slippage, a fundamental ambivalence, as a "metonymy of presence"—*of the same but not quite*.[14] Yet mimicry as found in Hauka, and implied in Andrade, is not solely a form of resemblance, but that of possession: it is a composite, a *monster*, the constitution of a body that is always already part-colonizer and part-colonized, a body of parts. Taking a bite, eating the other, is to ingest only a part; it creates an unstable form, a part-object referring us back to a fundamental gap, that violence so central to the colonial order. To take a bite therefore forces an encounter by not only violating a certain border, but also reconstituting (or regurgitating) the whole.

Accordingly, we may learn from the bite both the materiality of earthly matter, of affection and care, of what is available for sustaining the body, as well as the inherent force of the mouth to wound and defend, to appropriate, and to resist: to reshape the individual and social body through radical acts of ingestion. Biting is a negotiation with power.

Flows

To return to the vampire, Steve Pile highlights how Dracula is inexplicably tied to city life—not only does the vampire circulate among the flows of blood, drawing it out where it should not be, but also he features within the movements of economy and global trade, urban intensities, and the foreign. "Vampires, unlike ghosts, for example, are highly mobile in time and space, despite their reputed vulnerability to sunlight. Not only are they supposed to have superhuman senses and movements, they can also—under certain conditions—move great distances or lie in wait over long periods of time."[15]

From Transylvania to London, and back again, Dracula's journeys are emblematic of modern capital, where the attraction of the metropolis affords a plethora of opportunities for gain. "If the social figure of the vampire represents something real about city life, one of the more disquieting implications is that the city is itself vampiric—sucking the life-blood of its citizens."[16] Dracula's thirst thus demands a journey to the city, for "London's great crowds will act as the perfect cover for Dracula. In a city of strangers, the vampire will be just another man: just another stranger in a great tumult of blood."[17] Yet Dracula's pursuers throughout Stoker's narrative, in turn, follow the vampire according to the movements of information, tracking Dracula through England, and finally back to Transylvania. The narrative is marked by this continual movement, paralleling blood and mobility, and highlighting the city as a cosmopolitan body fully connected to (and fed by) the global network of the empire.

What marks *Dracula* is this dynamic of circulation, of blood certainly, but also of information, money, travel, and transactions enacted across and through the power of the empire. As Pile summarizes: "This, then, is the lesson of Dracula for understanding the imperial city: the imperial city does not simply belong to the coloniser, in a very real way it also belongs to the colonised and, further, to the foreign world beyond."[18]

Following Pile's reading of *Dracula*, as emblematic of a particular urban geography, we might appreciate the bite then, as Andrade's cannibalism captures, as linking skin and nation together: the bite is important precisely for its ability to bring into question the lines separating in from out, animal from human, stranger from citizen, slave from master. Every bite, as an essential movement of the body, drives us in and around the political economy of the nation state. *Dracula* thus radically conditions the bite as a possible strategy, like Andrade, for countering the power dynamics between colonizer and colonized, between diurnal and nocturnal life, between the logic and order of the empire and that of the bat.[19]

Vampiring then can be understood as a particular method of biting, one which brings the mouth *close* to one's enemy; undercover, vampiring is an act of trespassing, one performed to nurture an alternative body—whether in the form of the undead, as in Dracula's pack of victims, or for oneself, as Andrade suggests. The bite brings the foreign *inside*. Subsequently, it provides for a form of practice by which to relate to the other—to share in the materialities and socialities central to every meal; and further, it may show us how to navigate the "state of occupation" every society enacts onto its subjects.

Diets

Once in the mouth, the material devolves into certain textures and fluids, pushed and pulled by an array of radical agitations and gyrations to which we might say life is balanced, and to which, we might also consider, aesthetic form finds a deep hidden reference. A mechanics of transmutation, a geometry of formlessness—an awesome sublime, which if we were to glimpse would send us shuddering. Might the command "keep your mouth closed" give suggestion as to the intensities of the mouth in the midst of the chew? A violence wed to vital productions? A space of uncanny aesthetics?

Even as the digestive glands begin their work, the body attempts to find all possible sources, to incorporate this and that matter, as a total biological action; the oral in its most brutal, and most resilient. Such gestures form the basis for a deep relational contact with the world: like biting, chewing is the direct appropriation of materials *other* to oneself. An appropriation that plunders, destroys, colonizes, and engineers for the benefit of the body.

The chew is, of course, dramatically connected to the bite; yet chewing is already a step deeper, a step further in, with the mouth wrapping itself around a certain matter, massaging, and churning stuff in preparation for complete ingestion: to take everything inside, to the very core of the body. Whereas the bite is violent, the chew is sensual.

What kinds of base pleasures then are to be found in the chew? It seems, following this line of oral intensities, mastication figures as a prominent, voluptuous modality of oral delight. Is it because the mouth delves into one of its most acrobatic of gestures? All those movements—the stretching, the repetition, the modulations, and orchestrations—of muscularity and forcefulness: might they generate a deep, private vibration to open up the body to the deeper thrust of digestion? In other words, one of the primary if not essential choreographies of the mouth fully wed to sensual gratification, as well as animal satisfaction? A replacement for the lost object of primary warmth found in chewed matter?

In this way, the chew is intricately linked to eating. Already with the first bite we bring something into the mouth to labor over its processing, its incorporation, and its use. To chew is to already announce to the body the beginning of this greater process. Yet eating is not only a physical experience.

Rather, it is additionally linked to our deeper psychological and emotional life, in which chewing connects to self-image, practices of dieting and binging, and an entire network of social forces that often place great demands on the intake of food. As Susie Orbach suggests, eating properly enables you "to enjoy and digest not just your food, but to recognize and digest your feelings too."[20] Subsequently, the movement of the mouth as it takes hold of food performs in a volatile zone where issues of obesity, sexuality, and health are readily mobilized, to lurk always already in the chew.

Chewing incites not only the deep pleasures of food and the culinary, but also a network of related eating issues tied to the psychology of "looking good," as well as the pressures of emotional management. "As you take in the right amount of food for you, so you will be learning about how to cope with the emotional atmosphere around you."[21] All culinary delights then are balanced with the deep tangle of our emotional well-being, interweaving physical and psychological health, the mouth and the heart, into a complex relation that may also lead to madness. The case of Louis Wolfson gives entry into this complexity, in which language and food, eating and speaking, intersect. Wolfson's suffering experienced upon hearing or speaking the English language, his mother tongue, and chronicled in *The Schizo and Languages* ultimately led to a heightened paranoia around the intake of food. Subsequently, he would vacillate between fasting and binging, shutting his mouth to the powers of language and food, then suddenly gorging, "eating indiscriminately."[22] Wolfson must care for what enters the mouth; he monitors his throat as a passageway by which the mother tongue, and all related invasions, may enter to inflict the body.

Allen S. Weiss's examination of cuisine further highlights the sensual and imaginary expansiveness that eating comes to define. Delving into histories and recipes of French gastronomy, and its sheer extravagance, Weiss unfolds a deliriously poignant analysis of the workings of the culinary arts. In doing so, the pleasures of eating take us through a range of narratives, treatises, menus, and aesthetic productions, evidencing the degree to which the relation of food and bodily delight (as well as sacrifice and death) interlock. One such analysis leads Weiss to the work of Jean Genet, and in particular, instances where Genet meditates on the assimilation and incorporation of the lost loved body:

Since it was impossible that I bury him all by myself in an intimate ceremony (I could have taken his body, and why wouldn't the powers-that-be permit it?, cut it up into pieces in a kitchen and eaten them. Many scraps would certainly remain: the intestines, the liver, the lungs, and especially the eyes with their lids bordered by lashes, which I would have dried and burned, keeping the ashes to mix with my food, so that the flesh could be assimilated with my own), let him therefore depart with those official honors whose glory will rebound upon myself and slightly stifle my despair.[23]

Finally, Weiss concludes that it is through "ingestion" that "the world, as well as death, is most immediately experienced,"[24] and, in this instance, finds assuagement through the projection of cannibalistic fantasy. Genet reminds us that the mouth and the stomach are vessels by which to dramatize types of capture, seduction, and resistance; generative chambers in which dreams of life and death may be found.

The brutal adoration expressed by Genet comes to echo the more refined and highly symbolic gesture of communion found in the Catholic Church. The act of taking the body of Christ into the mouth, symbolized in "bread" and referring us back to the last supper, underscores the mouth and eating as tied to possession and belief—processes of ingestion that overcome any final disappearance.

Chewing is thus fully located at the meeting point of so many complicated negotiations and fantasies, psychic drives and social structures—in fact, it might be appreciated as a primary act of conflict in which food, and all its related politics and economies, enters the body to confront the deep interior echoes of what we hold close to ourselves, as a private emotional or spiritual core.

Matter

To return to the physical act of the chew, we can also appreciate its performance as bearing a fundamental relation to materiality—as an experience of raw matter. Chewing turns formed material into rough matter, a process by which one's mouth reveals a particular elasticity to the world around: by chewing we appropriate, process, mash together and, in doing so, produce yet another formal vocabulary—one always already on the way to energy, dissolution, and the formless.

We may witness this type of production in a work by composer Georg Nussbaumer, titled *Big Red Arias* (2004).[25] For the work, a group of singers are instructed to chew a piece of red chewing gum, slowly at first, while a conductor walks behind them whispering the words of the human organs: *liver, lung, tongue, kidney*, each whispered into the performers' ears to impress themselves upon their thoughts. Following this, the performers attempt to shape the gum into an image of the particular organ, pulling it this way and that, sculpting the matter through the mouth and its movements. The mouth is used to generate a miniature of the human organ, literally crafting raw material into a rather vague shape, imaging these unseen interior forms. The work concludes with the performers spitting out the gum objects, each appearing as mysterious blobs of uncertain shape, a sort of brute materiality caught between form and formlessness. The resulting photographs of the final globs produced by the artist give detailed focus onto the masticated material, highlighting them as crafted objects (Figure 1.2).

I consider Nussbaumer's project as a depiction of the chew in the negative; a literal impression capturing the actions of the jaw and the teeth in the midst of their intense productions. Wet with saliva, pierced, or stretched, the

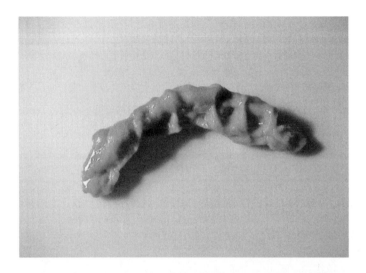

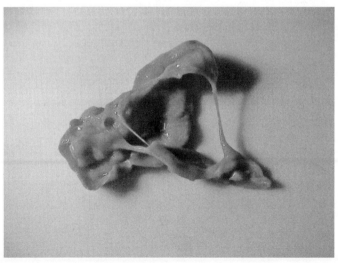

FIGURE 1.2 *Georg Nussbaumer,* Big Red Arias, *2004. Portraits of chewed gum, from a performance in Los Angeles. Photos: Courtesy the artist.*

series of masticated gum portraits puts on display the force of the chew, to produce a sort of visual lexicon, each blob revealing what generally remains out of view, that is, the severe productions and capabilities of the chewing mouth.

The chew can be appreciated as a fundamentally creative gesture, one that explicitly reveals how aesthetical production carries within its operations a sense for reworking, reshaping, and reconfiguring the conditions of given material. This perspective on the creative act already resides there in the mouth; while we may simply chew our food as part of eating, we might also marvel at the terrible beauty of the chewed article, as a production that radically strips away all sorts of finery, decoration, or even masking, to return us to the sheer vibrancy of the raw, while also suggesting a new state, a new figuration, a sublime there between the teeth.

Taste

Matter necessarily breaks down in the chew. To masticate by definition is to reduce stuff down to a base level, to make it easier to swallow and digest. By extension, to *chew on ideas*, for instance, is to explore the possibility of *It* going *inward*, to become a part of oneself. To figure a place for *It* within the structure of the body and its rhythms, beliefs, and projections. New ideas require some form of intake, and ultimate processing, a sort of manipulation so as to make more palatable the introduction of the foreign. The mouth performs a primary modification onto the world, not only its materiality but also its culture of ideas; it is from the mouth that we taste, acquire, negotiate, and produce worldly intensities. It is "taste" itself that comes to define the attributes of aesthetic pleasures and subjective judgments.

The chew is an extremely rich metaphor for life's more demanding issues, as well as for more abstracted thoughts, bringing forward our need to "chew it over" as means for deep reflection and decision making, for understanding and compassion. In this way, chewing can be appreciated as the basis for an aesthetic theory of great breadth. For the chew directs our attention to the essential elements of the organic; it casts all form into question only to give deep suggestion for what may yet come forward, as the promise of a future order, a future body.

Raw

The chew is a performative operation, bringing into contact the material world with the embedded vitality of bodily presence—in breaking material down, its essential elements are brought into play as fuel, as protein, an energy source for the generative sustainability of a body. But such relational contact, as Jane Bennett is keen to remind, is less hierarchical as may appear. Foodstuff is not without its own agency; its earthly presence contributes dynamically to conditioning the movements of not only the single body, but also our social and collective life. The chew may bring food inside, as raw material, but food may also migrate, contaminate, relinquish, and combat; it may fill us with unexpected vapors, turn us blue or red, make us run or fall down, delight us or drive us mad. It always puts us into potential contact with the foul and the dirty, infection and contamination, as well as the heights of animation. To chew, in other words, is risky business, turning oral pleasure into a project aligned with an uncertain future.

The forceful and energetic agency of foodstuff reveals the degree to which matter itself is replete with great dynamic, to level the field between human and nonhuman, as well as organic and inorganic. Accordingly, "Eating appears as a series of mutual transformations in which the border between inside and outside becomes blurry: my meal both is and is not mine; you both are and are not what you eat."[26]

Chewing, biting, and eating might be the essential means to imagine the possibility of becoming something other to oneself, where each masticating movement invites the promise of becoming other—the making of a body all the more defined by what it selects to put in its mouth, or what it ultimately rejects. In this regard, it is within the mouth that mimesis and alterity come to meet, where material transmutation both supports the sustainability of the familiar, of the same, while always already relating to the appropriation of what is different. A process that may also register the negotiations and incorporations passing between colonized and colonizer, the living and the dead. The difference that I put in my mouth is always prone to devolving the body, to contribute to an effective and radical transformation, which may reappear in the form of monsters or zombies, as well as through expressions of civic life.

2

Burp, Choke, Cough, Gag, Spit, Vomit

Although my attention is focused on the mouth, and the paralanguages and kinesics of orality, it's important to recognize the degree to which these are tied to the greater physiology of the body. As I'm suggesting here, the mouth is a fundamental site upon the body due to its operations as an aperture through which so many things, materials, words, and desires pass. The mouth is the very place where life finds bold expression, whether in the flows of voice (which are always our attempt to reach *the other*, even of oneself), the sensuality of eating, the voluptuous renderings of sexual intercourse, or even the soft murmurings that align us with spirits, ghosts, and the animal kingdom—the oral sustains, displays, traumatizes, and pleasures us.

In following such oral movements and choreographies, I'm thus led deeper in, to the back of the mouth, and further, into the throat and down to the stomach. The oral is such an expanded territory, a machinic assemblage, an elaborated signifying realm, which integrates these deeper regions, for what goes in the mouth may also come back out of it. Acts of burping, choking, coughing, spitting, and vomiting highlight the mouth as a vital passageway, an extremely volatile opening whose sensitivity to the materiality of the world balances us between life and death. The mouth, in short, keeps us safe while also putting us in danger.

Foreign

Choking immediately highlights the mouth as a bodily channel of entry and exit. Although choking occurs more precisely in the throat, the mouth is certainly the culprit, for in letting pass what should not be permitted the mouth throws us into convulsions. Foreign objects, excessive food matter, unspecified materials, or other mysterious items once let into the mouth may stick in the throat to ultimately kill us.

Such blockages send the body into fits, from uncontrollable gasping and coughing to sputtering and reeling. Choking is a violent undoing of the body that is often also unwittingly self-induced. Choking, in other words, is mostly in our hands, and while others may come to the rescue, administering the Heimlich maneuver or resuscitating us with CPR (Cardiopulmonary resuscitation), in the end we are deeply vulnerable to our own intake.

The sheer intensity of choking is captured in *Velvet Water*, the performance work by Chris Burden performed at the School of the Art Institute of Chicago in 1974. Indicative of Burden's interest in testing and pushing his body, *Velvet Water* consists of the artist attempting to breathe while submerging his head into a sink of water. While Burden and the attending audience occupied the same room, audience members could only witness the action through a live video feed transmitted to a set of five television monitors. Concealed behind a row of cabinets, the artist was hidden, leaving the audience to overhear his gasping and gagging alongside the silent, mysterious image. "The people in the audience knew that what they were watching on the monitors was really happening: they could hear the sound of his choking and gagging directly, live, right next to them. But Burden's use of closed-circuit television had the effect of objectifying the performance artifice, shifting attention away from his bone-chilling convulsions and onto the culturally sanctioned voyeurism and complicity of the spectators."[1]

Velvet Water stages the scene of choking, and appears within Burden's performance pieces of the early 1970s in which the artist forced himself into physically challenging situations. From confining himself to a school locker for 5 days to having himself crucified to a Volkswagen, Burden's keen interest in the limits of the body, and its potential objectification, is expressed here by way of the mouth. Probing and poking, confining and shooting, Burden aimed for possible ways of getting into the flesh, exposing weaknesses, challenging its shape and form, abusing its vulnerable contour. With *Velvet Water*, the mouth serves as the point of entry, and also weakness: the piece lasted for around 5 minutes before the artist collapsed, exhausted, and unable to continue.

Velvet Water operates as an amplification, a literal demonstration of the body confronting a primary limit—Burden's inability to breathe water reminds of the sheer vulnerability and fragility of the body. Such a primary view is further haunted by the work's reference to acts of torture, in particular that of "waterboarding" in which a prisoner's head is forcibly submerged in water as means for extracting information: *to cough it up*.

Loss

Swallowing is immediately connected to the ever-present possibility of choking. Yet it also points toward other matter, that of words. To "swallow one's own words" leads us to confront the social consequences of speech, as linguistic material with great effect. To speak too soon, or out of line, may subsequently come back in greater form; the words may return to us, to lodge themselves back in our throats, as well as our conscience, forcing us to regret their utterance. Swallowing is thus lodged within the oral imaginary to fully contour linguistic grammars with the movements of our physiology.

To "swallow one's words" is additionally complemented by the expression, to "choke on words." Captured in those moments of being overcome with emotion, usually while speaking in front of a crowd, "choking on words" brings us again to that zone of overlap between speech and the throat. In such instances, words truly become matter. One stammers or sobs, or loses confidence in midsentence—one is literally "choked up."

Choking thus occurs not only when something foreign enters to block the throat, but also when something rises up from inside, to make us tremble, gasp, or finally break down. In such moments, nothing comes out, but rather everything gets lodged in the throat. To be "choked up" can literally turn us red (as opposed to blue) with embarrassment. It may also bring others closer, in acts of sympathy, where the social circle closes to lend a supportive hand. In all of acts of choking, one is certainly pleading for help.

Such instances of swallowing and choking profoundly demonstrate the degree to which language is *stuff* with texture, weight, and density, and whose crafting requires so much physical as well as emotional energy. From such oral descriptions and experiences, we may glimpse the degrees to which the mouth and the throat are equally tied to language and food, speaking and breathing.

Alien

I'm interested to consider these instances of blockage, and by extension notions of incorporation as well as expulsion, as a specific oral territory. Coughing and choking, swallowing and vomiting define a *convulsed vocabulary*, which lends to describing mouth movements unquestionably connected to things *alien to the body*. From foreign objects and obstructions to contagions—as well as the emotional and social dynamics at play in the throat—this arena of convulsed movements comes to register the mouth as a deeply important exit through which alien substances are challenged, forced out and away. To literally *throw up*.

Returning to the overlap between words and food, we may further appreciate this relation by also considering swallowing as a greater process of incorporation and ingestion. The act of putting things into the mouth, or rejecting their entry, may register an entire ethos and the ordering principles of a certain ideology. To "swallow it" is to also accept the force of a particular belief system; it is to be "fed a lie," or to be brought up on particular ideals.

In this regard, it is by way of the mouth that all sorts of values are brought inside, to ultimately capture the body within the greater movements of power. Yet the mouth may also provide a certain opportunity for escape, a portal through which to additionally expel, by way of all sorts of agitated speech acts, logorrhea, fluencies and disfluencies, coughs and tics, and certainly through self-induced vomiting. Considering Chris Burden's *Velvet Water* performance, acts of inhalation and ingestion (as well as expulsion) may also be tied to a search for a different body, as an expression of what we may become, as well as how we may force out what has found its way in.

The convulsions defining this territory of the oral thus carry a profound relation to the body as the very site of socialization, a literal *embodiment* of all that surrounds and invades our individuality. They also highlight the degrees to which one attempts to negotiate external forces by way of the mouth. Continuing with this line of oral phrases, the expression "to shove it down the throat" fully reveals the way in which ideas, beliefs, and viewpoints are pushed *into us*, to influence and direct us into all types of behavior. We literally "regurgitate" what we have been fed. This finds terrible expression in the illness of bulimia. As an eating disorder, bulimia is deeply connected to notions of self-image, and the search for "the ideal body" so prevalent within our contemporary culture and often effecting women. Excessively eating large amounts of food, and then purging themselves through self-induced vomiting, bulimia patients reveal the degree to which consumption is deeply tied to the production of the self and the force of its idealization. "While we demand more rigor and have high expectations of what the fit, healthy, and beautiful body can deliver for us, there is an increase in symptoms, from sexual dissatisfactions to eating problems, fear of ageing, body dysmorphia, and addiction to cyber-disembodiment, which reveals how individuals struggle to make sense of the material source of their existence."[2]

Susie Orbach's examination of "bodies" in today's society emphasizes the deep pressures we enforce upon our bodies—to perform, excel, attract, succeed, endure, and charm. The body, as that fundamental material source of existence, is subjected to all sorts of exercises, surgeries, piercings, and treatments, as well as fantasies and projections. The desire for self-transformation may run multiple courses, often as an attempt to improve ourselves, or as a projection of a future self—we come to imagine various possibilities for how we might perform, which often gives way to a feeling for needing another body, fostering deep unease and dissatisfaction for what we have. While dreams may leave behind our physical bodies, they may also induce a sense for reconstructing them.

The acts of ingesting and regurgitating conditioning the mouth make palpable the connections between our bodies, our emotional and psychological life, and the powers that surround and ultimately feed us. The impressions we have of the world and of others may pass through all our senses, to influence our mental understanding and subsequent projection of ourselves, but the mouth is that literal portal by which in and out meet, to radically define, infect, or support the body. To eat, choke, swallow, and vomit are thus part of an elaborate physical mechanism that also balances and conditions our psychological being. This finds its ultimate consequence in the very lingering and ever-present fact that the mouth is always so prominently keeping us away from, or bringing us closer to injury.

Swallow

As I discussed in chapter 1, it is by way of the mouth, and its forceful appropriation of the material world, that we come to gauge our surroundings. Putting things in the mouth may also be about exploring and defining a relation to all that we come into contact with. Such perspectives emphasize once again the ways in which the oral performs in the creation of bonds between oneself and the world around, as well as their continual modulation. As Mary Cappello documents in her book *Swallow*, objects surrounding us perform within a greater psychic field and often lend material support to primary wishes. The way in which children put everything in their mouths, biting off doll's heads, or ingesting small toys, and even placing body parts into their mouths, immediately registers this dynamic interplay, conditioning all such things as substitutes for maternal presence and care, or as a relational frame to "test the extent to which the world can withstand" their physical presence.[3]

> All acts of swallowing are psychosocial at the core, not just cases of hysterical swallowing, because we don't come into the world self-integrated . . . but experience the body as a thing to be explored. We test the body by putting things into its orifices, and we test our relations with others by projecting onto the body's surface an idea of those relations . . .[4]

By bringing the world into the mouth, we seek out points of contact, of renewal, and of affirmation, as well as debate and negotiation. It is through the mouth that we come to know the world, and to test our self as part of it.

Swallowing is thus a process by which our physical bodies are also breeched, an experience that we may develop into opportunities for more intense, dramatic intercourses. The artist Alexandre St-Onge gives expression to such possibilities, capturing a relation to the world by way of the mouth and the resonances and vibrations occurring therein. As St-Onge suggests, the mouth is a potent space for "deterritorializing" language production, and in support of the emergence of what he calls "matter-meaning."[5] In St-Onge's work, the mouth is a generative machine for producing multiplicity.

St-Onge's sound project, *Une mâchoire et deux trous*, stages this primary oral drive, of exposing the mouth to what is around and placing what is external *inside*, to feel all such materiality there on the tongue, against the teeth, and deeper in. Consisting of what St-Onge terms "field recordings of the mouth," the work delivers a series of agitated sonorities: intense sheets of sonic hissing that bring the mouth forward. What we hear is the mouth ringed by the world around, a mouth choking on the intrusions of the city and swallowing all that passes by. The microphone literally captures this larger field of activity, to draw it closer, *all too close*. The mouth of St-Onge is magnified as a volatile cavity, a chamber in whose resonances we may detect the animate intensities that vibrate against and around us, and that the body incorporates as well as rejects.

Swallowing and related acts of eating and ingestion are inextricably tied to the imagination: if, as we know, we are what we eat, then acts of such incorporation are means to extend ourselves, to reinvent the body and its relations according to a mechanism of oral fantasy. As discussed in the previous chapter, desire is radically expressed by a primary oral wish—*to devour the other*, and in doing so, may also fuel the oral imaginary with the possibility of *containing* what may leave us.

The mouth is thus a site for dreaming, wishing, and fantasizing; it is, as St-Onge suggests, a generative chamber that extends from way down in and toward things outside us. An additional expression of these oral issues is to be found in the work of artist Charles LaBelle. *Disappearer—Shirt That Passed Through My Body* (1998–1999) appears as a men's dress shirt, yet divided and cut into 597 squares each measuring roughly 2 inches square. Each square has undergone a particular journey though, that of being swallowed by the artist and retrieved at the other end. Reassembling the shirt, LaBelle utilizes his body as a passageway, a literal thoroughfare whose hidden textures and liquids mysteriously surround the final object: a shirt ingested and then reconstituted, to stand hauntingly in the gallery space. The history of the shirt thus lingers in the soft creases, the stained folds, the blotched squares, each stitch reshaping the original and signifying all the more the rather fragmented whole. As the artist states: "I put something in my mouth quite aside from any nutritive need or gustatory aggression but only for the pleasure of a play of surfaces meeting, the acknowledgment that I am here" (Figure 2.1).[6]

I'm interested in LaBelle's statement as a suggestion for understanding the mouth in general: its sheer ability to relate an exterior world to an interior condition locates the mouth firmly at the center of our existential being. LaBelle's work underscores how the mouth is a mechanism within which a relation between "the whole" and its "parts"—what I might additionally term, "assurance" and its ultimate "fragmentation"—is continually negotiated, a site vulnerable to the fluctuations of input and output, and where fluids and materials may suddenly fall out, or drip over the tongue. His work is a performance that leads us directly into the alimentary canal; it occupies this extended tract to remind of the extreme porosity of the body. A fragmentation expressed equally in the works of Antonin Artaud, captured in attempts to rid his body of its organs, and resulting in a poetics obsessed with the corporeal:

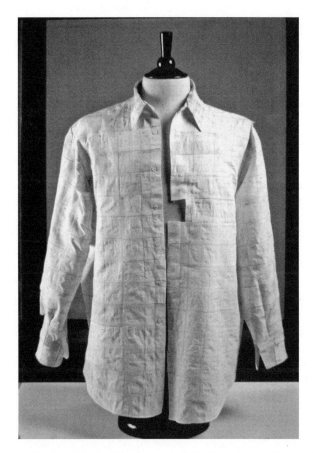

FIGURE 2.1 *Charles LaBelle,* Disappearer—Shirt That Passed Through My Body, *1998–1999 (men's dress shirt [size 40 regular] and iron-on mending tape). Photo: Courtesy the artist.*

When I eat, the gluttonous void of the bottom of the throat,
of the greedy orifice,
summons the alimentary bolus to monopolize it to the detriment of the
teeth and the tongue,
with which the uvula from behind has strange complicities.
But all that is of no interest of any kind,
for the tongue,
is an obscene hooker who in front is ready to follow the teeth in their
detailed work of mastication,
and behind,
even more ready to let herself be gobbled by the orifice,
and to push lewdly and treacherously food toward the orifice.[7]

In acts of chewing and swallowing, the mouth cuts into, breaks apart, and fragments the materiality around us. These are extremely physical actions that force a view onto the mouth as an organ aimed at dividing up the constitution of matter or form. A mysterious union of brutal violation and generative production thus defines the mouth, which ultimately captures the oral as that very place where the abject of the fragment and the sublime of the whole are never so far apart.

Education

Breathing, coughing, swallowing, and excreting . . . The mouth is one end of a greater bodily channel that starts there on the lips, those fleshy folds exposed to the outside and that quickly give way to the soft underside, the sensitive interior extended further into the flesh of the oral cavity. From the palate above ridged by the palatine raphe, the palatoglossal arch, and then again, the palatopharyngeal arch—a series of miniature gateways that announce entry, and that lead to the oropharynx, as that final point before plunging into the trachea. Deeper in, we immediately confront the epiglottis, that second set of lips through which breath is modulated, the first point of its sculpting and on the way toward sounding, voicing. Yet behind the glottis, the oral drops further into the body, to descend down the esophagus, or the trachea, depending (and upon which so much depends!)—how amazingly close do breathing and eating flow, like two canals carrying such different materials, to ferry two radically different economies—we can locate here the territory where coughing and choking reside.

The movements of swallowing and of coughing up force us deeper in, pulling the buccal surfaces back down and reminding of this larger biological whole. To bring something into the mouth's open space is in turn to initiate a greater operation, where an entire network of organs, liquids, and movements perform—as soon as something hits the tongue, the entire body is brought to the ready. Importantly, these physical attributes are forcefully connected to our psychosocial being, forming an epistemology founded on oral sensing and behavior. Is not the mouth a portal through which relations to things and people are developed and sustained? The very place where we learn how to care for ourselves, and through which so many lessons are brought down onto us, *into us*? By swallowing and choking we not only test and experience the materiality of the world, we further learn what to avoid and what to cherish, what we need and what we must reject. An education based on oral experience comes to inflect additional decisions of how to navigate through life's challenges and the innumerable relationships that come to define us. We may have to "swallow our pride" at times, to "choke on our words," or to "spit it out" when under pressure and to follow our "gut" when deciding on a course of action.

Puke

Swallowing and choking lead us into these deep performances and issues, revealing the degrees to which the oral assists in regulating our sense of self. With vomiting, this reaches an extremely dramatic peak. How horrible vomiting can be—that instant of the body, possibly in the midst of some terrible infection or illness, lurching forward to get rid of what has found its way in. Vomiting is the ultimate attempt to expel what is unwanted.

The artist Martin Creed gives us an image of the body in the midst of this single, convulsing expression. His *Work No. 610 (Sick Film)* (2006), running for 21 minutes, captures seven "performers" inducing vomiting, one after the other. Filmed within a white empty space, the video work isolates this single action, placing it as the central focus, a literal spectacle of the heaving body. Each performer is captured in the midst of gagging, coughing, spluttering, and hacking, all those micro-expressions surrounding vomiting and which give indication of its extreme physicality.

According to the critic James Hansen, Creed's film brings into question the very conditions of art production, and asks us to consider the ontological status of the art object. "Creed literalizes the expectation we have of art—something created in the mind (the inside) of an artist made visible for the outside of the world (created outside)."[8] Following Hansen, vomiting performs as a metaphor for the expunging and expelling of the creative individual, where the final object or work is thrust out from the artist's body in acts of production and exhibition. The work, in this sense, is a type of expenditure.

Such perspectives echo the idea of bodily excretions as primary creative acts, or gifts, often expressed by infants, and bring us to questions of sublimation and the abject.[9] As Allen S. Weiss acutely states: "Sublimated desire turns us away from [processes of the body and] its objects; desublimation entails the rediscovery of such lost objects."[10] Creed's film encapsulates a primary artistic drive toward desublimation and an overall celebration of "pure drive"—what Jean-François Lyotard theorizes in his *Libidinal Economy* as the overthrow of the signifier, "permitting the establishment of an aesthetics of production and not representation."[11] *Sick Film* notably stages this "aesthetics of production" by giving us bodies whose borders are breeched, disrupted by leakages and spillages. In this moment, such productions are fueled by a libidinal economy balanced by the mouth.

While swallowing and choking lead us into a relation with material things, vomiting pushes back up what has already gone in; a terribly mushy mass comes back out of the mouth, to splash and stain all surfaces. It is absolutely a substance that *abjectifies* its performer: one is immediately tainted by this outpouring. Vomiting reminds us of the sheer susceptibility of the body, and the potent force of what we may swallow or catch. Yet as

Creed reminds, such actions may also induce a certain appreciation and respect for the weaknesses we may experience.

Slosh

The mouth slackens, maybe during sleep, or in moments of drunkenness, to let loose a small seepage of saliva. It hovers behind the lips, to build up and then to slowly slip over. Drooling, in this way, is the opposite of swallowing; instead, the flow of intake shifts to exit, as a slow leak in instances of dribbling and driveling.

Interestingly, the act of driveling finds additional connotation in the term "drivel," which means "childish, silly, or meaningless talk or thinking; nonsense; twaddle." Drivel, or "silly talk," thus may be appreciated to contour understandings of drooling by locating it as an act inexplicably tied to "childishness" and "foolishness." To "drool" is to immediately fall short of the social order; it is to slip into foolery, appearing also in moments of sexual lust. To "drool over" someone is to let drip one's internal passions, that particular physical desire for another: *to be a fool for love* . . . . Thus we might draw a parallel between "drool" and "fool," suggesting a horizon of correspondence that casts the substance of spit onto a plane of discourse. Drool as a particular liquid marked by lust, foolery, and silliness—and further by "uncontrollability."

We further say, "I pity the fool." In this regard, we fall victim to our own drool and drivel, to the passions that threaten to seep over in moments of slobbering and that potentially overturn the boundaries that keep things in place. To drool is already the beginning of a possible rupture—it is a sign of an individual losing reason. In this way, the mouth may definitely give us away.

I want to underscore the micro-oralities of drooling and dribbling, and their related fluids, as being tied to all sorts of disturbances. From lustful tremors to the social choreographies of the fool, and further, to the breakdown of behaviors, this particular arena of mouth movements articulates an instant of loss: loss of wit, loss of consciousness (the slobbering drunk . . .), or loss of functionality that opens toward an uncertain future. As every swallow may ultimately undo us, the flow of saliva may seep over existing borders, of not only the individual mouth, but also that of relationships. It seems here that drooling, as that particular drop which might turn into a thread, or that might take stronger strides in the thrust of a spit, radically oversteps the lines between social bodies; it performs, as Christof Migone suggests, an intrusion onto the borders that keep all such excretions in their proper place.[12]

Migone furthers an analysis of saliva by way of Vito Acconci's *Waterways: Four Saliva Studies* (1971), a work that amplifies precisely this overflow. Consisting of a series of video works capturing the artist spitting into his hands, and sucking it back in, or sloshing spit around in his mouth, and letting it flow over the top of his hands to hang at the edges of his fingertips, each action amplifies this body fluid, leading us into the chamber of the mouth as a space of liquidity. Like Creed's *Sick Film*, Acconci stages the interior fluids as a leak usually held back, or one kept off-screen. With the artist playing with his own spit, as viewers we may certainly shudder, balk, or generally cringe, forcing us to witness a fluid body, a mouth letting it all hang out—a fool in the midst of questionable behavior. Spit is rendered unmistakably formless, nameless, and in this case, also noisy. Acconci's video is resolutely audible; a mouth swishing around its own spit may be heard to sound all the fluidity surrounding voice, giving way to the "allusive power" of spittle to draw us closer to what is usually unseen.[13]

Lubricant

Does not the mouth, and the sheer force of vocalization, fully rely upon such fluids? A lubricated interior so as to allow the vocalic its needed velocity? To slide up from below, across the throat and further, outward across the tongue and lips? Not to mention to facilitate processes of digestion? All such wet materiality supports the necessary performances of the self, as it speaks and voices, vocalizes and animates, eats and expels. As Migone identifies, language necessitates a primary relation to the substances and surfaces of the mouth, to that hole that is always vacillating and puckering, spiriting words with a great energy that may also *run away* with itself.[14] Voice relies upon these slick conduits and, in doing so, it also encourages their overflow in the form of seepages of desire, disquietude, or noisy excitements. While we may seek out smooth speech, the very spit and moisture surrounding it may also act as a platform for certain watery (dis)articulations, giving way to a salivated lexicon.

This is not to overlook how spitting is also firmly located within other cultural traditions, supplying us with a vocabulary of insult as well as methods for protection. Certainly, the act of spitting in another's face carries great meaning that fully bypasses the formation of words; its signifying power is so explicitly unspoken we need not dwell upon its interpretation. Instead, we are left stunned, shamed, resolutely insulted. This intensity of the spit is countered when it comes to protecting each other. In Greece, for instance, spitting around a loved one, in particular children who attract great admiration, functions to ward off the energies of the "evil eye." In this way, spit is a radically ambivalent fluid by being firmly located within the movements of the social order even while it's forced to its borders.

Belch

The obscenity found in spit is equally found in acts of burping. The burp is unmistakably rude. How many times we overhear a parent scolding its child for burping. How many times do we witness a child or young adult—or even adults—giving way to the particular act, to send friends and colleagues into a state of giggles as well as disgust. To burp is thus a small joke based entirely on a primary ambivalence; like spit, it occupies this unsteady territory. It is a mouth movement fully wed to a certain humor, one that breaks into the social scene with indefatigable force. We love it, and we hate it.

I take the humor of the burp as being resolutely tied to its sound; in fact, the burp is only identifiable through its audibility. Resulting from an air bubble in the stomach being released through the mouth, the actual sound is caused by the air or gas passing through the upper esophageal sphincter. A single, punctuated pop or an elongated croaking, the burp has an array of acoustical identities all of which are unmistakable. Within an Anglo-European context, it resolutely disrupts most social settings, letting loose both gaseous presence as well as crass humor.

Yet burping does have its place. The act of burping babies is not only acceptable, but also recommended to aid in a child's feeding. Letting out gaseous bubbles from a baby's stomach, burping can ease digestion. Patting a baby on the back and holding it over the shoulder assist in such releases, resulting also in spitting up. Thus exists the strange life of the burp: as a once encouraged act to adolescent joking and finally to its repressed disappearance in adulthood, and ultimate uncanny return.

In June 2012, Tim Janus from New York set the world record for burping. Sponsored by the World Federation of Burping (located in Geneva), Janus held a burp for 18.1 seconds. His expert burping was supported by various carbonated drinks, as well as controlled acts of air swallowing developed from years of experience. As he states: "I've been doing this my whole life, working in the backyards, working in the parking lots with friends, so I've got a lot of experience to draw upon. At the end what I try and do is to flood my system and draw out these last bits of air, push them all up from the bottom of my stomach to the top of my stomach so that I can produce one long quality lyrical note."[15]

Janus' poetics of the burp might be highlighted as an acrobatic appreciation for this particular mouth movement, suggesting that the burp is in fact an art form. He harnesses the physiological movements of the burp, controlling through various contractions so as to orchestrate this extended and reverberant sonority. Under Janus' direction, the burp further recalls us to that theory of aesthetic production highlighted by Lyotard, one that bypasses representation in favor of raw production, which in this instance draws out a certain brute acoustics, to equally provoke admiration and repulsion.

Sublime

The movements of swallowing, coughing, vomiting, spitting, and finally belching have provided a deeper consideration of the mouth as an extremely vital organ. This arena of bodily actions no doubt leads us away from the mouth proper, but it does so only to reinforce how explicitly it operates within a greater system, and how central it is to health and happiness, diet and desire, relations and productions. Such importance is also fully defined within a greater social order, which relegates the mouth's more fluid and messy matters toward the periphery. In this way, the more the mouth reveals of the body the more it oversteps social acceptability. Orality is thus understood primarily as a linguistic operation, and the mouth a site for the articulation of voice. Yet as I've tried to show, what is held back, repressed, or marginalized also returns to generate all types of sudden productions. It is certainly the aim of this lexicon to chart out these instances, and to locate them alongside the voice.

Accordingly, all such ambivalences of the leaking and excreting body find consideration in that particular discourse outlined by Julia Kristeva on the topic of the abject. For Kristeva, the abject, as "defilement and pollution," and as that which breeches the lines of a primal repression, haunts the sphere of the proper. Returning to Creed's *Sick Film*, LaBelle's swallowed shirt, and Acconci's spit expressions, the abject is precisely central to the creative imagination. What is prohibited returns in the form of those productions outlined by Lyotard, as a forceful assemblage of so many parts. As Kristeva states, "The abject is edged with the sublime."[16]

The beautiful and the ugly, the sacred and the profane, each functioning within a system whose logic paradoxically locates that which is excluded close to what is permissible. Sublimation, as Freud proposes, "is a way out,"[17] where the horrors of our own primary materiality, the stuff and mess of the inside, are held back and placed within a certain order that may also come forward, to make us shudder and reel, and to teach us of the volatility of our own existence.

In these interpenetrating dramas of the abject and the sublime, of excretions and cultivations, the mouth gives a radical performance. The ultimate orifice, our mouths are the site by which the messiness of the below is held back, captured, and restrained, capped by the articulations of an ordered speech—and the refinement of a language fused with precision—while also always giving way to all sorts of defilements, disfigurations, and vulgarities: regurgitated matter, cursed languages, profane exclamations, to "confront us with those fragile states where man strays on the territories of *animal*."[18] (I may point here to that strange act of washing the mouth out with soap, as a disciplining punishment against children using swear words.)

There is something trying to get out; it impels the body, throttles it with hidden energy and released in choking, gagging, and coughing: an agitated breath forced out of the lungs, scraped across the larynx, to push forth over the tongue, bringing all the wet air of those deeper regions back up. Yoko Ono's *Cough Piece* (1961) turns us toward this surge of the below, a 30-minute audio recording of the artist periodically coughing, which brings us closer to the respiratory, the phlegmatic, as the underside of the oral. Throughout the work we never know for sure what the artist may be choking on, what causes her irritation, or what may be forcing these surges of convulsed breaths. There is something *tickling* her throat which remains unclear, undetected, and unspoken—*something she can't get away from*, a below, or an off-stage whose absence or formlessness resides at the very center of the recording. It occupies the mouth.

These perspectives give way to a fundamental act of proliferation performed by the mouth—that multiplicity suggested by St-Onge—a cavity in which words and foods, breaths and languages, conversations and coughs are channeled and brought into various relations. A vessel equally occupied by the trembling matters of body and mind. Yet in following these "lower" expressivities of a mouth laced with its own wetness, and caught in all that finds its way back up, we might glimpse the force of the impermissible and the vile as they come to occupy the same palate by which we enjoy the finer tastes of culture—when the oral cavity wretches and convulses, vomiting forth and burping, coughing up; or when at times, like Acconci playing in the liquidity of spit, such scenes readily jar the syntax of normative behavior. Still, a curiosity reigns, a beauty even: while we turn away, we may also marvel at the matter that suddenly comes forward. These ambiguities are precisely at the center of sublimation, which forms atop all the filth of the below. As Norman O. Brown posits, "The concept of sublimation is a command to relate the human spirit (and its creations) to the human body."[19] Such a command might also invite an understanding of speech, and the communicativeness of articulation, that connects to the body in all its somatic tension and fluidity; the mouth, in other words, as a ground where the creativity of the spoken is absolutely fueled by, and inflected with, the powers of horror.

3

Cry, Scream, Shout, Sing

The mouth expands to widen its social horizon, broadening its reach, with the torso, a muscular chamber filling up and then thrusting out to shudder the air with vocal energy. These volumetric intensities bring us into the drama of communion, chant, and healing, as well as pain, suffering, and arrest. A sonority full of animation drawn out in the cry, the shout, screaming, and singing. Each performs to expand the scale of the body, inciting certain collective experiences. By bringing us up in volume, these particular mouth movements lead to a greater spatiality, one of crowds, communities, and even that of nations. Funeral songs to anthems, chain gangs, and pop groups, gospels to shouting matches—these raise the pitch on voicing, billowing out the lungs and the cheeks in harmony, as well as in moments of desperation.

Tracking these mouth movements, choreographies drenched in emotion, I'm reminded of so many songs whose particular force is driven by an enraptured voice: is not song that arena where the voice is so spectacularly displayed, fueled by so many breathless propulsions, fantasies, sexualities, and dreams? The singer, the crooner, and the bellower come to occupy a space of messianic figuring, embodying all that may drive us beyond ourselves, to incite metaphysical, social, and erotic gathering. How many times we collapse under the spell of another's song. One look to those wild images of early concerts by The Beatles, or that of Elvis, not to mention in the historical accounts of the shakers, and still today, in the gospel churches throughout Harlem or Atlanta, is enough to witness the power and glory of the song, and the ability of the singing, shouting, and crying voice to drive us into hysterics and collective rapture.

Aloud

Leaving behind the song for now, I start with the cry as a first step in volume. Reverberating from here to there, the cry demands attention. It forcibly resonates within the throat and mouth, expanding the lungs and exposing the voice to all sorts of bodies and subjects, societies and markets. I'm reminded here of the figure of the hawker on London streets (and elsewhere), that unmistakable voice crying out a multitude of announcements and numbers, from bananas to batteries, so as to inform and entice the passerby. Although, as Emily Cockayne reminds in her illuminating work on early urban life, the cry often resulted in "a hideous din": "As shouts were varied to attract attention, words degenerated into sounds, and many consumers would have had difficulty distinguishing one slurred yell from another."[1]

To hawk wares, to bargain and barter, the street vendor is a voice that sounds out through the acoustics of city streets, a vocalization that still carries in its reverberations a history of informal mercantile communities as well as criminal cultures. Peter Linebaugh alludes to sellers and their often poorly and petty criminal alliances in *The London Hanged*. In addition, Linebaugh notes that many sellers throughout the eighteenth century were women whose cries were illustrated in a deck of cards from 1754 called "The Cries of London." On the cards women are depicted crying out a variety of goods for sale, such as "sheep's hearts, livers, matches, muskmelons, shrimps, damask roses, cotton laces, peaches, apricots," etc. Such a medley of cries rising above the hubbub of the streets also contributed to urban songs, as Linebaugh suggests, captured in many hawkers' lyrical ballads sung out on the streets, in the prison cells, and as part of social banter and dispute.[2] The practical task of selling wares no doubt fuels the vocal imaginary, giving way to robust and idiosyncratic lyrics as well as twists of the tongue. As an observer in the eighteenth century noted, "Nay, so strangely infatuated are some very eminent Artists of this particular Grace in a Cry, that none but their Acquaintance are able to guess at their Profession."[3]

This rather public voice finds more official presence in the figure of the town crier, emblematic of this particular oral arena. Town criers were prominent throughout England from the medieval period to the nineteenth century (while a number still remain active).[4] Employed to announce important news, the crier would appear in town squares to proclaim a variety of information, from decrees by the monarch to obituaries, as well as more informal bulletins. "In the days before newspapers you would depend on the town crier to inform you of news of every kind. In addition to news, a town crier 'published' the Lost and Found and Obituary notices, just as newspapers do today. Indeed, the original meaning of 'publish' referred more to making public by crying aloud than to its later meaning of making public by printing."[5]

David Mitchell's important account of the town crier highlights how crying aloud performed as a primary means for informing a populace. Yet the town crier is not to be seen as a purely functional figure. Rather, the act of crying can be situated within a wider circle, alongside proclamation and preaching. To stand before a crowd and cry aloud is a fundamental social and political, as well as religious act; it forms the basis for civil society and the related freedoms to which speaking publicly attests. Mitchell's own practice as the town crier of Chester, England, continues the long-standing tradition while reminding of the dramatic powers of the crying voice. In particular, we might appreciate the crier, and the extremely related figure of the bellman, as the bringer of words, for instance as observed in the Bellman of St. Sepulchre. As Mitchell recounts, the Bellman of St. Sepulchre was employed to proclaim at executions held at Newgate Gaol and sought to encourage a condemned prisoner to repent:

> All good people, pray heartily unto God for these poor sinners,
> who are now going to their death, for whom this great bell doth toll.
> You that are condemned to die, repent with lamentable tears; ask
> mercy of the Lord, for the salvation of your own souls, through
> the merits, death, and passion of Jesus Christ, who now sits at
> the right hand of God, to make intercession for as many of you as
> penitently return unto him.
> Lord have mercy upon you;
> Christ have mercy upon you.[6]

The crying of the Bellman thus opened the way for possible redemption, aligning the cried word with that of the Lord and his merciful leaning. "The ringing of the bell, and the cry made by the Bellman of St. Sepulchre's, were indeed a summon, or more accurately, an invitation, to Heaven."[7]

Crying radically locates the voice as a public expression, a part of public life that also performs to inspire deeper concerns. In this regard, crying is as an administrative act that also seeks out the soul. On a more individual level, we also cry so as to *divest* ourselves, expose a secret burden, or expel some interior ache—to cry out in pain or in grief. Crying occupies these various territories, and as such charges them with emotional strain; it underscores the sheer *publicness* at the base of oral life, to ultimately announce: *something has happened.*

This finds its primal manifestation in the baby's cry, a sonority that most certainly communicates by its sheer force. A baby's crying is the first act of vocalization, one whose rending echoes break into the world in search of comfort, warmth, and assurance. Crying is such an essential vocalization that throughout life exclaims to the world these primary emotional states, of suffering and of want; its reverberations come to encircle a particular group, often giving way to consolation, support, and sympathy.

Crying of course is not limited to the mouth. Rather, it incorporates or requires the body. Yet, crying is notably linked to tears. The shedding of tears is so completely tied to emotional life, appearing in moments of intense happiness and despair, alongside the comic as well as the tragic. Tears come to occupy these extreme edges, to spill from our eyes as a release of inner emotion, a *breaking down*. Yet tears are also often accompanied by a range of facial movements, and in particular, by varying mouth movements, each conveying degrees of sadness and joy—like most of the micro-oralities I'm exploring here, crying is equally a form of *countenance*, a facial look. Sobbing, blubbering, and sniffling all punctuate the flow of tears with their movements, respirations, and soundings, pulling the lips down and often opening the mouth up, to expose the tongue in fits of desperation, happiness, or exaltation.

We may glimpse these expressions in a video work by the artist Bas Jan Ader. *I'm too sad to tell you* (1971) captures the artist crying, bringing us into an extremely intimate and yet uncertain scenario. As a form of self-portraiture, we are face to face with Ader; his eyes are closed and his mouth quivers now and again. An ebb and flow of emotion unsettles his appearance, with his head tilting back and forth at times. The occasional tear trickles down his cheek. Ader seems caught within an unsteady trance, on the verge of uncontrollable emotion or delirious with inner unease. His display of sadness catches us, as viewers witnessing a figure *at a loss*.

Although the work is silent, there are moments when we might hear his crying—it is there, like a lost soundtrack that comes to ghost the image. It surrounds his body as it trembles, with hands raised up onto the forehead, to cover the eyes for a moment.

Evoke

Do we learn the primary power of a raised voice through acts of crying? Lessons found in the sheer energy that passes through the throat and out from the lips, to burst onto the social scene? The cry, as that essential vocalization, sounds the body as a palpable and effective force, making apparent not only what is possible to say but also, importantly, with what emotion or beauty we might say it.

The powers of vocalization are highlighted by Michel Chion in *The Voice in Cinema*. Through an analysis of what he calls the "I-Voice," in particular, Chion alludes to the conjuring abilities of the voice, and how off-screen vocalizations may create powerful images. Such a view leads to deeper meditations on voice, and its essential operations. As he suggests, "Since the very dawn of time, *voices have presented images*, made order of things in the world, brought things to life and named them."[8] From reflections on cinema, Chion is led into the primary powers of voicing. Fundamentally, the voice *conjures* which it speaks; it may animate the inanimate, lending great power to the vocal imagination to affect "the order of things." In giving narrative, the voice may also capture the flow of life's movements, to direct our attention toward certain outcomes. To speak gives realization to particular freedoms—to embody the promise found in having a say. Yet it may also, through the same potential, arrest or injure the freedoms of others.[9]

The conjuring abilities of the voice can be found in the example of shamanistic traditions, where "miracle men" may heal the sick, damn the enemy, or address the gods through powers of articulation. Here, the cry is often chanted and sung, brought into particular rhythms and repetitions, as a musicality whose aim is to force open a conduit to the supernatural. As the physicist Fred Wolf observes: "Shamans invoked changes in nature by calling for them to appear. They didn't just call out, they sang the words. A word, when spoken in a certain way, invoked the thing spoken and not just a symbol of the thing spoken."[10]

Wolf's examination of shamanistic practices opens out to a series of observations and speculations that bring physics and shamans together, as well as the relation between vibration and healing. "Healing could simply consist of reinvoking those sacred sounds in the body. In other words, by singing or reciting the correct sounds, various parts of the body, out of harmony, could be brought back into harmony. Perhaps this is what the shamans do when they chant."[11] In understanding the world as a primary web of vibratory energy—where each object, body, or form contains its own particular "pattern"—Wolf sees in shamanism an important tradition of practices. "The key was the ability of the shaman to tune to my frequency of vibration and then absorb the illness from me."[12] Yet such abilities lie not only in detecting particular frequencies, but also in the acts of singing and chanting so as to conjure and transform existing conditions.

Energy

Although crying certainly calls for attention, to deeply affect the social scene, it is through singing we reach the central vitality of these volumetric vocalizations. There are moments when the body feels a certain energy, a particular melodic drive, to turn vocalization toward a musical gesture. I let the mouth open to this sudden impulse, one that sounds out a variety of resonating harmonies. This instant of banal song, of mundane musicality— that of amateur singing—expresses a particular quality of the voice, that of lyrical resonance. As a special sounding, singing draws the energies of the body outward, to fill the chest, to ring the mouth, and to flood the nasal cavity with vibration. The entire body seems to stand up, resounding with tonality, whether real or imagined, tuned or not. What I'm interested in is the mouth in the midst of such pleasure. This special instant of orality. What seems to mark this moment are the intensities by which body and sound unite to capture us in a certain weave, a *magic* found at the center of speech, for are not all words waiting to be sung? To resonate in a union of body and spirit, between each other, and toward collectivity?

Such pleasures no doubt are to be found in karaoke clubs. Of course, karaoke is a phenomenon inflected by all sorts of fantasies of stardom, of taking the stage and of emotional outpouring. Yet these extra elements only further highlight singing as a vocal that *takes us over*. That captures us, and that inculcates certain empathy: to witness song is often to sing along. It is precisely a mouth movement aligned with musicality, turning the spoken into vibration, resonance, and composed or raw energy. In singing, we externalize a part of ourselves distinct from the spoken self, that is, one touched by the powers of sonority, which affords a channel for affective change. As with the case of sound poetry (see chapter 4), singing aims for the "uniqueness of being" that voice so poignantly (and problematically) expresses.[13] Singing leads our speech into poetry and, further, into powers of collective transformation.

These potentialities are fully supported by singing's connection to fantasy, role playing, cross dressing, and general masquerading. Singing, in other words, leads us to the stage, to the *staging* of such potentiality, as that particular site where the mouth may twist or queer itself, to fill with so many alternative words and lyrical expressions. The stage is a space for the investigation of what I might call "dirty identity"—for posing, flexing, and inflecting the performances of the self with added imagination; to come out, to celebrate, and to finally announce a true or unique self, possibly, but one that might also only come alive there before a crowd, in the lights and explicitly, through a lyric that enables and frees, at times, a closeted self. It is equally showing as well as sounding.

Indian

The dynamics of singing leads us into various social settings and scenarios, underscoring the *publicness* originating in the cry: an emotional vocalization that extends beyond the semantic and yet brings into relief a space of communicative power. From weddings to funerals, birthdays to religious celebrations, singing often accompanies, if not lends to fueling the social narrative of passage or inauguration. One interesting example that I'd like to consider can be found in the Papago Indians of the Southwest United States. A tribe whose origins date back to the Aztecs, the Papago are a "singing tribe." Living in the arid landscapes of Arizona, in areas that due to their harsh and demanding conditions have left them quite alone, the Papago's ceremonies are shaped and driven by the magic of song. According to the Papago, songs first appear in one's dreaming, given as gifts by the Elder Brother, the spirit of all earth, and which are meant to be sung during specific ceremonies. What marks these songs are not necessarily their celebratory tone, but rather the power that they wield: each song is vocalized in *anticipation* of a desired event. In this way, songs and their lyrical content speak of what may come; they are sung so as to influence the materialization of events, for instance, the season of rain.

The example of the Papago highlights the metaphysical power of the singing voice. Like the chant or incantation, song must be appreciated as opening up a forceful and affective channel that aims explicitly to overcome the ordinary; song, as Adriana Cavarero suggests, as a bringing into relation.

> What is really at issue in speech, in my view, is a vocalic relation that convokes mouths and ears, making the uniqueness of the voices vibrate in their resonance. This resonance, the first matrix of every poetic song, does not exhaust its meaning only in determining the musicality of language. Rather, the meaning of the resonance lies first of all in the vocal relation to which the singular voices are called.[14]

This relational intensity promulgated by "resonance"—by that sounding of the voice—creates that special link, from one to another, and which we can continue to follow as a force that extends you and I toward *something more*.

Returning to the Papago, song can be appreciated as raising the mutuality found in vocal resonance to that of a communion with greater spirits: the resonance passing between singular voices is brought into a specific musicality aimed at the greater community, to the force of the natural world. "Magic will be worked if the description is vivid and if the singing or the recitation is done, as it should be, at the right time and with the right behavior, on behalf of all the people."[15] The ritual of the song may be understood to capture that conjuring dynamic of voicing, a resonance tuned to the particulars of a certain season and a certain gathering, and through which processes of transformation and renewal are evoked. To sing then is to capture the imagination of the other, to draw us into a resonating circle, and to raise such voice upward, toward all that may come to shape our culture, as unseen or mysterious force.

Singing brings us explicitly into the realm of the spiritual, the theological, and the metaphysical; in short, into rituals of transcendence, as well as that of sharing. Most religious practices have as part of their traditions an element of song and singing; song features as an enduring behavior that may overcome the various alterations, modernizations, or evolutions advanced within a given religion, functioning to cohere a particular constituency. Song, in other words, carries us through mundane existence. It is the voice that literally may rise above, to remain tuned to a greater lyrical presence.

Such power of song also appears in another important example, that of the songlines. Found in the cultures of aboriginal peoples of Australia, songlines act as geographical intensities linking people to the earth, its animals, and all forces of worldly presence, and especially, to the Ancestors.

So it was, on this First Morning, that each drowsing Ancestor felt the Sun's warmth pressing on his eyelids, and felt his body giving birth to children. The Snake Man felt snakes slithering out of his navel. The Cockatoo Man felt feathers. The Witchetty Grub Man felt a wriggling, the Honey-Ant a tickling . . . The mud fell from their thighs, like placenta from a baby. Then, like the baby's first cry, each Ancestor opened his mouth and called out, "I Am!" "I am—Snake . . . Cockatoo . . . Honey-ant . . . Honeysuckle . . ." And this first "I am!," this primordial act of naming, was held, then and forever after, as the most secret and sacred couplet of the Ancestor's song.[16]

Bruce Chatwin's account of the origins of the songlines opens up this first voice—this "I am!"—to that of animate life, where each first earthly being is born through its naming; a primordial call materializing into bird and flower, rock and water, dingo and cactus. Importantly, the *place* of this ancestral beginning is essential.

Each of the Ancients put his left foot forward and called out a second name. He put his right foot forward and called out a third name. He named the waterhole, the reedbeds, the gum trees—calling to right and left, calling all things into being and weaving their names into verses. The Ancients sang their way all over the world . . . They wrapped the whole world in a web of song.[17]

Vocalizing the world into being, the Ancients are the original singers; they embody or exemplify the primary, generative resonance of voicing by aligning the singular body with earthly and spiritual force—individual bodies with greater ancestry—all of which finds continual renewal, as well as contemporary modulation through song. In walking the earth, creating social bonds, hunting and gathering, and grappling with cultural change, the aboriginal peoples negotiate all these relations through the songlines: those original songs that brought everything into being and that afford the movements of social life a means for sharing knowledge, helping each across the great expanse of the continent, and supporting the existential traversals of individuals (especially those under threat).

Singing as they walk, each lyric evokes a link between this body and this place, a resonance not only between singular voices, but also between one voice and those that have come before, and that live on within each additional verse.

Siren

The power of singing, and its relation to place or territory, carries within it a deep political implication. As the example of the Australian aborigines attest, singing is a sacred rite by which entire communities are sustained. Such politics surrounding the singing voice finds a recent example in Israel where calls to ban women from singing in public have sparked protests. As Yakov Halperin, a religious member of the City Council stated: "The female voice is beautiful and it is fine for women to sing to each other but we do not want men exposed to the temptation."[18] The ultraconservative attack on women publicly singing has led groups throughout Jerusalem to stage public sing-a-longs, drawing forward debates on equality throughout Israel as well as the more general representation of women in public space.[19]

The gendered politics central to this debate leads us to the problematic ways in which women are often placed in the position of the "one without voice" and instead are aligned with the erotic force of nonsemantic vocalizations. As Cavarero argues, such equations bring us back to the mythological legacy of the Sirens' song, and the fact that singing here is imbued with the "monstrous" image of the tempting female (leading us to narratives of the hysteric). This image, for Cavarero, overshadows the actual speaking voice found within the original Homeric narrative, and ultimately turns "the feminine voice" instead into one that "seduces and kills, and that has no words."[20]

Transgression

Acts of singing then are central to practices of resistance, as well as appropriation; a type of territorial dispute is embedded within raising the voice. Singing may be a form of deep resonance and collective transcendence, but it may also provide a means for transgression.

In the practices of the Shakers this operates through the formation of a particular cosmology, where ritualized gatherings sought to create direct links to the heavens by way of all sorts of embodied expressions. "Trembling, shaking, twitching, jerking, whirling, leaping, jumping, stamping, rolling on the floor or ground . . . some barked and crowed, and imitated the sound of several other creatures . . . Also, hissing . . . rejoicing by loud laughter, shouting, and clapping their hands."[21] The Shakers' unique rituals of shouts and movements manifest also in their hymns, often combining "strange tongues" and "plain English," for example:

Lo all vo, hark ye, dear children, and listen to me
For I am that holy Se lone' se ka' ra an ve'

The lyrical fervor of the Shakers delivers a radical sonority, where glossolalia, collective singing, and the shaking body perform a deeply spiritual action, yet one that takes *possession* of the body. Song is utilized as a rending operation so as to raise the voice and connect the order of the community with the powers above.

Gospel further highlights this radical and enduring fever of song. As James Baldwin depicts in *Go Tell It On The Mountain*, moments of salvation are explicitly conditioned and supported through the power of singing.

> There was a great noise of praying all around him, a great noise of weeping and of song. It was Sister McCandless who led the song, who sang it nearly alone, for the others did not cease to moan and cry. It was a song he had heard all his life:
>
> > *Lord, I'm traveling, Lord,*
> > *I got on my traveling shoes.*
>
> Without raising his eyes, he could see her standing in the holy place, pleading the blood over those who sought there, her head thrown back, eyes shut, foot pounding the floor. She did not look, then, like the Sister McCandless who sometimes came to visit them, like the woman who went out every day to work for the white people downtown, who came home at evening, climbing, with such weariness, the long, dark stairs. No: her face was transfigured now, her whole being was made new by the power of her salvation.[22]

Singing is a primary, revolutionary force aimed at territories that might be conditioned by the social and political, yet also hover above the terrestrial and the earthly. In other words, singing is a vocalic force that steers us toward spiritual life, heightened rapture, and the intensities of transformation. To conjure, to lift up, to hold true. Therefore, to sing is to drive forward a certain confirmation of an order, yet one often in tension with another.

History

Estonia's "singing revolution" is another instance where we may glimpse the collective and transformative intensities around song. The important traditions of singing within the country were greatly repressed during the Soviet era and led to the formation of underground singing clubs. That singing was understood as subversive to the state draws us close to the ways in which song may spirit collective verve, to provoke both nationalistic pride as well as the courage to revolt.[23] Lyrical resonance and collective gathering hover behind this moment of the opened mouth, vibrating the single body into greater communion and belief. That such singing was to punctuate the independence of the country in 1991 is captured poignantly in images of people holding hands and raising their voices in unison against Soviet tanks.[24]

Singing thus brings us into a highly relational and expansive web, where single bodies link to local communities, to social and religious orders, and further, to metaphysical and transcendent powers. The instant of sounding the voice, to bring forth a lyric, a melody, a vibration of body and air, not of the spoken but of the compositional and the harmonic, the spirited and the angered, is an orality charged by the fevers of history and politics, friends and families, and nations.

Elaborating this view further, the work of e-Xplo at the Sharjah Biennial from 2007 draws singing out as both a space for memory and community, as well as that of political representation. Developed in the United Arab Emirates, their project *I Love To You* is a collection of audio recordings made of migrant workers singing. Focusing on the status of migrant workers, e-Xplo sought to draw attention to their rather ambivalent position within the region, not only for a type of critique, but also as a means for allowing voices to be heard. Singing enabled an articulation that points toward the specificity of the one who sings (bringing forward a critical view onto the context of this voice), while nurturing a feeling of self-presence, however fleeting. As the recordings reveal, the workers find comfort and joy in recalling a song from home, which also led to a renewed sense of entitlement. This lyrical instant, as a reverberation running *through* and *out* of the body, performs to reconnect them to something familiar, something *of their own*, opening up within their rather difficult conditions a feeling of assurance and community.[25]

Singing may provide us with an important means for *having voice*; when words seem to fail or fall short, subsumed by greater historical and political forces, a song may circumvent such difficulties to deliver a poignant channel for harnessing community and for challenging the orders of certain situations or ideologies. By using the mouth as a lyrical chamber, contorting it with often eccentric movements and unexpected phonemes, syllables of protest or of love, the singing body may disturb the genealogy of particular power structures, power languages, and discourses of the lawful; it may return us to traditions, some honored and others repressed, and it may also seek a break with what has come before, to search for new spaces of resonance for the crafting of another body, and another community.

Anger

The power of song, as I've tried to capture, wields an explicit force and magic, one that readily attunes self and other, as well as community and the spiritual. Song seems to pass through and around social life to open up and support so many channels of contact and communion. Singing as that powerful and empowering resonance that fills the body with energy, and which seems to cascade outward, as a vocalization tied to greater presence: to celebration as well as mourning, to passion and rapture. These intensities of song, and their political stakes, take on another pitch when shouted.

Within this territory of crying and singing, the shout as well as the scream figure as additional volumetric voicings. They raise the voice above normal conversation, to reach well beyond the single listener, and at times can rend the body with its forceful energy. Shouting and screaming bring us not to the generative resonance Cavarero identifies at the core of being, in the voluptuous power of song, but rather to the raw tensions found in needing or commanding each other.

To follow such tensions we may turn again to Israel, and specifically to the Golan Heights, and the area known as Shouting Hill. The Hill is located exactly on the border between Israel and Syria, one that prior to the war in 1967 stood firmly within Syria. With the subsequent division, families have been brutally separated, turning the Hill into a frontier across which the voice attempts to pass. Shouting to each other from across the border, a width of land roughly 400 meters wide at certain points, political dispute embeds itself within marriage celebrations, weekend visits, and family reunions, all of which are challenged by this gaping distance. Such personal events must negotiate this interfering border, an occupation of land whose violent logic is additionally heard in the shouting voice. The shout, while conveying particular information, resounds with the unmistakable brutality of national defense.

What interests me in the shout and the scream is just how explicitly the physicality of voicing comes forward, to perform as a direct conveyance of emotional struggle, pain, or anger. While singing resonates according to a particular musicality, contoured through melodic lines and structures, the shout of pain and struggle (not to mention the scream) is a sheer force of raising not so much voice, but its essential condition, its existential need: to manifest emotional presence. We may follow this intensity in the work of Marina Abramovic/Ulay and their performance work *AAA–AAA* (1978). With the artists facing each other, and shouting directly at, or *into* the other, repeatedly, the work confronts us with an obliteration of resonance. *AAA–AAA* is a brutal sounding, where voice operates more as a process of expulsion and extrusion, *release*. It is a surge of the body, with the mouth pushed open and giving way to an absolute thrust of raw vocalic power.

I do want to take note, for a moment, of the title of the piece, this triple "A" repeated or mirrored back to itself, two vocalizations face to face, or standing off in a complicated doubling—each voice trying to overwhelm the other. Yet the "A" calls forward not only the sound of the shout—a punctuated "AH!"—but also a first character from which language follows, the essential figure leading up to the name. "A" forms the primary and original mouth movement, the gaping mouth, the opening up—the cry, or the exclamation—a vocalic sound from which a concrete reference will follow: "*a* cat," "*a* building," etc. "A" is a foundational vocal event, which loops together the audibility of the shout and the primary act of naming, as well as that of the hungry body. This circle of the mouth, as a primary gape, performs as the first gesture of articulation, which contains that complex interweave of want and of self-expression, naming and needing.

AAA–AAA performs this fundamental articulation, brought up in volume and staged as an event. Although nothing in fact follows—there is no sociality here, no conversation as such, only an absolute exhalation that slowly tears the vocal cords, vibrating the facial bones, throttling the neck, with each body shaking. The two artists bring us directly into this essential moment, this existential vocalization, this first mouth movement, filling it with such audible and somatic force.

The work finds echo in Marina Abramovic's earlier performance, *Freeing the Voice* (1975). Here we find ourselves back to this essential scene of the shout, which like *AAA–AAA* is better described as *pure exclamation*. Although, in this instance, Abramovic is alone, lying with her head tilted back over the edge of a platform and facing outward, toward the audience, and toward a camera. She is prostrate, but also, upside down—both positions that no doubt articulate a *suffering body*, or a body in supplication. Certainly a body seeking transformation, obliteration, catharsis. The shout, which is at times more a scream, is forced out to rid the body of its own embedded energy. To free the voice is to also expel it from its bodily shelter, one defined by certain cultivation. It is to turn against language, encircling us within a raw vocality.

Arrest

I want to juxtapose these observations of the shout, as an elaborated or forceful cry—of suffering turned into sudden voicing—alongside the shout that commands; not the freeing enacted by Abramovic, but the arresting performed by the authorial shout. As Louis Althusser suggests, shouting, as that instant of raised voice, is also utilized by those who attempt to grab us from behind. Althusser's examination of the operations of ideology, as an arresting capture of the individual, is elaborated through a story, that of the moment of hearing from behind a voice that shouts—"Hey, you there!"[26] This voice is thus perceived, following the embedded and fully incorporated directives of ideology, as a voice that *hails* us: without even seeing from whom this voice originates, we hear it and readily assume our own guilt; we stop, pause, and possibly flinch, preparing ourselves for capture. Althusser's shout turns this particular mouth movement, this primary orality, of needing and naming, into one of command. As Althusser states, "Hey, you there!" directs us toward a fully scripted end, that of our guilt as a subject, a subject bound to an ideological apparatus.

The shout thus goes both ways: it empowers us, to demand from the world a certain sustenance, to announce ourselves as a wanting body, and also as a body not only with a name, but one that can also name the other; and at the same time, the shout is our suffering under such powers, of being arrested by the hailing of others, and also, by the authoritarian voice that is always already waiting—that already has our name on its list.

These shouting voices, that need, name, call or command, circulate finally in the recent Occupy movement at Zuccotti Park in New York City and the operations of the human microphone. In response to not being able to amplify a voice, the protestors would pass along an orator's words through a shouted repetition; from shout to shout, the words would be carried, so as to reach those farthest away. The action highlights the ways in which the shout, and all such raised voices, contends with distances as well as situations of unrest. These echoing shouts make us hear the voice as so readily caught, that struggles within the mechanics of need and ideology—the voice and its imminent arrest. The voicings of Occupy expose the shout to the weight of its own reverberations, for what may return in the wake of the shout, or the cry and even the song, are the critical tensions pitting law and lawlessness against each other.

Shatter

All such intensities of volume, that fill the mouth with fear and anger, longing and passion, expand the reach of the voice to rivet the air with emotional force. The shouts traced above—and all shouts, songs, and cries in general—no doubt have as their ultimate horizon that of the scream. To return to Edward Munch's *The Scream*, the mouth in the midst of such gaping emptiness opens the way toward hearing what is often so unable to be spoken of.

Munch's scream, so silent on the canvas, reappears again within recent demonstrations. In this case, not at Zuccotti Park, but in London, at St. Paul's Cathedral as part of protests in 2011. Although, in this instance, the scream is silently articulated, with protestors waving their hands for 1 minute to mark the passing of the imposed deadline for them to vacate the area.[27]

This rendition of screaming highlights the tensions surrounding the protesting voice in the public sphere, where decibel levels and the occupation of space may draw out the feverish limits of the political process. Yet screaming may also find its way out, to shatter the lyrical space of expression and articulation; while the scream is captured in such blood-curdling films as *Halloween, Texas Chainsaw Massacre,* and *Nightmare on Elm Street*— as a gaping mouth that expresses the core of horror in general, and that appears in all such horror films—it finds more considered expression in the project of artist James Webb, titled *Scream (Guernica)* (2008). Webb's screaming work additionally locates us within processes of national protest and history, in this instance in Madrid, at the Reina Sofia Museum, giving way to a sense for the emotionality so central to voicing. For the work, the artist recorded members of the museum staff screaming in front of Picasso's painting *Guernica.* If the scream can be thought of as that "presymbolic manifestation of the voice,"[28] here it aims itself at the artwork to force a tension between the image and the brutality it seeks to depict. The scream is mobilized as a means to unsettle the static image through a force of voice and its extreme audibility—to draw out its history in relation to the present, and to instigate a reflection on today's political situation. The work sought to utilize the embedded narrative held within the painting, and to animate its historical truth by way of a screaming body, so as to charge the public realm with a particular resonance: a force of angst, want, and desperation (Figure 3.1).

FIGURE 3.1 *James Webb,* Scream (Guernica), *2008. Installation view, with certificate of permission from the Reina Sofia Museum, plus audio recording amplified from concealed speakers, "MMXII" exhibition, the Johannesburg Art Gallery, 2012. Photo: Anthea Pokroy.*

Webb's *Scream* captures all the tensions and promises announced in the intense voicings I've been collecting here. From crying to singing, shouting to screaming, the raised voice resolutely calls toward a greater arena of collective rapture, social gathering, national spirit, and divine communing. The sonorous energies of such vocal outpouring is central to all such projects, energies commanded by the ability of the body to sound itself, to breathe so much melodic and emotional life into its vocality, one in turn fully contorted by a lyrical poetics: of journeys abroad and journeys home, of battles and salvation, of love and heartache. What we hear in such explicitly voluminous expression—whether in the tearing rupture of fright, in being overcome with passion or grief, or in that moment of collective song—is the edge of the sounded voice as it longingly aims to conjure more than itself.

4

Gibberish, Gobbledygook

At times, speech runs over itself. Words twist and tense under pressure, tripped up by inertia, or with urgency, perverted by nervous shaking or under the spell of secret pleasures, to produce slippages, ruptures, and even nonsensical outpourings. These trouble the trajectories of proper speech, to unsettle or complicate their meanings.

Voice is mostly constrained to the arena of communication, relegating the nonsensical to a periphery. At the same time, speech is to be appreciated as a movement that oscillates between sense and nonsense, between semantic voicing and its gibberish counterpart, each supplying the force of expression with material and drive. It is my view that gibberish, in being peripheral to voice proper, occupies a rather central position within the oral imaginary. Might we hear in the nonsensical a manifestation of an oral poetics underlying speech in general? Is not the "noise" surrounding verbal articulations a sort of raw matter supporting rather than undermining our faculty of speech? As Jean-Jacques Lecercle posits in his work on nonsense, or *délire*, "the abstraction of language is based on the material expression of oral drives," suggesting that language functions according to an inherent "corporeality" that is always prone to heightened expressivity, and madness.[1]

Uniqueness

The work of Adriana Cavarero provides a productive view onto the relations between sense and nonsense, speech and vocality, and what she refers to as "the saying and the said." This is supported by a critique of the philosophical legacies, stemming from the Greek concept of logos, that have withdrawn "the voice" from rational thought—a "logos" wherein only "the semantic counts."[2] Such legacies for Cavarero have ultimately relegated the primary phonation of voice to the periphery.

By capturing the phone in the system of signification, philosophy not only makes a primacy of the voice with respect to speech all but inconceivable; it also refuses to concede to the vocal any value that would be independent of the semantic. Reduced to an acoustic signifier, the voice depends on the signified.[3]

The challenge posed to such philosophical thinking aims to ultimately return us to an appreciation of voice beyond the strictly semantic, encouraging a deeper vocalic listening and discursive view. Accordingly, voice is mapped as an extremely rich and essential materiality whose sounding nature may support the semantic, yet importantly by remaining a force of corporeal presence, one leading out to a resonance of relation "to which singular voices are called."[4] Voice, in other words, is the very "uniqueness of being" that affords, in its recognition, the promise of joining together. "The voice, indeed, does not mask . . . It communicates the uniqueness of the one who emits it, and can be recognized by those to whom one speaks."[5] Voice is thus inextricably tied to identity, as the uniqueness that supports one in *having* subjectivity.

Cavarero's argument, while supplying a rich opportunity for recuperating "voice" as a primary sounding, as a process that need not arrive at the semantic, seems to also suggest voice as a "natural" property of the individual obfuscated by the directives of the rational and the reasoned. I would question whether her embrace of the "truthfulness" of voice, as that which gives way to our unique presence, also strips away the more playful and performative dimensions voice comes to wield. It is my argument that voice is neither fundamentally rational and reasoned *nor* primarily sounded and unique. The enactments of speech rather draw upon *and* debate with the semantic, finding support from the possibilities revealed when we open our mouths. In short, I'm interested in how the uniqueness of voice is often revealed when we play with words, impersonate others, parade the heterogeneity of our identity—that is, by enjoying the oral imaginary, which teaches us how to elaborate the spoken by way of all sorts of nonsense.

The relation of sense and nonsense, of the semantic and the sounded, is to be appreciated as the very fabric of voice, and it is the mouth's ability to flex and turn, resonate and stumble, appropriate and sample, which continually reminds us of the potentiality promulgated in being an oral body.

Poetry

The legacy and practice of sound poetry gives us extremely dramatic demonstrations of this potentiality. Intentionally aimed at overwhelming the supposed gap between language and body, words and their breath, sound poetry can be heard as a vital catalog of the choreographies of the mouth, and all the micro-modalities I'm tracing here. Its project, from text composition to *poésie sonore*, evidences how sound and sense intermesh, conflict, and ignite their operative dynamics, giving way to a voice in tension. As Velimir Khlebnikov wrote in 1920:

> What about spells and incantations, what we call magic words, the sacred language of paganism, words like "shagadam, magadam, vigadam, pitz, patz, patzu"—they are rows of mere syllables that the intellect can make no sense of, and they form a kind of beyonsense language in folk speech. Nevertheless an enormous power over mankind is attributed to these incomprehensible words and magic spells, and direct influence upon the fate of man. They contain powerful magic.

Khlebnikov's ideas of the "beyonsense" of language seek to recapture a primary voice, a "folk speech" from which words are no longer purely rational, but rather may perform as magical entities. As he further elaborates:

> Its strange wisdom may be broken down into the truths contained in separate sounds: *sh, m, v*, etc. We do not yet understand these sounds. We confess that honestly. But there is no doubt that these sound sequences constitute a series of universal truths passing before the predawn of our soul. If we think of the soul as split between the government of intellect and a stormy population of feelings, then incantations and beyonsense language are appeals over the head of the government straight to the population of feelings, a direct cry to the predawn of the soul or a supreme example of the rule of the masses in the life of language and intellect, a lawful device reserved for rare occasions.[6]

Khlebnikov's theories of language and the spoken parallel much of Cavarero's understanding of voice as a primary sounding, and the instantiation of individual uniqueness. Khlebnikov, in turn, sees in the dominance of Western logic an eclipse of the sounded, and what we might refer to as "the poetical." Much of sound poetry throughout the twentieth century adopts this conceptual position, seeking out a "lost voice" of the raw and the lyrical, a voice caught in the rather imperial directive of reasonable speech.

I'm interested to follow these appeals to the "predawn of the soul" and how voice figures on this horizon of recuperated words specifically through a reshaping of linguistic matter. Such work brings us closer to the mouth, and deeper into the performativities of the oral. It also evidences the voice as precisely a tussle between sense and nonsense, revealing the uniqueness of the individual as a figure shaped by the pressures of proper speech, as well as the opportunities found in *not knowing*—in the gobbledygook of experimental orality.

Ur

Cavarero's thinking finds expression in much of the work of sound poetry, whose critical relation to language is most often aimed at overcoming the explicitly narrow confines to which vocality is held. As in Khlebnikov's work, the "reign of the semantic" is understood to delimit the full potentiality at the center of voicing.

With Kurt Schwitters' *Sonate in Urlauten* ("Sonata in primeval sounds") or *Ursonate* (a poem written in response to Raoul Hausmann's phonetic poem from 1918, which starts with the line "fmsbwtözäu"), such articulations find particular form, whereby each vocable trespasses the scene of signification.

Structured as a traditional sonata with four movements, *Ursonate*, which between 1921 and 1932 saw countless revisions and additions, takes the listener through eccentric twists and turns of speech formed around a repetition of consonant and vowel sounds as seen in these first lines:

dll rrrrrr beeeee bö,
dll rrrrrr beeeee bö fümms bö,
rrrrrr beeeee bö fümms bö wö,
beeeee bö fümms bö wö tää,
bö fümms bö wö tää zää,
fümms bö wö tää zää Uu:[7]

In parts of the work, a series of articulations unfold that with each utterance adds and subtracts from the previous line, operating according to what Renato Barilli terms "electrolysis" where "the material of expression freed of semantic adhesives (lexemes and morphemes), is pronounced letter by letter, each of its various minimal components exploding in the acoustical space."[8] Thus we hear a slow deterioration of language whose pronunciation aims to formulate a new type of signification akin to that of glossolalia. Theorized by Michel de Certeau as "the beginnings of speech"—that primary voicing that punctures the mechanics of meaning making and the "institution of speech"—glossolalia is figured as a composite of the pre- and the postlinguistic: "Every glossolalia combines something prelinguistic, related to a silent origin or to the 'attack' of the spoken word, and something postlinguistic, made from the excesses, the overflows, and the wastes of language."[9]

A *speaking in tongues*, glossolalia suggests many aspects sound poetry comes to embody. From notions of the "holiest refuge" (Hugo Ball) to primitive voicing, or what Raoul Hausmann calls "mega-mneme" (great memory) at the deep center of voice, sound poetry mimics and mines glossolalia as an oral reservoir specifically bridging the pre- and postlinguistic—that is, the central origin *and* enveloping edge of language.[10] *Ursonate* attempts to return us to such a primordial form of speech, unearthing an imagined enunciation and unsettling what passes as language.

Gibberish may be heard as the instantiation of the particular pleasures of having words in the mouth, and all the excitations of self-sounding: to feel the passing of breath as it rises up from within to fill the throat and mouth, conditioned and contoured by the larynx, the muscular force of the tongue moving back and forth, to the final drop onto the lips, as sudden energy flows over to reverberate behind the ears, along the skin, and within the environment around. All such movements underscore the voice as an assemblage of signification *and* the corporeal, reminding of the material poetics of language.

Semiotic

Importantly, Certeau attempts to salvage glossolalia from "interpretations" that locate this speech back into the folds of meaning, and that ultimately hear within the broken syllables secret meanings. "Whereas glossolalia postulates that somewhere there is speech, interpretation supposes that *somewhere there must be meaning.*"[11] Rather than recover meaning in glossolalia to circumscribe the sounding body, Certeau seeks, as with Cavarero, to underscore the tension such utterances pose to language—as pleasures of prelinguistic mouth movements that unsettle the contours of meaning to suggest a project for a postlinguistic future. *Ursonate*, and sound poetics in general, can be appreciated to draw upon glossolalia as an imaginary center—a linguistic unconscious—to refigure speech according to primary utterance.[12]

Such views find support in Julia Kristeva's work on the semiotic. Kristeva's theoretical construct of the semiotic, outlined in her *Revolution in Poetic Language*, aims to capture "the drive" behind language and "the symbolic."[13] Poetic language is understood as the force of such drive, a transgression onto the territory of the symbolic; it enacts a certain unsettling of linguistic structures, and the inscriptions of the symbolic, to give way to what I might call "the wild." Importantly as Kristeva suggests, poetic language (*and the wild imagination*) performs by "imitating" the positing of meaning. In other words, by working within and alongside the operations of the symbolic, poetic language "mimes" the functionalities of meaning production; it necessarily *parades* as language while overflowing, through heterogeneous practices, the borders of signification.

Following Kristeva's view, it is clear that sound poetry, as gibberish stretching the mouth, aims for the operations of language, of the symbolic, by explicitly tracing over it, breathing into it, spitting on it, and pulling it apart. In doing so, it pries open a gap on the terrain of signification; it speaks through the oral imaginary, to rescue a disappeared voice.

Brute

The strategies of Schwitters, and others such as Hugo Ball, find elaboration in the developments of Lettrism (Isidore Isou) and Ultra-Lettrism (François Dufrêne, Gil J. Wolman), as well as in Henri Chopin's *poésie sonore*. Throughout the 1950s and 1960s, sound poetry would continue to create works that occupy the peripheries of language, speaking over and under the word and extending the oral as an extreme dimension, a highly elastic existential void. For example, François Dufrêne's Ultra-Lettrist works eliminate the remaining particles of language in favor of a corporeal, spasmodic performance, where noise is drawn out of the mouth through an exaggerated communicational thrust. His *Triptycrirythme* from 1966, for example, consists of guttural retching, recorded and layered to draw forward a body of phlegmatic intensity. The work is a voyage into the throat, an oral cacophony captured on the way in and out of the body. It wheezes, it spits, it moans and pants, it chokes, forcing out the movements of the vocalic mechanism into a reverberant noisescape.

In this regard, sound poetry must be emphasized as a cultural project that radically highlights the paralinguistic and paragrammatic arena I'm examining throughout this study. Its extensive dedication to unlocking the central vitality of the spoken, of all oral phenomena, provides a catalog for surveying the tensions of the mouth: sound poetry's conscious attempt to reinvent the operations of speaking, echoing the profound poetics of the glossolalic, evidences the intensity of the sounded body.

Paralleling Dufrêne's phlegmatic approach, the works of Gil J. Wolman equally leave behind the word and the letter in favor of hyperexpressions focusing on breath. His *La Mémoire* (under his general concept of Mégapneumes) from 1967 captures the artist exhaling and inhaling into a microphone to a point of tactile abrasiveness. The single drawn breath comes to reveal the individual body moving in and out of itself—a wheezing vessel full of animating energies that also exalts a primary poetical matter, that of the breath behind every utterance. As Dufrêne would state of Wolman in 1965: "the BREATH alone founds the poem—rhythm and outcry, that cry, content contained, until now, of the poem: of joy, of love, of anguish, of horror, of hate, but a cry."[14] This essential, anguishing matter exemplifies sound poetry's return to primary origins, breaking down language through an elaboration of oral actions. As Bachelard states, "In its simple, natural, primitive form, far from any aesthetic ambition or any metaphysics, poetry is an exhalation of joy, the outward expression of the joy of breathing."[15]

Sound poetry's brute vocalizations bring forward an unsteady and evocative weave between language and music, the poetic and the sonic, to open up a dynamic audibility lodged within the physicality of voicing. Twaddle, balderdash, hogwash, bunkum, and other acts of general gibberish thus find their point of optimal cultural reference in sound poetry. Out of the mouth comes an assemblage of paralinguistic expressions, forcing sense and sound into tense confrontation. The realignment of voice and its signifying energies, as an elemental force of giving presence and of sharing in worldly vibrancy, renders the mouth a dramatic organ: a mouth tensed by multiple drives, imaginaries, memories, and linguistic structures. The force of gibberish, as I'm following here, can be heard as the base of all utterance: a ground upon which speech is constructed, wielded, or exercised, as well as exploded.

Noise

Gibberish delivers a break onto coherence, and the communicative act. It necessarily ruptures the message, but it does so by letting in what I might call the *messy base of wording*: the noise *underneath* speech. Gibberish captures that foundational static out of which wording arises. As Michel Serres suggests, the background noise of the world may subsume human speech in its volume while also supporting the emergence of form—out of the noise, that primary babel, new language may appear.[16] Accordingly, it is my view that gibberish is an education onto the relation of sound to speech, sense to nonsense; it reminds of the primary phonetic noise by which we learn to articulate, and from which we might draw from again, in acts of parody, poetry, romance, or storytelling, as well as through the simple pleasures of a disordered semantic.

Here I'd like to bring into consideration Charlie Chaplin's use of gibberish in the film *The Great Dictator*. Produced in 1940 as a critical parody of Hitler, and the rise of the Nazi regime in Germany, Chaplin uses the voice as a primary vehicle for staging the brutal absurdity of the dictator's ideological views. This appears immediately in the opening scene, where the first lines spoken by the dictator (as well as by Chaplin, as this was his first talking film) wields an unforgettable force of effusive gibberish:

Democrazie schtunk! Liberty schtunk! Freisprechen schtunk![17]

Chaplin's nonsensical enactments throughout the film highlight language as a material susceptible to mutation, appropriation, and poetical transfiguration that no less delivers potent meaning. Such oral moves on the part of Chaplin reveal to what degree gibberish may perform to supply the thrust of speech with the power of critique.

Under the pull of gibberish, language appears as raw material, shaped and reshaped by the movements of the oral cavity, the guttural push of the diaphragm, and all the wet viscosity of tongue and fleshy cheeks. Words reveal their inherent breath and muscularity, and especially their sonority within the dynamism of gibberish. The spoken, as that vital channel by which self and other meet, and from which social structures gain form, if not intensity—the very coming into being of a subject—must be understood to be significantly fueled by its own periphery, by that which is excluded.

As Adriana Cavarero reminds, the primary sounding behind each word is a vibrant and elemental event that both supports language, and the profound delivery of speech, while also being relegated to an exterior of language. Yet it seems important to also hear in this "uniqueness" a fundamental ambiguity: while Cavarero hears this primary vocalizing as the opportunity for coming together, as democratic initiative, as shared resonance, such a voicing is also driven by the force of noise, and its uncertain trajectories; by hybridity, collage, excitation, and rupture.

Returning to Michel Serres, gibberish is precisely the noise of speech that drives the mouth and yet in return is repressed by its lingual functions. In other words, the voice is always in tension with the corporeal conditions essential to its sounding. The social and linguistic structures of language come to tune the mouth, locating it within a grammar of expressions intricately connected to the operations of speech. We might appreciate and understand "vocal noise" as that lost object—the *petit objet a* theorized by Lacan from which desire gains its motivating drive; through its relegation to the outside of language, noise operates behind the scenes, to supply the production of words, and related fantasies of voicing, with hidden momentum.[18]

Gibberish, and all such nonsensical vocality, is to be appreciated as the primary body of linguistic signification. Rather than hear noise then as outside any system of communication, we can understand it more as a central mechanism that must nonetheless remain invisible, or at least, unspoken. By drawing it back onto stage, Chaplin's canny speech, for example, proposes a complex theory: that gibberish is in fact aligned with the monstrous and the potentiality for violence. A noise whose destination is never certain, yet one tuned to the force of transgression, violation, and play.

By putting nonsense into the mouth of the great dictator, we come to hear in gibberish not only a critical vocabulary, a parody of fascism, but also how the return of the repressed (noise) may also lead to terrible actions. For what is so remarkable about Chaplin's emulation is how closely it aligns with the original.

Hitler speaks without notes, initially in drawn-out fashion for emphasis. Later on, words come tumbling out, and in overly dramatic passages, his voice is strained and barely understandable. He waves his hands and arms around, jumps back and forth excitably, and always seems to be trying to captivate his attentive, thousand-strong audience. When he's interrupted by applause, he theatrically stretches out his hands.[19]

Chaplin's nonsensical speech must be heard as a parody that also directs our attention to the terror of the spoken in general. I would emphasize that noise is always operating on this line, this difficult thread, between the barbarous and the poetical; between arrest and the emergence of form; between a return to primary origins—the "uniqueness of being"—at the center of the spoken and the awful ways in which "original" versions of the body can also unleash violence.

Although the "beyonsense" of language may give way to new figurations of the spoken, as a needed poetical slippage for the oral imaginary, it may also unearth the terrible force of abuse.[20] It strikes me as necessary then to hear in the rich primary sounding of the voice a medium also for disagreement, debate, and dispute. The uniqueness of being, and its energetic vocalic sources—the rich reservoir of the poetical—can form the basis for joining together, but also for breaking apart; for explicitly posing arguments, and establishing counter-publics, which more than ever may demand a thorough tussle, and deeper creativity, in finding the words.

Clown

I want to identify a potentiality at work in sound poetry and supported, in turn, by what Judith Butler terms "performativity." As Butler outlines, "performativity" is precisely a "reproduction of norms"; it is that mechanism by which power maintains itself, preceding the subject and reproducing through him or her its particular logic. Yet, importantly for Butler, in such reproduction exists the potentiality of things "going awry," to ultimately "produce new and even subversive effects."[21] Power is then always negotiating an inherent tension that pulls at its peripheries, agitating its limits, which in the case of sound poetry, and the force of gibberish, realigns the mechanics of vocalization toward that feverish territory of noise, "beyonsense" and *not knowing*—all signposts for the discursive limit of certain bodies.

Within this performative space of *not knowing* appears the possibility of a certain movement, not only of vulnerability and violation, but also of escape, parody, and clowning—that of things going awry. As Chaplin readily knew, buffoonery functions as an expanded platform—of bodily gesturing, as well as that of mouth movements, which can radically condition and contour a diversity of relational exchanges, and especially, ways of dealing with power: to push and pull within the dictates of the normative. His antics promulgate a steady catalog of maneuvering in and around the social structure, often slipping in and out of the law. The apparent "stupidity" of Chaplin's persona uncovers a potentiality in *not knowing*: by carving out a space to the side of the orders of language, bodily integrity, and social acceptability, one may gain certain elasticity, a means for bending and flexing within the strictures of ideology.[22]

In pursuing gibberish we can identify this as a question of the mouth. Returning to sound poetry, I would suggest that much of its creative work appears through a *clowning of the mouth*, a *not knowing* the words; if the mouth can be understood as that architecture by which words are literally shaped—where syllables take up residence—breath given form and language expelled, then to search for another linguistic order is to pull at that architectural container; it is tool and retool the cavity of the oral. In short, it is to turn the mouth into a clownish form—to *misbehave*. Such maneuvers also appear as the making of a potential—of new wording, which is equally new narrative, of the subject within the space of the social. It is to insert an X onto the line of the contract of language and power, knowing full well that we might be duped, but which might also give way to a new possibility for negotiation: to prolong that space between sense and nonsense (wherein identification resides) and in support of "who can be a subject."[23]

To return to Butler, and her outline of masquerade, of "gender performativity" and of queering the lexicon of bodily presence, I want to apply such views so as to underscore clownery as a mode of the performative. The clownish specifically gains definition by operating *alongside* a functional and stable body, adjacent to its productive actions and social participation. As Chaplin shows, clowning gains its power through its ability to turn the human form into something mechanical, something out of place and often at odds with "proper" performance. By standing in contrast, it carves out a space for more spontaneous and dissenting behavior.

As I map in the chapter on laughter, Henri Bergson's analysis of the comic gravitates around a number of points; one in particular focuses on the notion of the mechanical and the inelastic. The comic is driven forward at times by that moment of the body appearing disjointed, tripped up, or out of sync. Is not Chaplin's—and other's, such as Buster Keaton's—humor articulated through such instances of mishap, error, and failed articulation, of the stupid? In short, clowning is a gestural vocabulary based on *becoming other than (properly) human*, an other that is most often at odds with productive mechanics—of labor and capitalism, of normative behavior and gender identity. Clownery, in others words, articulates a vulnerable body. In doing so, it animates and reanimates the body *in parts*, a body coming undone: Chaplin's elongated shoes and shuffling gait, his twittering mustache, his blower hat and cane—these are not only props, rather they function as parts of his body that when animated come to life, to trip up others, to aid in foolery, and to provide sudden opportunities for escape, romance, and charm. Fragmenting the body into pieces, the clown, as the one who does not know, and who is vulnerable to language and power, is often unwittingly able to slip through.

Is not sound poetry, as that arena for extending the operations of the voice, calling forth a "right to speech" often undermined by the powers of language? A right to the verbalization of the "beyonsense" according to strategies of the stupid, the clownish, foolery, and mishap? And in doing so, expanding the public sphere toward that of the outcast or the underspoken?

Impersonation

Shifting to another figure of gibberish, and another cultural territory, I'd like to extend this study by focusing briefly on the topic of animation, and the character of Gerald McBoing-Boing. An animated character from the 1950s, Gerald's special talent for speaking only "sound effects" literally draws out the relations between voice and sound. In the first short film from 1950, we find Gerald, a small boy of 2 years, whose entrance into language is disrupted by his uncanny speech—in the place of words comes various sounds, such as train whistles, lions, bangs, and bonks. In response, Gerald's father attempts to correct the boy's problem by sending him to school, which lasts all of 1 day before Gerald is sent home for making "noise." Ostracized, Gerald finally runs away from home, to be rescued by a radio producer who hires Gerald to provide all the sound effects for his productions. From riding horses to gunfire, dog barks to bells ringing, Gerald soon turns into a radio star. His ability to voice an entire orchestra in a later film secures Gerald's fame as a genuine celebrity of the radiophonic.

While Gerald was becoming a radio star in the 1950s, Isidore Isou and Henri Chopin were recording their own paralinguistic experiments, aiming for the full breadth of oral capability, a sounded poetry. In some ways, Gerald McBoing-Boing may serve as the ultimate sound poet, a sort of mascot for sound poetry's project, where the voice is finally freed from the constraints of language to adopt a plethora of potential identities: to become pure effect. That is, to arrive at a state of pure animism—to become a *sonic body*.

As Henri Chopin's work demonstrates, sound poetry may focus on the mouth, as that oral dimension of possible utterance, but its productions unfold equally as extended bodily performances. With Chopin, the entire body shivers, quakes, and is doubled on itself through the use of microphones and the tape recorder. His works throughout post–World War II avant-garde culture are marked by this performative use of technology, fusing it with body sounds and gestures. The "body is a factory of sounds," Chopin proclaimed,[24] and it is precisely by amplifying, cutting, and splicing together that such a body is reshaped into a "postlinguistic corporeality"[25]—resulting "in a thickly woven fabric of sounds and supersonic rhythms . . . timbre, phonic thickness, body."[26]

What then might we discover in this expanded field of poetic sound, where the mouth cultivates new configurations? And that redraw the signifying lines between voice and language? While sound poetry searches for a zero degree of speech, to that primal breath and grain of voicing, the sphere of animation opens up another perspective on the topic of gibberish, that of impersonation, voice acting, and by extension, masquerade. It's my feeling that each cultural practice offers us a vital lesson in how to debate the very nature of voice, giving us the lead to reforming the mouth into alternative movements, soundings, and performances: sound poetry in the field of the existential—of primary myths, tensions, and in search of the first breath—and with animation, through a proliferation of fantastical characters and their vocal identities.

To expose this horizon instantiated by animation, I'd like to consider the amazing voice work of Mel Blanc. Working in the animation studios of Warner Brothers in the 1940s and 1950s, Blanc was extremely important in crafting the work of cartoons and their popularity. He was the main voice actor at this time, supplying the voices of such animation characters as Bugs Bunny, Porky Pig, Daffy Duck, Tweety Bird, Sylvester the Cat, Yosemite Sam, the Tasmanian Devil, and Speedy Gonzalez, among others. Having started his work in radio in the 1930s in Hollywood, Blanc soon became known for his vocal abilities of impersonation, leading to an array of comedy skits as well as characters. With his move in 1937 to cartoons, Blanc astounded audiences with his characterizations.

Interestingly, the diversity of voices Blanc was able to perform has as its backdrop the immigrant communities around which he grew up. As Blanc reveals in the first lines of his autobiography: "Even as a child, I heard voices. Now, I don't mean to imply that I was daffy, as in duck. I was simply fascinated by the way people spoke, particularly immigrants from other countries. And in the flourishing industrial center of Portland, Oregon, circa 1918, a medley of foreign accents caught my ear."[27] It was precisely these foreign accents encircling the young Blanc that captured his imagination and found their way onto his tongue, and eventually, into the mouths of numerous animation figures. Such oral circulations remarkably underscore the dynamics of impersonation, as a *speaking other*, to ultimately reshape the particular contours of speech and the self. Referring back to the works of sound poetry, might we hear in these poetical vocables an impersonation of an imaginary voice, that of the primary sound? A ghost in the mouth that drives the speaking self toward the fantastical, the brute, the existential, and the glossolalic?

I'm interested to introduce the figure of Mel Blanc as a further expression of what may happen to the voice when we speak differently. While for Cavarero such a voice may find its way toward relational resonance, in a song tuning self and others upon a horizon of conjoining, it might equally give life to a range of animated and funny figures. Acts of impersonation open the mouth up to adopt multiple personas, to collect together in the speaking body a chorus whose vocalic expressions are certainly more than one; a gibberish from which new voices may take shape, whether in the form of a daffy duck, a deranged leader, or a sound poet.[28]

Delirium

Gibberish performs as an extremely vital mouth production, allowing the full force of the body, as that vessel of absolute resonance, of animistic exuberance, of alien imagination, and of that "uniqueness" Cavarero outlines, to rise up and capture itself in various types of speech, and in the process, to contort not only the lips and tongue, but also the power passing between mouth and word.

Returning to Jean-Jacques Lecercle, his work evocatively renders the inherent "delirium" (délire) central to language—a delirium not of absolute madness, but one driven by the profound recognition of language's vital link to the body. "Instead of using language as a transparent and docile instrument, and looking through it at the world outside, they [delirious authors] focus their attention on its workings, on its dark, frightening origin in the human body."[29] The delirious work thus identifies the often-repressed origin of language, to revel in words as so much raw matter and whose potentiality resides specifically in its ability to generate correspondences across things, bodies, meanings, origins, cosmologies, graphisms, etc. Madness, yes, yet one that is compelled by the interactions of sense and nonsense, and the oral drives that may turn language into a base for radical poetics, as well as a vibrant social life.

5

Gasp, Growl, Grunt, Sigh, Yawn

Speech and voicing are inextricably connected to breath and breathing; the respiratory movements of inhaling and exhaling are the very operations enabling voice *to sound*. Yet these operations also figure in the lexicon of mouth movements, and oral expressivities; breathing and the thrust of the lungs occur in and around words, and the ordering of the voice, to interrupt, punctuate, and contour enunciation. Here we enter the territory of the throat, and the resonating glottal space, and lower, toward the vibratory regions of the diaphragm, the ribs, and the lungs. Gasping, grunting, sighing, and yawning—which also refer us to moaning and groaning, croaking and creaking . . . rasping . . .—all are punctuated breaths, strained respirations. Inhalations and exhalations shaped by various emotional and physical states, in response to external and internal events, and to aid in certain performances and labors. What also seem so pronounced in these bodily and oral events are their sonorous equivalents: each, in forcing and capturing breath, lead to an audible instant, a sound that immediately evokes.

Huh!

Something appears, to suddenly cause a fright; one is taken aback, there, in a moment of surprise. *To gasp* . . . that sudden inhalation sent quickly back toward the lungs, to sound as a rising note, unmistakably heard and jarring.

Gasping is fully aligned with certain external events or actions; an intensity of energy passes between the event and the body, from the world to the individual, materializing in this quick breath, and this sudden sound. Such drama can be readily glimpsed in various sporting events, most notably, at a tennis match. The quiet of tennis certainly lends to glimpsing the gasp, and in particular, as it circulates well beyond the single body and into the crowd. There is something extremely dramatic about the collective gasp—each body on the edge of its seat, enthralled by the game, each following the ball as it careens across the net, back and forth, sending the players into all sorts of directions. Something then happens—a missed hit, an amazing stunt, or an acrobatic move, *will he make it!* and the gasp arises: everyone inhales, quickly, sending the reverberations of so many clenched throats into the arena.

The gasp tunes itself then to the events around; or, it is rather tuned by the events, sharply plucked, like a string, at a certain moment to suddenly resound. The mouth, in turn, suddenly opens; or rather, it is *broken open* by the event, cracked by the scene. In this way, the gasp is extremely sympathetic, and reactionary, sending the body into a small violent jerk. Gasping is a form of identification, yet one that we may not want. We gasp in surprise, in fright, and in awe, suggesting that even while we look, what we witness is also *too much*. The gasp, in fact, is a moment of suspension: by inhaling we actually hold the breath, for a moment, to see what will further appear. Is this *really* what I see? What will happen next? We are literally violated by the external event, poked, and forced backward, for the gasp not only opens the mouth, but it pulls the shoulders up—we are *pushed* by what appears; we hold our hands up to our mouth as if to cover our sudden opening—to protect ourselves from what may come next, what may suddenly come close, all too close.

I'm reminded of countless film scenes where the gasp performs as the very pinnacle of suspense: everything glides over an uncertain time and space, maybe within a haunted house, with the main character looking frighteningly this way and then that way, through shadows, and especially around corners, until finally, something happens: a cat jumps forward, a knife appears, a body motions—to send the character (and us) gasping. The gasp finally confirms the suspense of the scene: it is a literal punctuation that sends us jumping. The gasp gives us away.

The quick movement of the gasp though is also given terrifying elongation in certain films, for instance, in *Invasion of the Body Snatchers* (1956). The climax of the film must certainly be highlighted as that moment when the character of Miles looks down onto the face of Becky, exhausted after running for their lives from "the others," those who attempt to capture and take over their bodies—in this instant, when he suddenly kisses her only to realize she is no longer Becky, no longer the one he loves, but rather, she is *other*, taken over by an alien form. Here we are given an extreme close up of Miles' face, with hair disheveled, beads of sweat dropping across his cheeks and forehead, and then suddenly, with his mouth opening, aghast at the realization: that all is lost. The scene lingers for some seconds, and we are left not to hear his surprise, in the form of sudden gasping, but to witness it as a mouth opening, quivering, unable to speak. This scene of the gasp radically echoes that other gaping mouth captured in *The Scream* by Edward Munch—a painting whose hauntingly vague figure continues to reverberate through time, with this open mouth, a gaping void, whose dead silence suggests a scream, a shout, a cry and also, a gasp: hands thrown up around its face, the figure literally shivers with existential uncertainty, aghast, breathless, struck dumb by the unknown in front.

Gasping is a moment of breathlessness: not only may we gasp in fright, but we may also gasp when in need of breath. *Short of breath*. This breathlessness is precisely the fundamental operation underneath the gasp; the sound of the gasp is the sound of a body reaching a terrible threshold, one unquestionably marked by horror, fright, and death. The fright at the center of gasping parallels the fright of this breathlessness: it is the moment of glimpsing the end, the fall, the crash, punctuating the very punctuation of the gasp—with its sudden inhalation, the sound of the gasp rises quickly, to end in an abrupt "choke." The thrust of gasping, as the fright and threshold of the end, is thus described precisely in this sonic breath, as the literal "last gasp," contributing to this lexicon the reverberations caught there in the throat, and whose small sounding is so greatly meaningful.

Raw

In tandem with the gasp, grunting also performs as a raw orality, as an instance of dynamic breath. It also highlights the mouth firmly as an expanded oral chamber, where voicing may operate more as vibratory thrust than sounding syllable, more as bodily expression than worded act. Interestingly, grunting locates such expression close to that of the animal kingdom, and in particular, to the pig. In reading dictionary entries, grunting is most often referred to as "making the half-nasal, half-throaty noise that a pig makes." While whistling brings us closer to birds, and biting to the bat, the grunt is particular to the pig, and to the orders of filth, mud, and the lowly.

Grunting mostly captures an instant in human endeavor close to physical exertion, occurring in moments of labor, as in sport, as well as in sexual intercourse. To grunt occurs clearly to the side of intellectual work, articulating in its sudden vibration a body close to the ground or in the midst of intense action.

This can be appreciated by recognizing how the grunt is a rather "unvoiced" oral sounding, a vocable lodged in the larynx. Physiologically, it is a forced expiration against a partially closed glottis, allowing for the lungs to maintain a higher volume over a longer period of time. Accordingly, the grunt appears commonly, like the gasp, in the game of tennis. (The concentrated silence of the tennis match makes for an optimum arena for witnessing in detail such athletic soundings.) Numerous tennis players are famous for their grunting, which can even lead to reprimand due to its loudness and intrusiveness, for instance, in the case of Monica Seles at Wimbledon (1992).[1] Yet grunting here is not only about disruption. Rather, it functions to maintain a player's muscular rigidity in the trunk of the body, especially just before making a shot. Timing the rhythms of play to one's breathing is essential, also experienced in any type of physical labor. Controlled breathing allows for directing intensities, and grunting appears as a sonic register of this, where the energy of breath is held in the lungs until the optimal moment of release and attack.

With closed mouth, grunting vibrates the throat; it is an exhalation of a breath held inside, and then released up into the back of the mouth. It sounds as a closed-off reverberation, a force of the laboring body. Yet we might speculate on the degrees to which grunting, as a particular mouth movement fully tied to exertion and forceful thrusting, may also spur us on, toward those realms of physical intensity: in other words, might the deep thrust of the grunt felt in the chest and behind the mouth encourage us in our lower habits, a vocable participating in the play of human form and its erotic strengths, and whose soundings bite down onto language? Gasping and grunting align us with fright and force, and the vulnerabilities, strengths, and passions of being a body; as such, they each perform as intense exertions in and around the oral, specifically tuned to disciplined and suspenseful actions in which language is left behind.

Beast

Grunting is also closely related to growling and its deep guttural sounding, leading us further into metaphors of animality. Such intense vocalizations (and metaphoric resonances) are put to use within death and black metal, as well as grindcore music. The vocal technique known as "the death growl," prevalent within these musical genres, connotes not so much the pig, but rather, the realm of the undead; we move from the pigsty to more dramatic fantasies of monsters and beasts. In this regard, the death growl delivers an unmistakable *beastliness*, which is played out not only in vocal styles, but also through a repertoire of dress and makeup: death and black metal fans are often marked by a particular "gothic" fashion, with bodies draped in dark cloth, faces painted white and hair dyed black, all of which registers a particular affiliation with the zombie.

The band Napalm Death, from Birmingham, England, has been important in the development of grindcore music, as well as the related death growl vocal style. Their debut album, *Scum* (1987) is full of such growling, with singer Nik Napalm (and later, with Lee Dorrian) perfecting the grunt and the growl. Lyrics such as—"A vision of life/On television screens/An existence created/From empty dreams"—are forcefully growled to sound out a nefarious vocality, a bolt of absolute guttural corporeality. This finds its ultimate expression in their song "You Suffer," which is held by the *Guinness Book of World Records* as the shortest song. Clocking in at 1.3 seconds, "You Suffer" captures the intensity of the growl in a single unapologetic thrust. The growl here is fully supported by the attack of drums, guitar, and bass, which thrash underneath this vocal matter. A shot of pure intensity, "You Suffer" unquestionably sums up the power of the throat.

Grunting and growling thus move between the metaphoric orders of the pig, and of slovenliness, to that of the undead and a general beastliness that brings us close to images of the devil (a figure central to black metal). Is not the growl and the grunt mobilized in various films precisely to capture the extremes of evil? To produce a voice explicitly beyond that of human morality? The devilish voice is certainly of a growling nature. For instance, the figure of Bain in *The Dark Knight Rises* (2012) no doubt gains much of his haunting intensity through his heavy granular speech (accentuated by his mysterious muzzle). We can also recall the more familiar Darth Vader, whose deep voice is punctuated by an extremely amplified breathing, all of which sound from behind his metallic mask to signify in pure form the haunting presence of an evil body. This is not to overlook the terrifying guttural voice from *The Exorcist* (1978), jarringly spoken by the possessed girl Regan to unleash a narrative that brings god and the devil into forceful contact. Strength and death, animals and zombies, possession and radical evil come to produce an altogether different orality, one close to that of a raw and mutated nature: a lowness of pitch evoking the lowness central to abject form, of haunted bodies and all that lurks down below.

Grunting and growling are thus mouth movements aligned with *possession*—of extreme strength and athletic moves, as well as of demonic intensity. Their explicit sounding immediately signals physical (inhuman or superhuman) exertion, locating the mouth well back into the chest, and back toward the ground. (There is nothing angelic about a grunt . . .) Grunting, in this regard, is more a bodily sounding of all that resides prior to voice, and the fuller articulations of the mouth. It is a compressed breath, a tightened throat. Hence the characterization of the beastly and the monstrous: grunting and growling locates us well behind the frontal vocalizations of language.

The grunt and growl find additional crafting in the work of Runhild Gammelsæter. A Norwegian singer and artist, Gammelsæter is most known for her work in the metal bands Thorr's Hammer and Khlyst. Yet the experimental range of her voice work is captured prominently in her solo album, *Amplicon* (2008).[2] Throughout the 11 tracks, Gammelsæter combines an incredible range of vocalizations, bringing the essential growl of black metal into conversation with more melodic, sonorous, and experimental techniques. Here, the grunt and the growl expand toward a broader grammar; *Amplicon* can be heard to harness the grunt as a poetical voice, whose lyricism seems to unsettle any strict dichotomy between human and animal, between angel and devil, and between the animate and the dead.

The abjectness expressed by the grunting voice is suddenly flushed with a sublime energy, leading to an extremely ambiguous articulation of voice. Gammelsæter forces a rupture onto the conventions of the death growl, performing against any stable referent or vocal body. Her voice instead comes to model a chameleonlike vocality, bringing the pig and the princess, angels and beasts into conversation, and rendering the mouth an instrument for the production of multiple identities.

Tired

The body falls back, pulled by a sudden movement—of chest and lungs, throat and jaw, opening to draw in breath, and then to expel, an action that also integrates the arms, the shoulders, often outstretched, in parallel correspondence to the jaw, all brought together in a fully choreographed event. We know this movement, this sensation, this break in the general rhythm of breathing and being.

Although gasping and grunting are full of sudden energy, either in moments of fright and surprise, in the labors of the body, or that of monstrous imagination, yawning, on the other hand, is a lapse in energy. It is slowness and tiredness that fills the mouth with an elongated and rather limp expenditure.

The yawn though is also an extremely dramatic mouth movement, one that can capture the whole body, now and again, throughout the day and night, to announce through such unmistakable body language that "I am tired." Yet that's not all: as we know, the yawn unquestionably signals to the other, even without wanting to, that "I am bored"—we may protest, we may follow up the yawn by insisting to our friend or colleague otherwise, but it's no use. The yawn radically signifies, as a paralinguistic gesture interjected into conversation, by bearing a noticeably visible and audible movement. Its kinesic quality can be seen to put on display a rather ambiguous communicative force: while the yawn certainly signifies, we may always fall back upon the excuse of physical, and therefore, uncontrollable tiredness. In the yawn, I am thus caught between my body's own physical needs, its unconscious patterns, and the dynamics of a conversation, which may also lower the body's rhythms, to embarrassingly draw the yawn out. The yawn accordingly is "read"—like all forms of body language—by our interlocutor as some inner symptom whose outward expression fully signifies.

Social

I dwell on the yawn because it is such an unmistakable mouthing, signifying through an extremely dramatic oral event. It is a profound mouth movement within this arena of heightened respirations, and their various orchestrations.

An interesting expression of the yawn can be found in the sound works of the Brazilian artist Raquel Stolf. As part of a larger body of work, *Céu da boca*, focusing on the relation of voice and mouth, words and their sounds, which the artist has been developing since 2007, Stolf has recorded and composed various mouth movements and oral soundings, including that of the yawn. "This project is a kind of (auto)study that combines fictional (and concrete) exercises about hearing/listening and editing my own voice (with its constituent vertigo), other voices, and other soundscapes 'empty of voices'. The work involves also some interests in movements, pauses, and situations on/inside/of/under the mouth: eat, yawn, sneeze, speak (some word or nothing), and breath (some air or some word)."[3]

The particular work, "Bocejos e um espirro," focuses on the yawn (with the integration of a sneeze); it captures a series of yawns and composes them one on top of the other, to create a polyphony of exhalation, a continual *emptying out* that seems to move us, with each yawn, across its auditory field. In this way, the yawn turns into a sort of topography, with its peaks and valleys, its depths and surfaces, dramatically shaped by the body, its breath, and the mouth, as that primary cavity. ("Yawning" in fact also denotes a "gaping cavity, or wide expanse," drawing out a correspondence between oral space and geography.) With each yawn we feel the weight of the body, leaving itself, almost falling—a descending rush, toward its final collapse, or repose.

Stolf amplifies the yawn as a mouth movement full of compositional structure—how it orchestrates a range of oral movements and reverberations. As part of these movements exist others, that also rise up in an attempt to mask the yawn's sudden appearance. While we may try, the yawn is a force that is difficult to squelch—the body tries, at times, to suppress the sudden break, the rising movement as it starts from deep below, to trickle up from the back of the mouth and finally, to pull the head back and the mouth wide in its unmistakable intervention. But mostly, it fails.

Such elaborated movements of yawning are also interestingly extended through its rather contagious nature. It is almost certain that if a person yawns in public, another is sure to follow. As Robert R. Provine states, "Yawns are propagated, being passed from one person to another in a behavorial chain reaction. This mindless connection involves social behavior of the most primal sort."[4]

Studies indicate that such contagious yawning may be the result of an instinctual need to keep alert. For instance, pack animals are often seen yawning while at rest, such as lions or dogs, which may send a contagious signal throughout the pack designed to encourage watchfulness, like a ripple that literally affects those around to cause them to yawn in response. Others suggest that yawning is a form of empathic behavior, functioning to perform within social circles: contagious yawning passes much quicker among friends and family then in the company of strangers. To share a yawn with those we are close with is to encourage intimacy, to draw together in a sympathetic, echoing bodily expression.

Yawning though also leads to feelings of embarrassment. To push the yawn back down is to regulate the body according to certain perceived decorum; even without being directly in front of another, the yawn is often subdued. For instance, riding on the subway, we drift along in silence, watching other passengers, maybe flicking through a book. Then, we feel it—the yawning sensation stirs, and we surrender to its composition. Still, we feel compelled to quiet such display by drawing our hand in front of the mouth so as not to reveal, in such unabashed openness, the back of the throat, or to announce our tiredness, or sense of deflation. The yawn, in other words, seems to require a primary act of repression: to literally suppress its uncontrollable intrusion. Is it because yawning exposes the mouth in all its gaping excess? Or that its contagious potential performs an elemental form of infection? The yawn as some sort of secret?

> The air itself is one vast library, on whose pages are for ever written all that man has ever said or even whispered. There, in their mutable but unerring characters, mixed with the earliest, as well as the latest sighs of mortality, stand for ever recorded, vows unredeemed, promises unfulfilled.[5]

Within this "aerial library" then might the yawn also perform, to litter its pages with the outpouring of a certain miasma, that of all the particles expelled through its exulted breath? Contagion may generate and support a ripple of empathy, to nurture the flows of common life, but it may also contaminate the social body. The gesture of covering one's mouth when yawning is an etiquette that may also minimize the threat of infection.

Present

The mouth, in particular, is called forth to represent the subject, the name of this body, as well as the agreements that govern its behavior. From laughing to spitting, whispering to lecturing, wheezing to coughing, the mouth is always held within a multitude of negotiations particular to social life. It must open up continuously, and without end, to participate, to perform, and to contribute, not to mention sustain the individual body; at the same time, it is always prone to slipping, to breaking in with too much, to *mouthing off*, or to leading us into uncharted territory. From speaking to oneself ("is he crazy?") to laughing too much ("she's so loud!"), the mouth is that physical organ responsible for the project of the self—its presentations, its liberations, and its struggles. It navigates the line between center and margin, proper and improper, order and disorder, to catapult us forward, through languages and soundings, or to sabotage our integration.

To return to the yawn, it is clear that such a seemingly uncontrollable act can undo any number of conversations—is it even conceivable to yawn in the middle of a job interview? In this way, we might wonder if the yawn is precisely a mechanism for leading us *out* of situations we don't want to be in. Whether in moments of boredom or tiredness, yawning seems to keep us on guard, pulling the body into all sorts of stretches and extensions so as to prepare the muscles and our alertness, to draw us out and make us attentive to what might lie in wait, elsewhere. It announces we are tired, but it does so by keeping us awake. This can be seen to occur also in moments of nervousness. Often when we are nervous, we yawn, which may aid in bringing energies forward, to keep the body flexible, to bring air into the lungs, and to announce to ourselves that things are about to begin.

Recently, studies have also suggested that yawning is a process of regulating brain temperature. Conducted by Andrew Gallup, a research associate at Princeton, tests indicate that people yawn more frequently in ambient temperatures lower than their bodies. The hypothesis "proposes that yawning is triggered by increases in brain temperature, and that the physiological consequences of a yawn act to promote brain cooling . . ." Furthermore, "the cooling effect of yawning is thought to result from enhanced blood flow to the brain caused by stretching the jaw, as well as concurrent heat exchange with the ambient air that accompanies the deep inhalation."[6] Following Gallup's proposal, the yawn can be appreciated as a further instance of the mouth performing to regulate and negotiate relations with the world.

As with gestures of biting and chewing, kissing and, of course, breathing, the yawn allows for regulating one's situational conditions—it pulls in what is outside, and let's out what is in, to modulate the intensities of being a body in particular places, and in this case, within particular temperatures.

The mouth, as that point in the body of dramatic opening, is the very site through which self and surrounding interpenetrate. The voice operates within this larger vocabulary of oral gestures and movements, choreographies and modalities, giving expression to inner moods, while also exchanging with the outer environment. I question the yawn then as solely a physical act, as a physiological regulator. Rather, its circulation through numerous social situations evidences a complexity that starts to suggest the yawn may be a mouth movement explicitly aimed at resisting or combating social life: signaling our deflation in the face of another, or preparing us for imminent attack.

Rest

In exploring the various productions and exertions of the mouth, it becomes apparent that each carries within it a high degree of ambiguity. Whether in whispering, biting, or laughing, or indeed yawning, each unfolds varying meanings that are often antithetical. Such ambiguity indicates a particular condition of the oral in general, as one always already extending and diffusing the semantic by way of the body. As Paul Ekman's studies on facial expressions attest, the subtle differences found in the appearance of the smile, for example, articulate extremely varied meanings, from anger and fear to joy and worry.[7] Extending this across the entire field of mouth movements, we find that each twist or turn of the mouth, each flexed pucker of the lips, conveys a range of emotions, psychological intensities, biological needs, as well as social conditions. Although speech communicates much of the identity of the individual speaker, from physiological attributes, social positions, or ethnic backgrounds, as well as emotional being, the mouth is an extremely sensitive register of our affective state or moods, and their oscillations. Our sense for being in a certain time and place, surrounded by others, or alone, is expressed by so many tiny gyrations, expressivities, and paralinguistic flourishes, silent and sounded, gestural and articulated, noisy and sensual, that encircle and prick the mouth.

In this regard, the mouth and the voice inflect one another, extending or shutting down each, in moments of mute embarrassment (tongue-tied) or in sudden displays of heightened appeal (to speak from the heart). We might glimpse such dynamics also in the sigh. Sighing is such a gentle expression that no less carries great communicative energy. It turns the lips into soft curtains blown back by an exhaled breath and whose audibility is heard as a descending note. A dramatic *rest*. Starting from the back of the throat, the sigh carries forward as a slow build up of breath whose sudden release gives way to sound—of all the energy of the body collapsing. Sighing is an articulation that makes palpable the very sensation it expresses, that of despondency and loss, of letting go or of giving up.

It is no wonder then that the bridge connecting the courthouse and the prison located in Venice is referred to as "the bridge of sighs." Passing over the Rio di Palazzo, the bridge connects the new prison with the interrogation rooms at the Doge's Palace and was given the name by Lord Byron. As the final point before a prisoner's entry into the cell, the bridge offers a view of the lagoon through its small windows. It literally functions as the last view of possible freedom, ultimately inciting a prisoner to sigh. The sighing bridge carries all those sensations of loss and emptiness experienced and embodied by the prisoner: as a body soon to expire from the movements of social life.

Loss

The resounding connotations of the sigh are additionally located within the experience of melancholia. As Naomi Segal suggests, the bereavement for lost love central to melancholy may lead to the "incorporation" of the lost object of desire; the *body of the other* is held onto, as a sort of "phantom limb or second skin."[8] In this way, we bring the lost love into ourselves, in acts of conservation, to live within or through our own body. We literally *hold onto* that which has disappeared.

In complement to this interior life, Segal also seeks to follow its expressions on the outside, upon the skin, recognizing how "love enwraps" while "loss flays."[9] Love, in other words, plays out through a psychophenomenology of the flesh. This relationship between inside and outside produces an extremely volatile state, one that interweaves interiorized conservation with an externalized imaginary: we may feel "the pain" as if in a lost limb, in the expressions of an imaginary friendship, in an emotional process that attempts to materialize the lost body, directly on our skin. (To wear, or to continually touch the clothes of a lost love are also examples cited by Segal.) Thus "mourning and melancholia" channel into a desperate creative output; what is lost is given form in objects, things, and productions—a tactility that extends the interior pressures out across one's skin, so as to touch within our hands the body that has left us.

While for Segal we may "keep alive" what is lost through the making of a "shared skin," I'm interested to also hear in the sigh, an act of melancholic identification, as a vocalization that literally lets out what is held in. As an oscillation between tension and release, the sigh gives way to a concealed breath, a breath that literally blocks the throat; it leaves the mouth as a sudden exhalation that pulls the shoulders down, that drops the head to leave one in sudden despondency. Yet sighing is a type of "rest," one that also lets out what cannot be held onto; the resignation of a grieving body, it produces a form of conclusion, or resolve, however unbearable. It literally exteriorizes, and in doing so, may give shape, in the form of a breath, to all that we can no longer have.

Sighing is the sound of the body as it vacates itself, as it experiences the sensation of a creeping loss, of something *falling through* oneself to resolutely exit out of the mouth. In this sense, the sigh is a sort of rehearsal of one's dying moment: it shadows the body's ultimate gasp, that final sound and respiration.

Pressed

The intensities of all these respiratory events bring us closer to the relation of the lungs and the mouth, and the extensive terrain of the oral. They refer us to a history of feared contagion, as well as imaginings of the uncivilized. The improper vibrations that may pour out at certain occasions in the form of a grunt, a gasp, or a groan, or certainly even a yawn, come to map the peripheries of the spoken: the timed rhythm of respiration supporting the flow of words (as well as all other exertions) is also tuned to extra-expressive soundings. Their significations come to reveal a body, a subject in the throes of labor, sexual excitement, beastly expression, as well as fear and boredom, nervousness, or longing; a subject on the verge of transgression, loss, or rapture. These paralinguistic and kinesic gestures lend so much emotionality to being an expressive body. In this regard, they might suggest a sounded phenomenology of the mouth, functioning as primary voicings or respirations under the line of speech. In their sounds we might locate the point at which the body is impressed upon by the sudden weight of the world, by the surprises that lie in wait, and by the labors that demand our energy and our excitement. I hear all these small breaths and guttural vibrations as currents that ride under the voice and that communicate so fully without ever becoming a syllable.

6

Inner Voice, Self-Talk

In thinking about what to say, I hear the silence within. It starts as an unidentifiable collection, a hesitant murmuring—I see it almost as a darkness that begins to move, an uncertain matter in pursuit of form. Something starts to develop, to gain definition, dim at first and then slowly, mysteriously brightening, and suddenly, words appear. They break out of this darkness to bubble up, and reverberate as an inner voice: that is, they speak before I do. I can almost feel them, these words tickling the back of my throat with their soft, restless hands. In this moment, the silence within becomes palpable. Nothing stirs from my lips; no sign can be found there, not yet; no motoric semblance or physical energy passes from the mouth. Although, at times, irrefutably, a breath threatens to fill the mouth and pierce its cavity with a certain pulse—the voice wants to follow these interior, linguistic apparitions; it craves to billow out and be heard.

The drive is there, the voice always already connected to language, on the way toward the social, toward you. Words and voice are inextricably linked, bound together, a couple entwined. I hear this inner movement, these words before speech (and that also drives this writing), and in this hearing the voice longs to vocalize, to be articulated.

This inner sound radically situates voice well behind the mouth, within an ambiguous mental space, flexed by a silence whose resonating energy drives thought forward. Yet, can we call the inner voice, this silent wording, a voice at all?

Auditorium

I'm interested to linger here, within the uncertain interior of the body as it speaks silently. That is, to listen in on the *inner voice* as a voice that remains within our minds while directing so much of what happens on the outside. The inner voice is never a single voice though. Rather, it appears through a variety of registers, in a variety of volumes, at times only a soft murmur while at others as a full articulation of words, for instance in moments of reading to oneself. In reading, we follow the words and unmistakably "hear" them in the back of the mind, hovering in a sort of nowhere space. Our voice sounds within, as a shadow to the words on the page—*can you hear them now, while reading this sentence?* I hear them even in writing this: I'm searching for the words, one after the other, to cohere a sentence, to conjure the next step; the words come to "sound" in my thoughts before they fall onto the page, before they send my fingers tapping onto this keyboard.

Steven Connor explores the experience of silent reading precisely as a question of space; as he states, the stirring of the voice within is "the creation of an auditorium or *arena of internal articulations.*"[1] Importantly, for Connor, this auditorium of internal articulation is also to be appreciated as "not quite inner"; rather, this particular voicing generates a "new amalgam" of sound and space to which "there is no consistent visual or sonorous correlative."[2]

It is my interest to hang onto this new amalgam mapped by Connor, and to follow it through questions of not only sound and space, but also the ways in which inner speech, as well as related self-talk, enables forms of navigation and inhabitation—how the auditorium of the inner voice fully assists in orienting ourselves against the pressures of life.

Unsound

To search for words is to already stir the silence, to drum it up so as to extract a knowable and nameable flow, what is not yet an idea but more a thrust of possibility. All this movement, all this language, hovers as a deep matter—a resonant body full of voice; a voice full of silence. The inner voice as *unvoice*. It speaks to me, as if I am its partner, its quiet listener. At the same time, I already know your inner voice is sounding, as a resonating mutuality. In following these words, within the quiet page of the book, your mind tumbles with vocables that have first appeared as a stirring within my own.

What might we call this, this silence that sounds within? What type of speaking actually occurs within this auditorium of the "not quite inner"? Within this quiet resonance? The inner voice, as a subvocalization performs *under the skin*, to support while also haunting verbal articulation. In this regard, it is my view that the unvoiced and the voiced partner in a complicated doubling, to hinge onto the linguistic socialities of speech the unconscious fevers and emotional states that flit through the body. I may pose the unvoice as not a voice out front, but behind the face, yet one that assists in *bringing us forward*: a shadowy voice operating "behind the scenes" to give animation to the movements out front, while importantly lending to life within. An oscillation that, as Connor suggests, unsettles the fixity of inner and outer.

Denise Riley's important work on inner voice also explores this vocal dynamic. For Riley, the common notion of inner voice as "the voice of thought and conscience" central to our moral behavior too readily undercuts how it is also fully tuned to social life and the circulation of language as a public material. "Our thought is not secreted in a realm apart, in some innermost and sealed chamber of our being. Thought is no 'internal' thing and does not exist independently of the world or of words."[3] Instead, as Riley suggests, "conscience comes from the outside" and is importantly a question of "importation," not to mention "interpellation."[4]

> For inner speech is no limpid stream of consciousness, crystalline from its uncontaminated source in Mind, but a sludgy thing, thickened with reiterated quotation, choked with the rubble of the overheard, the strenuously sifted and hoarded, the periodically dusted down then crammed with slogans and jingles, with mutterings of remembered accusations, irrepressible puns, insistent spirits of ancient exchanges, monotonous citation, the embarrassing detritus of advertising, archaic injunctions from hymns, and the pastel snatches of old song lyrics.[5]

Riley's vertiginous account of the "inner" definitively punctures that sense of enclosure the word comes to imply; in contrast, "the self" appears more as a "membrane" impressed and pressing back onto the world around.

The inner voice addresses me as a type of vocal body, one whose shadowy articulations bring the spoken voice to life. It is not an essential voice, on the contrary; it is always linked to the concrete world outside. It is a type of madness driven by all the interactions, experiences, and sensations occurring around and within. The forcefulness with which the inner voice stirs must be recognized to unsettle understandings of "the spoken" as that which appears in front of the body, as an emission. The inner voice does not emit; rather, it hums along. It pursues numerous trajectories, haphazardly, while gaining feverish momentum at times. It is an operation that emboldens one in negotiating the intensities of being a subject, commanding as well as enabling types of reflection.

Subsequently, the unvoice importantly sets the scene for self-sounding, and for self-reflection; it may not expose the individual, within the social field—not yet—rather, it is the *preparation* for such voicing. In this regard, the unvoice may be aligned with what Jean-Luc Nancy describes as the primary resonance by which self becomes itself; the "pure resonance" in which the body is brought into relation.[6] A becoming-different, one differentiated by this resonance of oneself: to hear oneself, *as a body*, a cavity, sounding to oneself *as* another.

Subvocal

In tracking the dynamics of voicing, it is clear that the unvoice definitively *ghosts* the spoken. The history of the modern voice is a history of the split subject, the multiplication of consciousness, identity as always already divided, and by which voice is an operation that transverses these divides. It travels, migrates, and transgresses, negotiating the complex web of inner drives, outer structures, and all the emotional topographies of personhood. The unvoice is captured by such histories, central to their narratives, motivated by the image of the interior self and contrasted with notions of "the public." An interior precisely as that which is in relation to an exterior (theological, societal, familial, etc.). If voice is the thing that can go outward, into the world, it can also go inward, like a hook to extract and give shape to the murky inner world—of dreams and fantasy, of wishing and longing, to act as a guide.

The inner voice finds its amplification in current research in subvocalization technologies being developed by NASA. Scientists at the Ames Research Center in California are working with small, button-size sensors placed under the chin, and on either side of the throat, to pick up nerve signals occurring from subauditory speech. "A person using the sub-vocal system thinks of phrases and talks to himself so quietly, it cannot be heard, but the tongue and vocal chords do receive speech signals from the brain."[7] The technology is being developed for use in spacesuits, as well as for the purposes of remotely controlling devices in deep space exploration, though it could also find more ordinary application, for instance in telephone technologies. We might imagine a subvocal device that enables "telepathic" communications, particularly within noisy environments. A technology extending the reach of mobile networks. I understand such developments as extremely prescient of future modalities of communication, where we might speculate that voice as we know it may no longer be the same; rather, voice may be understood increasingly as nerve signals whose pulsations and charges can be sent through any number of digital devices. In this regard, the slow dematerialization pronounced throughout the modern may certainly, and finally, take over the human body, ushering in those disembodied vocal phantasms of previous radiophony, yet now as part of everyday life, as a silent speech full of communicative potential.

These technologies might also underscore the degree to which the voice is an internal movement, a "sound" that actually reminds us that hearing is firmly located behind the ear, in the back of the throat, within our neurological center. While we may learn how to speak by moving the mouth, fitting breath and word together within the architecture of the oral, the voice takes root within the mind, in the depths. It blossoms as an interior force, partnered with the mouth and the ear, and yet also partly separates from its physical mechanics, and whose autonomy may find greater future expression.

While Denise Riley proposes that our inner speech is precisely a "voice without a mouth" and partnered with an "inner ear," I'd counter such a view to suggest that if there is an inner voice and an inner ear, then surely there is an inner mouth. As I've tried to show, the mouth as an organ is not a single entity; rather, it is an elaborate system of parts, a highly charged, flexed, and performing assemblage that extends from the lips down to the gut; though this is already to limit it to its physical dimensions—we know well how the voice is already an expanded geography pricked by an entire constellation of psychosocial, sexual, and linguistic elements, which would suggest that the mouth equally starts and ends where our relationships take us. In this regard, the mouth is *all through our body*.

Madness

The experience of hearing voices leads us to the state of madness; verbal and auditory hallucinations, while symptomatic of certain conditions, such as schizophrenia, more generally inflect the very notion of the inner voice with an element of terror. The inner voice is always already prone to mad expression, toward the periphery of the rational.

But there is another dimension, that of depth, the depths of the body, where another language emerges, raucous, violent, full of consonants, and unpronounceable sounds, of screams and hoarse whispers. This is always threatening to emerge from the orifices of the body, to overcome and destroy the fragile language of the surface, to plunge the subject who is made to utter the sounds into the deepest madness: it is the scream—or breath-language of schizophrenia.[8]

Jean-Jacques Lecercle's description of the "depths of the body" that always lurk, poised behind the surface, as a "breath language," gives us entry into the slippery territory of the inner voice. Hearing voices within may assist in finding the words, but it may also unsettle the clear delineations that mark us as subjects; the inner voice always threatens to expose the central truth of individuality, as one of fragmentation.

The experience of hearing one or more voices in the head is captured in the entertaining film *Stranger Than Fiction* (2006).[9] The protagonist of the film, Harold Crick deals with the sudden appearance of a voice in his head and who turns out to be a fiction writer inadvertently narrating his life through her new novel. The voice, in other words, is Harold's own narrator; a voice-over that speaks to Harold his own thoughts, describing his actions as well as emotions, to the point of eventually predicting his own death. This playful use of the schizophrenic condition (in the film Harold actually sees an analyst, who diagnoses him with schizophrenia)—this narrative ultimately opens out onto reflections about life, relationships, and work, as well as dreams of the future. Subsequently, the voice in the head leads Harold to radically transform his rather dull life, from working as an insurance agent to a life of risk and uncertainty, that is, one full of love, generosity, and the promise of happiness. In other words, the inner voice supplies Harold with the courage to be *emotional*.

Stranger Than Fiction is yet another narrative of the split subject, a narrative of doubling that reveals to us how reality as we know it is only a construction whose design, in this case, is up to us to realize. Harold's inner voice—his narrator—is precisely a productive rupture, a second body (a repressed voice finally breaking in . . .) that supplements his own, and whose interference disrupts the patterns of the real to let in passions and possibilities, fantasy and the imagination. In this regard, the lesson of the film might be that it is precisely by tuning into our inner voice—the unvoice which at times requires deeper listening—that we might live a more fulfilling life.

Although I would also like to raise the critical question: is the inner voice to be trusted? Might the voice in Harold's head reveal the degree to which the inner voice is defined by the incorporation of a certain imperative, drawn out by a particular ideological value system, which in this case might be heard to emphasize happiness as only coming from an independence from the institutional and the mundane? That is, one that equates happiness with individual choice?

Michel Foucault's analysis of power, and the technologies of the self, readily suggests that the inner voice can be heard as one embedded logic among others by which ideology and power enact forms of subjection; conditioned by the structures at large, the inner voice might be a voice that returns us again and again to a certain administrative dynamic, *keeping us* firmly in place.[10] The inner voice is that sound whose radical influence literally directs us into forms and functions of a particular social order—to abide by the law. Yet it may also move us to challenge, manipulate, or seek out new routes toward pleasure and fulfillment. As the unvoice, I'd suggest it is also prone to mishearings, mad revelations, and spirited hauntings, all of which may paradoxically support a poetics of inner vocalization in negotiating the powerful grammars that define this voice and how it operates.

Sleep

The silent, inner voice is paradoxically an articulated figure; a second, shadowy body that at times may come alive, here and there, to extend our own. We are prone to particular slippages according to the pulse and tremble of inner speech, that quiet murmur just behind the throat, and which may also suddenly appear, out here, to affect and influence, to loop through the soundings of voice all that lurks behind with what is waiting in front. That is, to break out and into audibility. This audibility may be heard, at first, in sleep talk. Paul Dickinson's thoroughly evocative audio work, *Sleep Talk Recordings Vol. 1*, captures the speech that leaks out in the middle of the night.[11] Developed over the course of 1998 and 1999, Dickinson had himself monitored and recorded at a sleep center in Chicago. The subsequent recordings capture him speaking aloud, resulting in highly suggestive fragments of talk, murmuring, exclaiming; a nocturnal diary that literally ghosts the diurnal body located within the sociable movements of the everyday. As one transcription reads:

1999, November 1:

A gu zillz a wupa zed
yer up yer head
mmmmmmmmm—hyello
gone be a lill
piss what I dill
gettin' oola from yoot[12]

Eavesdropping on Dickinson's punctuated bursts of speech, this particular voice can be heard to occupy or spirit a liminal territory, a zone defined both by the social order of speech and the unvoice of the interior; a type of hybrid form laced through with interior and exterior forces. Dickinson's work gives radical suggestion for understanding the mouth as a space fully occupied by both interior and exterior, language and the body—the mouth as always already multiplying the trajectories and overlapping of words and corporeal drives.

How often the mouth moves as if by its own volition, not only during sleep, but also throughout the course of the day. Usually in the midst of some personal thought, or quiet, random remembrance, the mouth may suddenly part, propelled by this interior movement of the unvoice, to break into self-talk. What comes forward is usually only a fragment; a series of words that may also form into sentences, and possibly, a full monologue. This vocalization is fragmented, dipping in and out of audibility and often also monitoring itself so as not to be caught.

Erving Goffman gives an account of self-talk by underscoring the varying social taboos surrounding it, and how "to be seen walking down the street alone while silently gesticulating a conversation with an absent other is as much a [social] breach as talking aloud to ourselves—for it is equally taken as evidence of alienation."[13]

Self-talk is thus prone to censorship; it carries within its movements a sense of unease, as if such vocalizations must occur undercover, hidden from the gaze of others. Yet self-talk is precisely a speech that *must* come out:

this voice reaches out, it spills from my lips; it needs to be heard even if addressing only myself: it falls from my mouth to be caught by my ear. In such self-hearing, I speak to myself as if I am two. I feel myself as *another*.

Such movements express the greater ontology of talking, as an act that forms the basis for social contact. That is, talking is always already *conversation*. To talk is to enter into a social sphere with another, even if only with oneself, an imaginary friend or an alter-ego. Self-talk is precisely the making of conversation, as if *in preparation*. As Goffman states:

> With self-talk one might say that a sort of *impersonation* is occurring; after all, we can best compliment or upbraid ourselves in the name of someone other than the self to whom the comments are directed. But what is intended in self-talk is not so much the mere citation or recording of what a monitoring voice might say, or what we would say to another if given a chance, but the stage-acting of a version of the delivery, albeit only vaguely a version of its reception.[14]

The notion of impersonation gives suggestion for understanding self-talk as a talk in preparation for another; whether such a conversation in fact ever takes place is not so much the point, but rather, self-talk seems to psychologically prepare us for its possibility, and its imagined dialogical flow. Here I'd suggest that to talk to oneself is a vital rehearsal of the self that allows a space for acting out what we might be while in front of others. It is to rehearse as a body separate from others; it is to project the voice, as a narrative. In this regard, self-talk sets the scene for a doubling movement: to suddenly become two, as speaker *and* listener, so as to expose and explore one's singularity. It is to entertain the difference that I am.

Self-talk radically affirms the construction of identity as being embedded within a social process, as a part of those who are *over there*, whether in the form of the family, or throughout a multiplicity of social circles. The demands to be individual, to speak for oneself, no doubt condition the voice as a central movement of identity and its construction. It is how *I* exist, yet an I always already more than one.

Rehearse

Questions of self-talk appear as an important yet often uneven theme within psychology, child development work, and research in audible verbal hallucinations. Here the theories of Lev Semenovich Vygotsky (1896–1934) remain key, and continue to be debated and referenced within contemporary studies in child development and questions of "private speech."[15] Vygotsky's research early on raised the issue of private speech in children, and highlights a number of important perspectives onto its function. For Vygotsky, the cognitive development of a child reaches a crucial stage around the age of 3 years when specifically "speech and practical activity, two previously completely independent lines of development converge."[16] The acquisition of speech coincides with an increase in motor functions, and a deeper experimentation in play as well as task-oriented gestures. At this stage, children develop the ability to talk aloud as they undertake such activity, often commenting on their own activities, singing or humming along, or making announcements that accompany their gestures. For Vygotsky, the emergence of these speech acts by performing a vital assistance in a child's development, giving support to their skillful management of objects while also announcing or "communicating" what they cannot do. This, for Vygotsky, exemplifies what he identifies as the two main areas of speech, that of "socialized" and "private" speech. Private speech is defined as thought spoken out loud and develops as "an externalized self-monitoring system, that plans, directs and controls behavior."[17] Importantly, for Vygotsky, private speech is "parasocial," in that it already indicates a will *toward* communication.

Vygotsky's view on private speech was developed also as a critique of the related work conducted by the psychologist Jean Piaget. For Piaget, private speech, or what he called "egocentric speech," need not perform on a "communicative" level at all. Rather, private speech indicates a lack of communicative intent and "signifies a still undeveloped ability to take, or imagine, the perspective of others."[18]

Here I'm interested in the understanding that self-talk functions as an *enabling* form of self-management, as a speech *in rehearsal* of itself. In other words, self-talk as self-education, a sounding that assists in exploring what the self can be. A type of echolocation designed to enhance orientation. As David Stoop outlines in *You Are What You Think*, we talk to ourselves so as to achieve a particular outcome—"the things we say determine the way we live our lives."[19]

For Stoop, self-talk is vital to emotional and physical health; it affords an important channel to negotiate the challenges in life, and to project a positive outlook. Feelings of anger, depression, and guilt, in particular, are identified as arenas of emotional labor that find support through self-talking. Accordingly, self-talk becomes a central platform from which we replicate existing patterns—of abuse, anger, or fear—but also, and importantly, from which new patterns may be developed. "What we must remember about self-talk is that we do not create it; we simply recognize that it is already there. The challenge is to learn how to change our self-talk and point ourselves in the direction of positive growth."[20]

Help

Stoop's understanding of self-talk as a transformative potential echoes the deeper understanding of voice and the power of the word to alter reality. Evidenced in various cultural traditions, in particular within religious and spiritual traditions, acts of voicing (as noted in chapter 3) may conjure particular forces—to utter a certain word may call forth a specific spirit, for instance, to open the way for an effective change in existing patterns within the social order, or also, importantly, for a particular body. Healing powers are centered around not only the touch of certain mystics, witch doctors, or shamans, but also the pronouncement of a given word or phrase that, through evocation, summons certain transformative mysteries.

These traditional and somewhat occult vocalizations have found a place within our contemporary psychological environment, supporting the need for self-healing and self-improvement. This can be glimpsed notably in the phenomenon of self-help guides that often take the form of audio recordings. Self-help recordings, since their prominent emergence in the 1980s, are based on giving guidance for self-improvement, self-control, and self-empowerment. From how to lose weight or how to overcome particular fears, to how to take control of one's life, self-help recordings perform such directives through the use of sound and vocalization. One interesting example can be found in the Inner Talk series. The series, defined (somewhat questionably) as "thought modification programs," consists of audio recordings of "pleasant, easy listening music or nature sounds" that are additionally mixed with "positive background affirmations" on various topics, such as "building confidence" or "improving intimacy."[21] Listening to the recordings, the sonic atmosphere assists in dropping activities of conscious thought, allowing the subconscious to become more susceptible: "While the conscious mind enjoys the pleasant music or nature sounds, the subconscious mind recognizes and receives the powerful, life-changing affirmations."[22] Much of the power of such "technology" is found not only in the reception of the message, but also how the spoken voice locates itself within our "inner talk." By adopting as our own the affirmative pronouncements of the recorded voice—such as, "Today I have positive thoughts . . . There is nothing to fear . . . I blame no one for how I am feeling . . . I refuse to see myself as a victim . . . I look for the growth that all experiences offer me . . . I am in control of my life"— we're able to recall its original messages, to restate or respeak this original voice, but as our own, and at later moments in life. The self-help process is thus no doubt strongly supported by the use of audio recording: the spoken voice we listen to, in fact, performs as a form of self-talk; in other words, we listen to this imaginary and invisible figure talking to himself or herself, and incorporate not only its messages, but also importantly its capacity to properly self-dialogue.

In another example, the self-help publication *Self-Regulation through Private Speech*, self-talk becomes the very subject matter of the recording. As the opening statements reveal:

Self-regulation is developed through self-promotion and by using your private speech tools, or self-talk tools. This tool is an amazing gift that we have and can help you find answers to many problems. When you learn to use this tool you tap into your subliminal mind, which in this area is hidden messages. The messages are there and arrived from your experiences and knowledge gained in your past. You want to make these tools your best friend. We face many problems today, which include many underdeveloped people failing to find their way in life. This is because a part of a person is developed rather than a whole person. We all must develop a whole person so that we can work through life successfully. But what is a whole person. A whole person makes up our spiritual, mental, emotional, and physical self.

We build this person by developing self-regulation and our private speech, which can talk us through darn near any problem we may face. Therefore, we must start building today to create that whole person. What it takes is you putting forth the effort, and a will to learn a few strategies and techniques that will guide you to self-regulation and private speech.[23]

Running at 2 hours and 50 minutes, the recording addresses the issue of private speech from various angles, such as constructive thinking or self-growth, free will, and awareness, thereby aims to provide a listener with tools for achieving "wholeness." In this regard, self-talk is argued for as an essential practice.

Repeat: *I am a proud soldier now that I conquered my fear: I do not have to be nervous or tense. I find it easy to relax. My ability to overcome my fear will give me greater self-confidence and regulation in all areas of my life. It will give me an increase in my sense of self-control. I will manifest faith and self-confidence. Instead of worrying about my fear, I will adopt the ability to take control of it. I am in control of my fear and I will conquer it.*

What you are doing now is utilizing your private speech to affirm what you can accomplish. Affirmatives are great mechanisms that you want to work each day when using private speech to give you confidence to succeed.[24]

I'm interested in how self-talk functions precisely through a sense of embodiment, a type of materialization that must sound within the mouth. It is a vocal process that requires externalization, a resonance passing across the tongue, and outward. In self-talk, this appears as an enveloping and immersive promise: that to open the mouth is to incite the necessary flows between self and surrounding, to sound out and enfold ourselves in the transformative power of speech.

From traditions of evocation to self-help recordings, self-talk is a process of channeling particular forces for self-transformation. Such enactments further echo the practice of mantra chanting. Originating within Hindu traditions, the mantra is a sacred word or expression chanted as part of meditation. Each mantra, while being adopted by individuals, is highly impersonal. Rather, mantras exist as sacred phrases connecting us to a greater cosmic order. Specific mantras are chosen, or given, according to a person's individual needs or character, and are chanted so as to channel us toward this greater, universal presence. In meditation, one recites the mantra, repeating the phrase so as to bring it through the body and outward, to resonate through the mouth (chakra). The mantra's power is precisely in this repetition, in the sounding dynamics, and aims to enfold or release the body into a greater spiritual realm. Thus the mantra wields the primary force of self-talking, as a speech that leaves the body so as to bring it closer to harmonious balance. A form of communion, and of management.

Self-talk continually surveys, negotiates, and transforms existing boundaries, which may constrain us to certain negative patterns or loop us into various power structures. The "impersonation" Goffman describes is thus not only a form of acting in preparation for particular social interactions, but also a means by which we direct ourselves as inner beings—the construction of an imaginary voice, if not the imaginary itself as it exists in articulated or worded form, and always marked by an inner silence and its conjuring reverberations.

Secret

Self-talk can be heard to split the self, turning one into *another*, as well as to hold oneself, so as to literally wrap the body in its own vocalizations and the primary power of voicing. To unfold the subject within, to let the voice out so it may return, and in doing so, open the way toward visions of a possible future. I get to know myself through this voice; even while it samples and incorporates, this voice is mine and no other's; I recognize it as it speaks; it is a voice reaching out only to fall back upon the flesh—to embrace oneself, yet as two sides, an inside and an out. A body in the present, and a body appearing on the horizon, as a suggestion for new beginnings.

I have to linger further over this movement, to follow its soft folds, its mysterious sounding. What I might call, *the secret voice*. Speaking to myself occurs undercover and out of bounds; a speech spoken, or half-spoken, only for my ears, and which no one else must hear. Whereas for Vygotsky a child's self-talk announces to nearby adults that which the child may need help with, or that calls for positive affirmation, as an adult, speaking to oneself appears as a sort of embarrassment. I speak to myself when walking down streets, making sure no one sees my mouth moving. Maybe this voice can only sound forth, to take place, by remaining close to myself, unobserved? By hovering in the mouth, just behind the lips; a vocalization that is essential while remaining *out of place.*

Goffman's observations on how self-talk appears as a speech out of place, as social taboo, bring us close to the mouth as that place on the body where so many forces resonate. Might self-talk appear as taboo precisely through its alignment to the power of conjuring, as the potential of a channel through which different spirits may pass? To move the lips without participating in social conversation, but only for oneself, immediately performs a radical suggestion—that we are tuned to the unseen, the invisible, the ghostly, and that whatever I am speaking must be operating on some unspeakable level. As Vygotsky suggests, speech divides into two branches, one for social communication and the other for private articulation. Thus private speech is somehow outside the space of social life, as a sound that rubs against the grain of communication proper. Self-talk might suggest that, in fact, I am in need of more: help, direction, and guidance; to speak to oneself is to already announce that something is wrong—I am full of thoughts, burdened by some emotional imbalance, or haunted by the spirits of terrible memory. Self-talk is thus an indication of trouble *within* and therefore occurs to the side of public life.

The rhythms and motions of this "speaking to oneself" find their expressiveness in the musical work of Robert Ashley, and in particular his *Automatic Writing* (1974–1979).[25] The recorded release of the work (Lovely Music, 1996) is a mysterious collection of utterances that seem to tumble forward, hovering within a surrounding web of distant tonalities, murmurings, and paragrammatic vocables. A type of drifting speech that cascades in and out of focus, suggesting a line of thought, but more, a dream that searches for partial form. Ashley speaks from inside a particularly mesmerizing environment, as if haunted by memories—of other voices and languages, and especially his own. The voice ebbs and flows, like a movement appearing from deep within to envelope us in an extremely private space. A space of breath, of overhearing, and of self-talk.

As Ashley comments, his interest in "involuntary speech" stems from his own habit of speaking aloud, which for him brings forward a relation to Tourette's syndrome, and that sudden uncontrollable urge to speak out, and usually with great force. For Ashley though, involuntary speech and music have a connection, which finds articulation in his compositional interest in the rhythm and sound of words.

Involuntary speech draws an interesting connection to self-talk and gives a certain complication to its seemingly functional operations. While self-talk is often explained as an instant of directed speech, no doubt much of its energy derives from the involuntary, unconscious movements of the oral imaginary. In other words, to the unvoice, as that voice behind voicing and that tempts the mouth into speech. Self-talk and involuntary speech form a spectrum of self-utterances, weaving together conscious articulation with unconscious sounding, as a proliferation of speech filling the mouth. They trace over the often thin line between the private and the public, locating the mouth firmly on the border of "legality." As Ashley states, "It is against the 'law' of our society to engage in involuntary speech. That's why we are embarrassed to talk to ourselves. That's why Tourette had to leave the room."[26]

His self-talk captured in *Automatic Writing* appears under the breath, words half-formed, to outline or to trace something that cannot be fully spoken aloud, yet which finds its way out and toward articulation, as it must. As a shadowy phonation, a musicality of vocables and of phonetic playfulness, *Automatic Writing* is all such taboo amplified.

Schizo

Self-talk produces a purely private geography, yet one that is neither inside nor fully outside, neither fully audible nor without volume, but rather is manifest in both. It is both a distancing, a throwing of the voice, toward an imaginary conversation, and a self-affirmation of one's inner life, as total privacy. It is privacy and publicness together. In this way, self-talk exemplifies the voice in general, as finding definition in the space of the mouth. A tight space between speech and hearing, kept to the self, and close to the skin, and also, thrown outward. Self-talk brims over the line of the lips, to touch the body with its own self-hearing. In this way, to speak to oneself fulfills an image of schizophrenia, as based upon the "domination" of a certain linguistic structure in which speech is always one of "productive reason" and social communication; at the same time, self-talk and all such related involuntary enunciations suggest a disruption of such a matrix—as an expression of "desiring production," a libidinal antagonism onto the field of signification. As Gilles Deleuze and Félix Guattari propose, subjectivity under the spell of capital functions within a primary dynamic of fragmentation that is then housed within the lines of a certain Oedipal matrix in which the unconscious is circumscribed by a familial model, as well as stretching and breaking, through an overflow of "desire" such principles and interpretations. The alternative model of "schizoanalysis" ultimately mapped by Deleuze and Guattari aims to recuperate the immediacy and singularity of "the schizo" in favor of radical "deterritorialization" in which self-talk (and related gibberish) certainly performs.[27] The amalgam of inner and outer, private and public, resounding in that ambiguous auditorium, produces a proliferation of spoken trajectories whose destinations are always contoured by excess, slippage, profanity, madness and the poetical.

I want to hang onto self-talk, as that self-regulating and private activity that may enable forms of development and cognitive extension, but which also contains the core sensuality of voice, and the related troubles or eccentricities of its expression. That is, the primary pleasures in speaking forth, in enunciating, as Cavarero suggests, and that fundamentally states the "uniqueness of being," but that also appear as "illegal."[28]

As Steven Connor outlines, a primary *self-pleasuring* rides along with the voice—the flexing and vibratory caress that speech promulgates within and through the body as the voice rises up from the diaphragm and through the throat to the oral cavity, all these movements that can be appreciated as a form of self-sensing: to feel oneself as a body, *through* the body.[29] In this way, the voice supplies us with a rich, immersive audibility fully tied to bodily sensation, and the silence within, whose palpability finds its reach by leaving the mouth, by a thrust of the oral imaginary as it parts the lips. Voicing is so pleasing precisely because it is something we create, as a fundamental exhalation, excretion—a gift, a power, an emanation brought up from within. I wonder then if self-talk can be appreciated as a form of *self-embrace*: a sense for sensing oneself, not as an enclosure, but precisely as an *unfolding*: a doubling that opens oneself up, to *oneself*, and that rehearses the moment of social contact, of finding conversation, and of not being whole, and therefore alone. To take pleasure in being a self, as a subject brought to life precisely by coming out, and also, by going in. Such pleasures of the self might give us joy in feeling not only in control, of our selves and our thoughts, our being and its development, but also in sounding the body as one in touch with itself: touching itself according to the pulsations of the mouth, which may appear out of place, against the lines of social behavior, precisely through the ripples of the sounded and unsounded voices that no doubt tune themselves to greater powers and experiences.

7

Kiss, Lick, Suck

As part of this lexicon there must be room for considering the mouth as a deeply erotic organ, an agile and agitating figure stimulating the intensities of sexual experience. These are the movements by which the mouth expresses itself fully, when orality surrenders to its corporeal nature and gives way to all those surrounding vocables—*syllables so fully abandoned*—that appear in these instances of sex, but also, the quivering and shaking movements that pucker the mouth, or send it toward wider expressions. While we may imagine other organs as central to acts of love making, it is the mouth that may be highlighted, whose performances and behaviors are intensely multiple and multiplying of our sensual embraces and excitement.

In the midst of the many conversational and vocal expressions of social life, the mouth functions as a central site around which desire, longing, fantasy, and lust gravitate. It is onto the mouth that much of our sexual and loving imaginings are often placed; in the tiny instant of kisses, that condition the routine of relationships, through to the deep push of intercourse where the mouth is deftly operative. Discourses on the voice thus need to be filled (or flustered!) by these deep erotic charges surrounding orality and the spoken.

As an extremely articulated orifice, the mouth supports any number of erotic drives, giving way to an entire range of sexual and sensual enactments. The mouth appears across the entire spectrum of physical contact, from the delights of words to the erotic charm of lips and tongue, and to the various oral performances that send us shivering. In this regard, voice as that dramatic vehicle by which self and other relate is always already located within an erotic vocabulary—of sensual gesture and movement, lustful fantasy and desire, deep physicality and sex. How close are the choreographies of speech and sex, radically inflecting the mouth with such voluptuous excess.

Here we encounter a range of mouth movements, from licking and kissing, tonguing to sucking—these are the most obvious, the one's that can be named out of the plethora of sensual mouthings (what I might call the "hottest"). For it's important to remind that even throughout this lexicon the mouth presents a range of exercises and expressions beyond definition. These erotic movements appear as intensely sensual mouthings, locating lips and tongue against the surfaces and depths of others, and leading out to the relational fevers by which we learn to give pleasure, and to express love.

Moist

Accordingly, within this space of sensuality and erotic experience we also come closer to the sheer physicality and moistness of the mouth—its various physiological attributes become highly active, and these scenes of sensuality bring out the mouth as an assembly of deeply flexible parts. For instance, the tongue is such a *flexed thing*, moist and glistening, hot and gregarious, loving and enticing; it may extend, like a projectile, or sudden appendage, out of the mouth to break the seam of the lips. It may delight with so many subtleties, or unfix us with its sudden invasions. In this regard, it is one of the most expressive of bodily parts, full of life and vibrancy, full of knowledge of the dramas and secrets of bodily pleasure, and the tastes by which so many of our exchanges are driven.

To enter into the mouth, according to the performances of the tongue, is to recognize the degree to which moistness presents itself, as a condition. The mouth is deeply wet; it is full of saliva, that viscous secretion integral to bodily functionality, and which also comes forward when licking, kissing, and sucking. All such movements and gestures rely upon spit; this wetness of the mouth is a central referent when it comes to sexual excitation, and it is from such moments that we might learn the dynamics of the mouth, as an extremely wet space, a cavity whose reverberations are always conditioned by its dampness, or lack of. To lick is to essentially *give* wetness. In the throes of sex, our tongues race around, to moisten and draw excitement forward with its licking.

Licking is also central to the kiss. As the ultimate choreography of the mouth, the kiss brings the entire sensual life of the body there onto the lips. It focuses all energy onto this thin line, intensifying the pleasures of the oral by bringing two mouths together. The lips promise entry into deeper pleasures, deeper intimacy.

There are certainly a variety of kisses, ranging from the small peck of the familial good night kiss to the broad spectrum of passionate kissing where the entire mouth and all its surfaces and muscularities participate in this moist drama, leading us into a deep labyrinth where the mouth may become an entire universe. There may still exist words here, but language certainly slips—even attempts at a semiotics of the kiss tremble when confronting its movements and all its scenes, its pleasures, its unfathomable wetness.

I understand the kiss then as the most erotic of mouth moves. I will elaborate on the kiss from this perspective, fixating on the most dramatic of kisses, the most passionate, where kissing gets carried away with itself. That is, where the world disappears within this wet contact. *Romantic kissing*.

Desire

As with the whisper, the kiss certainly brings us closer. It starts with closeness yet quickly takes a radical leap: the kiss is *breathlessness*—a double breath, shared breathing. It brings the entire body onto the lips, to dissolve into another. I am literally lost in you, navigating according to your lips, and their responsive pressure, murmuring and soft surrendering. The kiss is the absolute form of mutuality: it is to say, *there is nothing or no one else in this moment*, only you and I. In this way, the romantic kiss is the absolute collapse of distance; there is no perspective, only the movement of a vanishing point rushing in, suddenly, to overtake the self. What architecture can stand against the proposal that every kiss makes, that of creating an altogether perfect form of enclosure? In bringing two mouths together, the kiss creates its own dwelling, a privacy that always already exceeds itself. "I like the feeling of breathing someone else's space, sharing with them the basis of life, i.e., air."[1]

Within the space of two mouths together, along the touching of lips, language falters: there is literally no room to speak, for the mouth to find words, to even take a breath. The kiss is a form of drowning. Yet the movements and intensities of such disappearance also affirm an oral imaginary that speech secretly revolves around: love. Might the kiss articulate the very hidden core of all speech, that of longing? The wish to be finally enclosed within a primary warmth? Does not speech secretly aspire to raise one up *for* the other, as the object of desire? To find wholeness in the longing and desiring expressed by another, for oneself? How often speech longs to leap forward into a kiss!

Adam Phillips addresses kissing in this way, as central to our "oral education." Following Freud's analysis of kissing, Phillips understands the act of placing our mouth against another's as stemming from early experiences of "tasting the mother"—the fact that "our first and most foremost relationship to the world is an oral one." The kiss thus returns us to "the primary sensuous experience of tasting another," though in a way that also "disappoints."[2] Again, in accordance with Freud's view, the oral intensities of tasting the mother, and experiencing her ultimate withdrawal, come to fill the mouth with an enduring absence. Aspects of oral gratification participate in negotiating this absence, this lack, yet the desire to kiss another seems to articulate, for Freud, not only a desire for the other, but precisely the desire for self-sufficiency, for wholeness. It is the removal of the breast that turns us toward ourselves, toward our own mouths, as the source of completion: of finding alternative means not only for pleasures, but also for supporting the fullness of our body. Thus kissing brings us back to the point of rupture, to the site of this primary absence, and this wish; it is in the mouth of another that we search for our own completion, where the emptiness of the oral cavity is forever haunted by the impossibility of kissing oneself. "Desire, [Freud] wants us to know, is always in excess of the object's capacity to satisfy it. The object of desire . . . is resonant, finally, because it disappoints; and because it disappoints it can be returned to."[3]

Such perspectives of longing and desire underscore the mouth as lacking: a hole from which not only speech emanates, but also within which a mechanics of fantasy operates. As Lacan poses, it is from that which is missing—that symbolic cut—that we are brought into the dramas of fantasy, of representation, and in line with objects of desire.[4]

Along with the gaze, Lacan places the voice within the psychoanalytic repertoire of "drive objects" (which also include breast, feces, urethra, and penis). As a drive object, the voice is intimately connected to the operations of desire, which perform precisely on the level of the unspoken and the unspeakable—to that which cannot be articulated, and yet which surges forth. The voice as *petit objet a* is thus a negative, an empty or vacant space, an object that "represents the limit of that which is thinkable or expressible in discourse."[5] Lacan's enigmatic theory of voice is predicated on these operations of lack, signified through an emptiness, a nothing around which desire circulates, and is provoked.

While Lacan's theory understands the voice as object, I'm more interested in reinforcing the mouth as that point where the voice is most alive—both as a silence, an emptiness, as the unsounded, as well as the fully articulated body, the one that entices, prolongs, and excites the mechanics and oscillations of the erotic. In other words, as the zone that is most occupied by the fluctuations of longing. If the voice pokes and pricks me into being, into the pressures of subjectivity; if it empties me out, or overwhelms me, then it must be the mouth to which desiring productions turn and by which they proliferate—as the whole *and* the hole. In other words, by *lying in wait* for the voice, my attention anticipates a mouth whose movements may put me at ease, or which may anguish me further; a mouth that may open for me, or that may also close shut.

It is my argument that the voice, however diffuse, phantasmic, or acousmatic, is never truly without a body; even as an "invisible" presence it comes to *suggest* a body, an identity, an image, or a material thing. The voice, in other words, sets the scene for a body to come, and it does so by referring us to the oral imaginary wherein the voice finds so many expressions and animations—from experiences and memories of tasting, licking and biting, chewing, sucking and crying, to the pleasures and pains words come to enact. It is the mouth that locates the voice so completely within a greater experience of orality and desire, politics and poetics, and to which we continually return—to sustain ourselves, to pleasure ourselves, to negotiate, and to surrender.

Rapture

Is not the kiss a first step toward greater sexual contact, toward the plenitude of fulfilled desire? By placing our mouths together, is not the kiss a voluptuous space boiling over with passions and wishes? The kiss as a choreography *in the making*, and toward which all our bodily rhythms and vibrations, fevers and hesitations are drawn, pushed back, and then drawn again, as an orchestration. Following Catherine Clément's work on syncope, does not the (first) kiss initiate a greater flow of passions (and disappointments) soon to follow, performing as a type of "musical" moment that draws us forward, suddenly, enraptured and in anticipation, where the lips literally unfold against a greater pull of longing for what is soon to disappear? Syncope, *fainting*: the musicality which "accentuates delay," immersing us in a duration or a time signature haunted by oblivion.[6] Two rhythms meeting, two forces rubbing against each other, to produce a beating of hearts, a pulsing of imaginations, a rubbing of skins, which in their coupling seek out a figuration of harmony, a composition of intimacy. "Syncope always provokes this sensation of reunion"[7]—a beating whose movements, of ascension and descension, of oscillation, or counterpoint, are given form there on the lips, and in the small pressings of mouth upon mouth. Our speech, in other words, is so fully tuned to the heart and its rhythm.

In this way, kissing may be the horizon to which speech gravitates, when the mouth, as that point where subjectivity continually negotiates the meeting of in and out, is awash in the pleasures of intimacy, of losing one's own limits in the sensuality of togetherness. For is not speech always a searching for the other? A materialization of fear and longing though sublimated, literally articulated—that is, cultured into language, aiming for assurance and belonging, recuperation and retrieval of the intensity of our *first kiss*, our first fainting.

Tino Sehgal's performance work *Kiss* may be seen to bring such intensities out in the open. Presented in 2010 at the Guggenheim Museum in New York, Sehgal's work occupied the main atrium of the museum throughout the day, presenting a couple stretched out on the floor kissing. As with much of his work, *Kiss* gently disrupts the normative operations of a museum space by inserting a live and temporal action. While kissing appears within any number of visual representations and media platforms, the physical presence of a couple kissing, holding each other, within such feverish sensuality, reverberates within the emptied out Guggenheim with an extremely suggestive energy.

As the critic Holland Cotter notes: "[Sehgal] thinks that production is ceaseless and technology destructive. His art is a response to these perceived realities as they play out microcosmically in the context of the art industry. His goal is to create a countermodel: to make something (a situation) from virtually nothing (actions, words) and then let that something disappear, leaving no potentially marketable physical trace."[8] *Kiss* can be appreciated to accentuate experiences of intimacy, locating that sense of closeness in the museum so as to deliver us from the pressures of consumption, artistic and other, and the mechanics that place value on that which is marketable.

Sehgal's work, and this sensual rebelliousness, finds complement in the writings of Franco Berardi, specifically on the level of the economic, through his attack on the "financialization" of social life and the subsequent loss of the erotic, social body.

. . . we have lost the pleasure of being together. Thirty years of precariousness and competition have destroyed social solidarity. Media virtualization has destroyed the empathy among bodies, the pleasure of touching each other, and the pleasure of living in urban spaces. We have lost the pleasure of love, because too much time is devoted to work and virtual exchange.[9]

To recuperate the possibility of a new form of solidarity, in support of the "social body," Berardi's call for "the general intellect and the erotic social body to meet on the streets and squares"[10] sets the scene for the power of the kiss: the kiss not only as the individuated act between two, but also a general movement of erotic freedom. To found a new form of sensuality, the sheer privacy of kissing may drive forward a radical invigoration of public space, and of public life. Kissing here, as the expression of a body in freedom, performs a resistance to the "financial mafia" and all the mechanisms that place emphasis on market forces.

Of course, Sehgal's *Kiss* (and other such ephemeral works—as well as the "erotic body" in general) also fully participates in the movements of the contemporary "creative economy," where "immaterial" productions are also inscribed within the market to support new forms of capitalism, and under which sexed bodies are extremely susceptible.[11] Yet what interests me about *Kiss* (and Berardi's proposals) is how it might refer us to a larger history, in which the closeness of mouths, and the spirit of intimacy, sought to enact a type of political demonstration.

Initially, we may return to earlier moments, for instance in the late 1960s, where the display of freedom and resistance found expression in gathered, sensual bodies. The tradition of the "love-in" embodies this erotic potentiality. First appearing in opposition to the Vietnam War in the United States, the love-in captured the social energy of the "sit-in," as a form of political demonstration, interweaving it with the "love-and-peace" ethos of hippy culture. The love-in articulated a greater position, also tied to notions of economy and capital, for as Abbie Hoffman sought to remind, the body and the expressions of love are first and foremost, free.[12] They are our own to give and to share with others, whose public display might be said to steal time and space, if not the air itself, from within the structures of moral (and capitalistic) society; and the expressions of intimacy, of sexuality, were primary articulations of such freedoms—that love and the sharing of the body could not be quantified, placed within the registry of the administrative system or the military complex. Especially, by locating such expressions in public, out in the open, kissing becomes an enactment of a primary transgression, as well as an articulation of hope.

Subsequently, the kiss is a particular mouth movement that may also carry the full weight, and potentiality, of a (collective) body in revolt; that is, the manifestation of a radical pleasure whose expressivity can be wielded as a tactic in the social struggles of contemporary politics. This was given more recent expression in the "kissing protests" held in Ankara, Turkey in 2013. In response to transport authorities who castigated a couple kissing in a subway station, protesters called for "free kisses" and staged public kissing throughout subway terminals.[13] The passion of kissing is thus conditioned by a sociopolitical dimension found on the tongue, in between the lips and in the feverish charge of two mouths holding each other; and one whose shuddering and fainting musicality may also perform to reinstate the softness of a generous and intimate life.

Attachment

Returning to Freud's view on kissing, I want to move closer toward the act of sucking. While kissing performs a range of movements, bringing us into the finer choreographies of the erotic, with sucking we enter more fully into those primary oral experiences. As Freud suggests, kissing may be haunted by early experiences of tasting another, in particular that of the mother's breast; essentially, experiences of sucking. We might appreciate the kiss as a sublimation of the suck; with lips tracing over another's, the kiss elaborates not only those oral pleasures found in sucking, but also the simple and direct mouth movement sucking performs. Even the word "sucking" brings us back down, toward a more base level—it is such a direct word, whose sounding immediately conjures forth a deep wetness. Hence the use of the word as an insult; to say, "You suck" leads us into an interesting twist, for the word slips from an act and toward a trait; it suddenly, and mysteriously, taints us. "You suck" seems to carry its vulgarity precisely by capturing us as "the one who sucks," as the one who occupies this lower level of behavior, marked by this primary and rather unspeakable oral drive.

Originating in the phrase "go suck an egg," "suck" as an insult brings us closer to the intensity of the act, as well as its lingering reverberations. To be at the mother's breast is an extremely deep form of attachment and immersion; it sets the scene for the primary dynamics we develop by which experiences of gratification and loss, love and destructive impulses, are formed. As Winnicott suggests, "Psychologically, the infant takes from a breast that is part of the infant, and the mother gives milk to an infant that is part of herself."[14]

The psychoanalytic work of Melanie Klein elaborates this view by way of what she terms the "good and bad breast." It is precisely the experiences we have while feeding from the mother's breast that "initiates an object relation to her," oscillating between the good and the bad breast, that is, the breast that provides and which is always there, and the one that pulls away, or is absent. "The various factors which enter into the infant's feelings of being gratified such as the alleviation of hunger, the pleasure of sucking, the freedom from discomfort and tension, i.e., from privations, and the experience of being loved—all these are attributed to the good breast."[15] Of course, this relation is dramatically one of dependency, leading to feelings of fulfillment and plenitude, of attachment, as well as frustration, longing, and detachment.

Sucking comes to perform as an extremely vital channel for infant development, a literal site of "oral communication" that no doubt embeds itself not only in the balancing of "libidinal and destructive impulses"—the positive and the negative, that captures our psychosexual life—but also the feelings we have for the mouth, the body, and the oral. If it is through the mouth that we establish such elemental patterns, such foundational emotional structures, then it is from the mouth that a great many future longings and experiences are defined.

These elemental dynamics of the mouth are poignantly elaborated by René Spitz in his influential paper, "The Primal Cavity" (1955). Through his work as a psychoanalyst, Spitz investigated early infant development and specifically analyzed how the mouth functions as a highly active, if not essential, mediator—a constellation of "surfaces"—between the infant and the external world.

> . . . these will be the first surfaces used in tactile perception and exploration. They are particularly well suited for this purpose because in this single organ, the mouth cavity, are assembled the representatives of several of the senses in one and the same area. These senses are the sense of touch, of taste, of temperature, of smell, of pain, but also the deep sensibility involved in the act of deglutition. Indeed, the oral cavity lends itself as no other region of the body to bridge the gap between inner and outer perception.[16]

Interestingly for Spitz, this "bridge" of perception is expressed most profoundly in the act of sucking, and what he refers to as "the sucking reflex"—an innate action that, like clutching, "takes in" a surrounding material or object. Sucking appears as our first form of directed behavior; it provides the vital link between a newborn and a mother, conditioning perception and functioning as the mediator for distinguishing between what is inside and what is outside, what is good and what is bad. This "oral discrimination" performs an essential contouring to the emergence of subjectivity, as it will lead directly into "the separation of the self from nonself, of the self from the objects, and in the course of this road to what is accepted and what is rejected."[17]

As Klein further outlines, it is through the act of sucking and feeding that a number of primary fantasies are formed. The absolute dependency on the breast locates us within a constant flow between the good and the bad, the offered and the denied, to such a degree that the impulses to love or to hate are unquestionably interwoven. In this way, fantasies of admiration and hatred circle around the breast, leading equally to libidinal and destructive impulses: "These processes underlie, I think, the observable fact that young infants alternate so swiftly between states of complete gratification and of great distress. At this early stage the ego's ability to deal with anxiety by allowing contrasting emotions towards the mother, and accordingly the two aspects of her, to come together is still very limited."[18] These contrasting emotions open out onto fantasies of "devouring the breast," of "scooping out the mother's body," as well as "diving in," of deep warmth and attachment.

The reflex of sucking and the primary dynamics of the oral are to be appreciated as forming the very basis for the delineation of the self; while for Lacan, the instant of recognition of one's body operates through the ocular, that moment of gazing at the mirror, signaling a certain break—a narcissistic wonderment at oneself as a separate animate presence[19]—the "oral discrimination" performed by the infant seems even more significant, and pervasive, as setting the conditions by which "recognition" takes hold. The mouth develops as the very point of physical and emotional negotiation by bringing parts of the world directly in while also rejecting others; and from which experiences of deep attachment are found, yet one's that are also prone to painful absence. Before we can even fully see the world, we have already plunged into the difficult movements of self and other.

Dream

These oral dynamics, as I've tried to suggest, appear as a weave of direct, physical experiences of matter and material—a certain pragmatic ground of corporeal work—and that of more imaginary constructions. The mouth, in this regard, captures the reality of all the substances it encounters, and transfers this—rematerializes it—within what we might call "oral dreaming." As Eric Rhode suggests, the mouth is also a "dream site"—a space of unconscious drive, a haunted space—wherein tongue and teeth replace the breast and the nipple, and the oral cavity itself performs as a maternal uterus. Within this uterine cave a range of creations are generated—words are magical productions born from acts of insemination, where the tongue may penetrate the throat, and the teeth may provide nourishment for these birthed syllables. The infant may "claim its mouth, and not the mother's womb, as the site of procreation," thereby relating "the act of procreation with the ability to [orally] dream."[20] The mouth-dreamer channels acts of symbolization through the oral cavity: the profound coupling of mother and child, enabled through the breast, turns the mouth into a mythic stage; performances are dramatized, and narratives unfold that integrate teeth and tongue, saliva and breast milk, nipples and the mother's skin, casting them into a cosmology of attachment and loss, conflicts from which an infant may learn how to imagine and dream through acts of sucking and tasting, ingesting and digesting. Fantasy is thus fully regulated by oral contact.

Elemental

Returning to the fevers found in kissing, and the erotic sensations experienced in licking, it becomes clear the degrees to which the mouth acts as a central part of the body for *finding connections*, if not our most primary ones. All the movements and micro-oralities I'm exploring here lead us both to the heights of passion as well as the essential relationships by which we love and care, share, hold, and take.

Is not the mouth the very part of the body by which to negotiate that sense of wholeness found in primary experiences, as well as the projection of lingering fantasy? A part balancing the whole; a hole teased by the whole, and which continually expels and exceeds itself, even while trying to hold in? Here I'm reminded of the work of Monique Wittig, and her publication, *The Lesbian Body*. Written in 1973, the work radically unsettles language with the material force of a "body in writing." Paralleling the work of Hélène Cixous, and her notion of "écriture féminine," as a methodology for shifting the patriarchal ordering central to Western discourses, *The Lesbian Body* is rife with an unfolded or fragmented body—a body equally whole and fragmented, conjoined and at a loss. It is a text where the personal pronoun is literally divided typographically as well as by an erotic charge, of lesbian sexuality, to locate us within a dramatic breaking point, a body pulled apart by love and oral dreaming.

I have access to your glottis and your larynx red with blood voice stifled. *I* reach your trachea, *I* embed myself as far as your left lung, there my so delicate one *I* place m/y two hands on the pale pink bland mass touched it unfolds somewhat, it moves fanwise, m/y knees flex, *I* gather into m/y mouth your entire reserves of air. Mixed with it are traces of smoke, odours of herbs, the scent of a flower, irises it seems to m/e, the lung begins to beat, it gives a jump while the tears flow from your wide-open eyes, you trap m/y mouth like a cupping-glass on the sticky mass of your lung, large soft sticky fragments insinuate themselves between m/y lips, shape themselves to m/y palate, the entire mass is engulfed in m/y open mouth, m/y tongue is caught in an indescribable glue, a jelly descends towards m/y glottis, m/y tongue recoils, *I* choke and you choke without a cry, at this moment m/y most pleasing of all women it is impossible to conceive a more magistral a more inevitable coupling.[21]

As a reader we are forced into this linguistic and corporeal scene, tossed into a multiplicity that leaves us without a center, and that places the physicality of sensual life onto the page, to which the mouth is profoundly operative.

Such work opens up a territory imbued with an overlap of language and corporeality, discourse and fantasy; Wittig's literary work is precisely a language that moves through the body, dragged across the elemental passions and primary drives that always lurk within, and that fill and flush the oral and the spoken—to produce a *sticky* discourse. As Julia Kristeva poignantly states: "Through the mouth that I fill with words instead of my mother whom I miss from now on more than ever, I elaborate that want, and the aggressivity that accompanies it, by *saying*."[22] By saying, and also through an array of oral gestures and expressions that always rotate upon a highly erotic and sexualized axis. It is this axis—one steeped in the penetrative poetics of a *writing the body* that can equally be a *speaking the body*, and that figures the deep oral imaginary always already in the mouth.

8

Laugh

Laughter dramatically moves the body. In small ticks and gyrations, as well as convulsions and fits, laughter pulls the mouth this way and that, to bare the teeth or toss the head back, to hold the belly or even slap the thigh—all as an expanded gestural event. The laugh *vibrates* us—we *shiver* with laughter—as a force expelled from deep within to break onto the scene with a certain infectious potential. (Like the yawn, laughter is a type of corporeal energy that immediately passes through social circles, to induce sympathetic ripples.) Laughter throws itself at others, riveting the air with its exuberance.

The bodily intensities of laughter are captured in the video work by Sam Taylor-Johnson titled, *Hysteria* (1997).[1] Over the course of the 8-minute video, we witness a woman laughing: her mouth wide open, eyes closed, head tossed back, and then forward, her body swaying, succumbing to an unseen interior force—a phantom? A terror? Unbearable joy? As viewers we are allowed to witness, or scrutinize this intimate display, recorded, and also slowed down and silent—we cannot hear the laugh, only stare into this gaping mouth, with the tongue pushed back and the pharynx exposed, all the teeth in full view. At some point, the woman appears to lapse into crying: how close the two are, laughter and tears. Such is the unsteady and energetic zone of laughter, with the body susceptible to so many pressures and expenditures (Figure 8.1).

Taylor-Johnson's video uncovers the laugh as an extremely excessive mouth movement; so completely does the body collapse from its own convulsing energy. At some point in watching the video, I certainly wonder: *will she die of laughter?*

The physicality of the laugh though also sends its corporeal force away from the individual body to enter dramatically into the social. From the smile to the giggle, the small laugh to the boisterous one, the casual guffaw to the uncontrollable chuckle, laughter passes *across* the body to modulate, sculpt, and radically choreograph relationships. It is a deeply social sound, explicitly

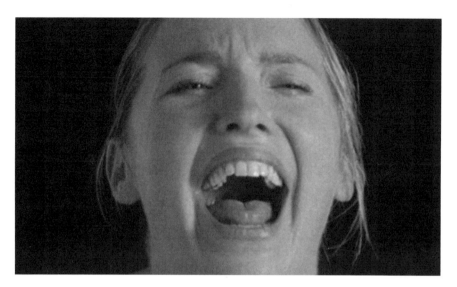

FIGURE 8.1 *Sam Taylor-Johnson,* Hysteria, *1997. Laser disk, shot on 16 millimeters. Duration: 8 minutes. Copyright Sam Taylor-Johnson. Courtesy White Cube.*

performing as a responsive sonority to those around: one continually laughs in dialogue with others, and as part of innumerable situations that punctuate and orchestrate the everyday. This extends particularly through laughter's "contagious" effect, which so immediately takes hold and gives shape to social synchronization. This contagious effect is rendered with great hilarity and madness in the film *Mary Poppins,* when Uncle Albert and Bert sing together "I Love to Laugh," which causes them to levitate; hovering near the ceiling, their mad-capped laughter eventually spreads even to the children, who join in on the infectious zaniness. The contagion of laughter—also appearing in historical accounts of "laughing epidemics"—leads us into an extremely complex territory. The mouth here is balanced between the socially warranted *and* the dangers of taboo, between shared languages and the rupture of their rationality. (As Uncle Albert demonstrates, laughter borders on oblivion.) With laughter, the movements of the mouth exceed so many limits, to occupy and break, as well as reaffirm the edges of the social order.

Identity

I would like to extend the laugh, as an extremely prominent mouth movement, as well as an intensely social sonority, into questions of identity and the operations of looking and listening; to follow existing resonances, which announce a deeper view onto embodiment. Discourses around feminism, in particular, have located the ways in which identity is (over) determined and subject to power relations that are often driven by "the field of vision." Immediately, this can be captured by delving into Luce Irigaray's *The Sex Which Is Not One*, a text riddled with "the (female) body" and its "fluid mechanics"; a mechanics put into contrast to a "phallic logic" within which "the predominance of the *visual*, and of the discrimination and individualization of form, is particularly foreign to female eroticism" (my emphasis).[2] From such a characterization we are given a discursive structure to unfold a generative dialogue that runs across the senses, the body, and the inscriptions that cite one into subjectivity and that charge the interaction of sight and sound. As Jacqueline Rose proposes in *Sexuality in the Field of Vision*, "we know that women are meant to *look* perfect, presenting a seamless image to the world so that the man, in that confrontation with difference, can avoid any apprehension of lack. The position of woman as fantasy therefore depends on a particular economy of vision."[3] Thus sexuality is captured by the gaze; female sexuality comes to occupy a space of the observed, of the looked upon, of exhibition, while its male counterpart is constrained by its presupposed search for self-affirmation and conquest expressed in the penetrating look. The operations of desire are defined then by a certain patriarchal logic, a phallocentric dynamic by which language and the law turn. Accordingly, *to look is a serious matter*.

In contrast to the examinations of the field of vision, Paul Carter concentrates on the auditive, stating that sound operates through an "erotic ambiguity," thereby suggesting that forms of representation, identity, and sexual and social relations gain in flexibility according to auditive structures.[4]

As found in the visual–sexual thinking of Rose and others,[5] much feminist thought appropriates or locates a potentiality in the properties of sound and audition, as well as that of "musicality." For instance, Julia Kristeva's formulations of the semiotic fasten onto corporeal attributes characterized by the rhythmic, the pulsional, and the fluid, which lend identity routes toward flexibility and ambiguity—"musicalization pluralizes meanings," she writes, thereby setting the scene for transgressing language and all the signifying practices enveloping and radiating from the subject as a stabilizing "natural" order.[6] "Musicalization" rather supports embodied drives and libidinal charges to equip the force of articulation with pulsional potential— that is, a *heterogeneity* that unfolds subjectivity, as forces of individuation. Kristeva's theories are, in turn, echoed in Irigaray's search for an elemental transformation of sexual difference. Defining the feminine according to a fluid mechanics in which flows, ruptures, immersions, and drifts disperse the "named" subject, Irigaray embraces the embodied peripheries in which identity may formulate a radical and productive ambiguity: a fluidity that necessarily drifts from the normative scripting of the proper and the named. Cultivating and sculpting such openings and fissures, she crafts a vocabulary infused with the temporal and the evanescent, the dynamic and the inchoate.

Such linguistic engagement is echoed in Hélène Cixous' conception of "writing the body": "So for each text, another body. But in each the same vibration: the something in me that marks all my books is a reminder that my flesh signs the book, it is *rhythm*. Medium my body, rhythmic my writing."[7] To *write the body* is to rupture or complicate the conventional dichotomy of the rational and the emotional, reason and the fevers of desire, through the intensities of a primary vibration. Such collapse—this writing the body, this language dragged through bodily logics—supplies Cixous with potent flexibility in writing against the grain, literalizing on the page the promise of fluid identity, amorphous sexuality, and a body in motion.

The semiotic rushes, the embodied fluidities, the primary vibrations, all greatly lend to feminism's attempt to resituate and reposition the discursive limits of identity, and to disrupt the logic of the phallic, to ultimately play havoc with optical power and readability. The production of identity and sexual being is exposed as a *politics* of the sensed, and the sensible, in which legibility, observation and apprehension encircle and define the subject. In contrast, the fluid, the rhythmic, and the vibratory all give way toward a horizon where the structures and reasonings of the seen diffuse; the erotic ambiguity of the auditive, as that which is always already unfixed, lends support to the marginal and the peripheral, and to the emergent.

Henri Lefebvre interestingly parallels such thinking in his seminal *The Production of Space* when he makes claims against the perception of space as pure visibility.[8] For Lefebvre, the production of space must be understood as integrating and involving the sheer tactility of embodied relations, which are most exemplified in rhythm further mapped in *Rhythmanalysis*: "At no moment have the analysis of rhythms and the rhythmanalytical project lost sight of the body. Not the anatomical or functional body, but the body as polyrhythmic and eurhythmic . . . the living body has always been present."[9] Through the dynamics of rhythm Lefebvre charts out the importance of those in-between spatialities, the informal operations of a social life nestled in the gaps of the urban grid and that come to beat out their own modulations onto the visual coherence of a city plan.

In conjunction, we find alternative answers to the problematics of the optical also in what Marshall McLuhan and Edmund Carpenter refer to as "acoustic space." Characterized as boundless, without center and determined by its own momentum, acoustic space is again an opening or break onto the operational and functional often defined by what is most apparent.[10] The auditory intervenes onto the fixity of space, and the inherent politics that often control and regulate according to a transcendental optics. In contrast, the auditory is understood to assert an ambiguous and temporal status onto the order of things. From sexual relations to identity, spatial form to city life, auditory thinking and sonic materiality seem to supply the dynamics of relations and their ideological play with potent elasticity.

The proposed liberation found in the auditory grants energy to forms of identity and relations that may support Rose's challenge to the "economy of vision." It finds further articulation again by Luce Irigaray when she proposes "laughter" as the dimension of desire that may overcome the "seriousness of meaning" promulgated by "the phallic," as well as by which "to escape from a pure and simple reversal of the masculine position"—in short, for Irigaray, one must "not forget to laugh."[11] Here I want to grab hold of this notion of laughter, as it breaks into this discourse on sexuality, identity formation, and the interstices existing as fault lines in the economy of vision, and to carry it further into the sphere of orality and this study of the mouth. If the mouth can be underscored as the vital channel through which individuals come to perform within a social space, and from which they are (literally) called into being as a subject—the mouth allows the voice to appear, to enact, to claim—as well as enabled to call back, in so many ulterior shapes and meanings, we might locate the rawness of psychosexual energies in the laugh.

Comic

The laugh is certainly the product of a social dynamic, as well as an important participant in its very formation: it establishes a bond while charging that bond with complexity. The laugh appears across a wide spectrum of interactions, moments of gathering, intimacy, and even being alone; it punctuates, conditions, and elaborates, through its propulsional energies, what it means to be a social body, affording important contact and sharing, and independence, alongside that of the spoken.

The laugh though may also locate us within an array of contentious, rapturous, and volatile exchanges, explicitly through a sort of "violation." From the superiority of one to another (to laugh down at someone), and the forced laugh that covers up and masks buried pain (to laugh in spite of oneself), to the shared recognition of unspoken yet agreed upon discriminations (to laugh collectively at the tensions embedded within social norms), and the radicality heard within the corporeality of "busting a gut" (to laugh in the face of oppressive systems)—such a medley of scenarios underscores that laughter and humor are rapturous by often appearing where they should not. To be *out of place*, to follow uncanny juxtapositions—the comedy derived from two dissimilar things coming into contact—or to uproar in the face of another's tragedy, laughter is intrinsically *disjunctive*.

Comedy is built upon this dynamic. Comedians know how to be obscene—to introduce that which must remain off-stage, smuggling in the vulgar and placing the passions in the spotlight through a set of linguistic and gestural moves. The comedian is a magician of the lowly and the base, using it and being used by it, in a type sorcery of humor: puncturing holes onto the codes of society, piercing the heart of the matter through various calisthenics, the comedian knows how to be out of place with himself or herself, to poke fun at the body, and to perform one's own embarrassment— to *slip up*, precisely.

Such maneuvers paradoxically interrupt while also nurturing social life, if not its most primary of drives. For Freud, the mechanism of "joke work" is bound to a reservoir and expenditure of psychic energy that is balanced through the telling, the sharing, and the ultimate production of laughter, which *requires* an audience, a listener. The joke teller seeks us out so as to share the joke while experiencing cathartic release through the other's laugh, as an essential psychic discharge. "In laughter . . . the determinants are given for an amount of psychical energy, used until then for charging, to be freely released."[12] Joke work acts to charge and release, to contract and punctuate, psychic energies and related social behaviors. "A joke depends on the audience to release an inhibition in the teller, which then enables both the teller and audience to laughingly enjoy their close brush with forbidden pleasure."[13] Continually circulating within our exchanges, laughter contours conversation with such feverish energy.

Freud's analysis of jokes and laughter is given critical reading by Moshe Halevi Spero in his article, "The Joke Envelope." For Spero, joke work functions as an important psychic mechanism, linking us to childhood experiences of sound, noise, and the "uncontrolled" nature of the laugh. "From early development onward, powerful states of manic exuberance, laughter, and gleeful aesthetic rapture are experienced as pleasurable *and* painful, requiring sensitive containment lest they overflow and overtake the infant mind."[14] Subsequently, jokes come to act as means for such containment, as an "enveloping" container by which to revisit these primary experiences, to return to the rapturous instant of exuberance and intensity, of feverish breaks and ruptures, while explicitly housing it within certain borders. The "joke envelope" acts as such a container, serving within the "work of humor" and the pleasures of the laugh to assist in negotiating the "auditory crises" experienced from before. The auditory rapture of the laugh thus "sonifies" the presence of "archaic memories," of those experiences of absence, breaks in the continual flow of sound (for instance, the absence of the mother), the repetitions of sound (that might refer us to overhearing parental love making), the cries of pain, etc.[15] The ruptures thus signified through such auditory intensities or gaps return in the form of the joke, delivering us from the pain of the remembered and into the flood of a laughter shared.

Humor delivers us to such unsteady experiences; it dramatizes through jokes and antics to poignantly reveal what is blatantly apparent; it shuns convention through coy maneuvers, trespassing while at the same time occupying an already familiar territory—the comic is a space defined by invasion, overstepping bounds, smuggling in gestures, usurping control that is also fully inscribed and warranted within the social.

What the laugh proposes, through its radical gregariousness or subtlety, is an affirmation of embodied being, taking secret pleasures (and plotting secret wishes) in full view of the social center—Irigaray's proposal of laughter can be understood as just such a *political force*. To my ear, the laugh is a form of public display that is potently disruptive while being absolutely acceptable; it treads across lines of social etiquette while formulating, in its moment of quivering and trembling excess, routes toward mad expression and bodily recuperation. For every laugh plunges us into such joys precisely by appearing in and among others, as it scrapes against existing structures and social bonds, moments of shame and embarrassment, as well as within the often-trembling uncertainty of what to do next. Of course, social situations are precisely bounded by conventions of acceptable behavior, and this is exactly what humor and the comic thrive on. Humorousness plays havoc with convention, social norms, the acceptable and the unacceptable, surfacing where it should not be, and in doing so, producing a form of renewed sociality—for the crowd takes pleasure in observing acts of transgression performed onto itself. The joker, the buffoon, and the comedian flirt with the vulgar, allowing us to enjoy and partially accept the tragedy of our own seriousness.

Covert

At the same time, the forcefulness of the laugh—as so much psychic, emotional, sexual, and social energy—can also lead to arrest, to a trespass far across lines of instated ideology. As Christie Davies chronicles, political jokes were extremely operative during the Soviet period, offering important "areas of freedom and social escape from socialist hegemony."[16]

> For those living under socialist tyranny jokes were special. They were a means of communication, a way of expressing one's alienation from and in some cases disgust with the entire political, economic, and social order; they were a welcome reminder that socialism was a mere social construct and not the inevitable order of things. They were a way of testing and achieving interpersonal trust.[17]

Additionally, within Nazi Germany such "whispered jokes," or Flüsterwitze, were important in opening up the rather oppressive atmosphere. Yet such jokes and laughter also carried great risks, and at times led to arrest and deportation to the camps.[18] Laughter can thus be appreciated to function firmly within the social environment while remaining extremely suspect to the powers above. As Hélène Cixous provocatively states, "all laughter is allied with the monstrous."[19]

Mikhail Bahktin identifies the power of laughter by recognizing its political dimensions, most poignantly expressed in traditions of carnival. "The inversions and suspensions permitted and legitimized by carnival represent substantive challenges to authority, therefore offering the possibility that comedy, invested with the spirit of festive and carnival traditions, may also be an expression of popular discontent."[20] The laugh is a primary expression of possible rebellion, a marker of the people in whose expressivity we might locate the future. Yet, following Bahktin, what is so crucial for an appreciation of laughter, as that vital animation of the body, is how it remains unclear and ambiguous, as well as pointed and unmistakable. It occupies an extremely slippery zone of signification, whose physical and social energies move in the cracks of the dominant system. As excess, as expenditure, laughter may reinforce this particular order, and at the same time, it may already be instigating change.

These dynamics of the laugh are additionally examined by Georges Bataille, through meditations on the religious and the sacred, and finally, according to what he calls "nonknowledge." As he suggests: "The strangest mystery to be found in laughter is attached to the fact that we rejoice in something that puts the equilibrium of life in danger."[21] Laughter explicitly locates us against the peripheries of knowing, leading us to confront what Bataille terms "the unforeseeable."

> We laugh, in short, in passing very abruptly, all of a sudden, from a world in which everything is firmly qualified, in which everything is given as stable within a generally stable order, into a world in which our assurance is overwhelmed, in which we perceive that this assurance is deceptive. Where everything had seemed totally provided for, suddenly the unexpected arises, something unforeseeable and overwhelming, revelatory of an ultimate truth: the surface of appearances conceals a perfect absence of response to our expectation.[22]

For Bataille, laughter delivers us to experiences that remind of the limits of understanding, putting into suspension what is known. Such perspectives ultimately lead Bataille to align laughter with the religious, and with transcendence, with experiences that become "divine insofar as it can be one's laughter at witnessing the failure of a tragic nature."[23]

In contrast, Henri Bergson's enlightening study suggests laughter as not only what breaks with understanding, but also what may mend the social order.

> Laughter appears to stand in need of an echo. Listen to it carefully: it is not an articulate, clear, well-defined sound; it is something which would be prolonged by reverberating from one to another, something

beginning with a crash, to continue in successive rumblings, like thunder in a mountain. Still, this reverberation cannot go on forever. It can travel within as wide a circle as you please: the circle remains, none the less, a closed one. Our laugher is always the laughter of a group.[24]

For Bergson, laughter is explicitly a social project. "Laughter must answer to certain requirements of life in common. It must have a *social* signification."[25]

The social significance of laughter finds its place within a "life in common," circulating in and around social exchanges to contour instances of "imbalance"—of that which breaks and undercuts the common—with a "corrective." "Society will therefore be suspicious of all inelasticity of character, of mind, and even of body, because it is the possible sign of a slumbering activity as well as of an activity with separatist tendencies, that inclines to swerve from the common center round which society gravitates: in short, because it is a sign of an eccentricity."[26] At this point, laughter functions for Bergson as a corrective targeting the gestures, movements, and formalities that capture social life in a net of repetition, of rigidity, in "slumbering activity." What Bergson suggests is that laughter supplies a vital elasticity—a reinstatement of the common, of a social life of movement and flexibility—buttressing as well as intervening onto the formal expressions of bodies with its giggling.

The nonknowledge of Bataille is rather overturned in Bergson, as laughter seems to operate precisely in the center of what we all know, rather than on the edge of knowledge. In other words, we laugh at what is unspoken, and yet so obvious.

Punctuate

Laughter can be appreciated for supplying us with a medium, for rebelliousness, self-indulgence, joy, pleasure, and the raptures of letting oneself go—an opening up that floods the body with such emotional and physical energy, to come pouring out of the mouth. It conveys self-presence by being outlandish in the face of convention, as a gesture withstanding the pressures of staying in place. Yet, as I've also tried to suggest, the laugh grants us *entry*—it not only opens onto a certain danger, as Bataille suggests, but also performs as a mode of participation within social life, within the common, as a way of being with others. It is an extremely important audible rivet piecing together relations; and it does so by "punctuating" the flow of speech: "During conversation, laughter by speakers almost always follows complete statements or questions. Laughter is not randomly scattered throughout the speech stream."[27] The rather ordered recurrence of laughter within common speech—inserted within the rhythms of conversation, and forms of group behavior, as a modulating energy within the ebb and flow of sharing—seems to appear as a somewhat "concluding" event, lending a punctuated contour onto the passing of conversation. This interaction, between speaking and laughing, begins to suggest a dichotomous view in which "the expression of cognitively oriented speech" is contrasted with the "more primitive, emotion-laden vocalization of laughter."[28] Is laughter then a break or accent aimed at balancing the often-reasoned order to conversation, words, and speech, with its bodily and vibrant energy? To literally fill the mouth with an alternative matter? A release of tension that maintains a steady introduction of what is always already central to social life? And might such punctuation, and emotional delivery, also echo with the dangers mapped by Bataille—that the punctuating vitality of the laugh surrounding conversation flirts with what lies on the peripheries of the rational? The trace of carnival always embedded within social life?

This push and pull may highlight how laughter wields a dramatic ambiguity. Is not the laugh a paralinguistic gesture, an extremely rich mouth movement, whose meaning is always in question? That is, a pure vitality whose coordinates and destination are forever shifting? "In releasing laughter the joke liberates laughter's double purpose of threat and bond."[29] A double consisting of rupture *and* recuperation, danger *and* affirmation. The laugh may unsettle the territories of language by communicating a surprising pleasure; it may counter structures as they bear down onto individuality, and in doing so, to return us to each other, as subjects full of desire, and of archaic memories. The laugh literally *affords* the individual a potent means for transgressing the limits that are always surrounding, either in the form of social etiquette or something greater, as an unbearable circumstance against which the laugh may provide a sudden release or route. An escape by which we may also find another form of community.

Echoing Paul Carter's notion of an "erotic ambiguity" inherent to sound, we may hear the laugh as a potent slippage that escapes via the mouth to activate the entire body—from the diaphragm and the pit of the stomach to slaps on the table and stomps of the feet, an entire embodied and acoustical movement that produces social connections while also alienating others.[30] A sensual performativity that affords the subject an element of play. Laughter, and the clownish, supplies a certain vocabulary, a grammar of body forms that evidences possibilities for navigating the tense pathways of social life. As Alenka Zupančič outlines in her extremely rich analysis of comedy, "the flaws, extravagances, excesses, and so-called human weaknesses of comic characters are precisely what account for their not being 'only human.' More precisely, they show us that what is 'human' exists only in this kind of excess over itself."[31] Laughter is a route out of often-difficult moments; it is a channel—for ambiguity, for escape, and for return, of what is enduring.

The laugh is thus a project for the future, for it may be heard to disrupt the plane of social space, enthralling and annoying at one and the same time.

It builds communities out of thin air, as a contagion spawning unexpected connection. It rivets the social with humor, pleasure, cruelty, and potentiality. It modulates and breaks, only to reaffirm.

Hysteria

Returning to issues of identity, and the operations of the powerful look, for Hélène Cixous the laugh is just such a potent proclamation on the field of desire and power. In her essay, "The Laugh of the Medusa," she traces the narratives leading to an understanding of hysteria, where the forces placed upon the female body by the examining male doctor leads to symptomatic spectacle: contorted expressions, locked limbs, gaping mouths, speechless, or telling lies, these come to be identified as expressions of repressed desire—women, in other words, are guilty of secret wishes.[32] As Janet Beizer argues:

> The doctors' representation of hysterical voice is a caricature of culturally accepted perceptions of female voice, for if human voice is situated between mind and matter . . . woman's voice is skewed so far to the side of corporeality as to all but deny the other end of the connection. The voice of hysteria that sings and cries to the medical men, laughs and burps, meows and barks, grunts and babbles is the negative double of accepted patriarchal speech: devoid of the control and signifying clarity of adult language, it is replete with the affective and sonorous properties that the doctors renounced when they entered linguistic manhood.[33]

In this way, the female body is called upon to perform for an audience of male physicians, in this scene of looking and the authoritarian gaze demarcated by such powerful interplay: to observe the hysterical body, the medical gaze performs its own unconscious wish to witness the feminine in all its power, its secret magic, and its erotic animality. The gaze, for Cixous, locates hysteria as that very display of feminine power defined as enthralling and threatening, supernatural, and demonic.

Within such a scene, Cixous also locates a potentiality in which the performance the body is called upon to enact is, in turn, a stage for subversion or escape. The hysteric disrupts familial bonds, and the relationships that keep "woman" in a proper place, by becoming a spectacle—displaying that which is looked for, and that which must also remain out of view. Such havoc finds expression through words, but also through the body, in which gestural articulations—of tics and squirms, hardened limbs, and convulsed gyrations, as well as through those "sonorous properties" Beizer points toward—prolong the scene.

As part of this vocabulary of uncertain passions, the laugh enters to be heard, as Cixous hears it, as both obstacle and irruption. The laugh unsettles diagnosis by turning back onto the medical gaze an ambiguous gesture—for the laugh instantiates a sense of agency, giving expression to a madness that is difficult to read. It signals the potentiality that the scene is being directed not by the analyst, but by the other, the woman on the couch. Thus the laugh gives the hysteric a weapon, a mask, a gesture, and a vocality that can be heard to problematize, resist, or transgress the arresting maneuvers of language and the look. It specifically teases and pokes the "seriousness of the phallic" mapped by Irigaray, which "claims to state its meaning" as truth; which claims to speak *for* desire, a "discourse about sexual pleasure, and thus also about *her* pleasure."[34] In other words, the laugh affirms the hysteric symptom while suggesting recuperated agency.

We might witness this rupturing laughter in the video work by Sam Taylor-Johnson discussed earlier. *Hysteria* shows us, in extended detail, a laughing woman whose presence is difficult to read: what causes this laughter we never know. Rather, the laughter is but a sign, an expression whose mute rendering leaves us guessing. I take this uncertainty as key, and as an echo to what Cixous is claiming: that as viewers we are intentionally dislocated, unsettled, our gaze put into question, as the very source of the scene. In other words, the woman both laughs for us, and *at us*.

Laughter is captured as a potential means for deflecting the authoritarian gaze of patriarchal meaning. In this sense, it's important to also extend this further, not only as a dynamic within female sexuality, but also within the performances of masculinity. Does not the clownish, and acts of shenaniganery, delineate a field of faltering masculinity? A site where humor and laughter perform to release the male subject from the script of a certain performance, a certain expectation, a certain truth? Every clown is a sort of faltering man—here I would generally claim the clown as a male figure, just as the hysteric is generally cast as a female subject, though each no doubt can be occupied and experienced by each gender—a performing body unable to follow through with the obligations of malehood. The clown, the buffoon, and the fool may perform as a spectacle, but their role is designed specifically to unleash and support that intense auditive rapture at the very core of laughter: to find a route toward a future liberation.

I'd like to suggest that laughter is a territory sounded out and shaped as a zone of *dispute*. In this way, it is my interest to recognize in laughter an extremely central performativity: in its enactment, laughter both calls into question the lines of a social order while reinstating others; it gives way to the forces of danger, of the *incommensurable*, aligning us with the irrational, and the spirited vitality of the nonsensical—madness, foolery, shenaniganery, and clownery—while also figuring a set of actions and agencies that operate through the common and the sensical. Laughter, in other words, makes sense while explicitly entertaining all that lies in opposition.

Seen

I want to move away from these greater discursive perspectives, to return to the scene of laughter and to the ways in which we laugh throughout everyday life, that is, the common laugh. Laughter, on a fundamental level, is a sudden irruption onto our countenance; it is in many ways our most active and dynamic facial expression. As an instant of sudden facial animation, the laugh also shifts and modulates the face-to-face encounter, that is, the tensions of the exchanged look. Does not laugh, as an incredibly dynamic event, unsettle the drama always already present in the operations of appearance—in the functionality and answerability found in facing the other?

Returning to the "field of vision," and the powerful operations of the ocular, it's interesting to finally consider laughter as a mode of negotiation, a greater corporeal and psychic expression by which to modulate and shift the presence of the other's gaze. To agitate, for an instance, the lines that surround us and that fix us. How often we giggle, smile, and laugh throughout a meeting, a conversation, an exchange (even, a medical examination); free from any actual "joke," these occurrences do much to shift the borders of being *in front*, of and for another. A sort of restlessness or nervousness lurks behind the laugh. Returning to Bergson, laughter supplies the body with flexibility. In such moments, we may be laughing so as to unsettle the field of vision, and the economies that work to fix us as an object framed by a certain view or facial presence. A type of fidgeting, laughter vibrates the materiality of this body, this subject, and this mouth always so pulled by language, while in the thick of social meeting, to flex and inflect how we are seen.

9

Lisp, Mumble, Mute, Pause, Stutter

Only later do the words come.

First, there is the movement, not as sounded expression, nor as a fully realized articulation; not yet. More a soft animation unfurling from the deep knot of memory to suddenly float and then capsize into breath; at this instant, this indescribably slow revelation, a line starts to make its way. Back to front, to the side and then over, down and back again—the line whose wavering pulls forward a set of words; not even, more a mist of thinking from which I begin to hear the preceding moment, the initial gap, when the words held themselves back in search of form. That is, a moment of pause and hesitation, of uncertainty; *before* the word that would start the line tumbling forward and over itself, as an opening, for the other.

It is my interest to hang onto this hesitation, this gap, to occupy the prolonged moment, this *being on the verge of speech*. In such a gap we might detect the life of the voice, its arrival, as a slow irruption between the lips, and which irritates the air in front with sudden force. With this pause, this gap we might capture the body as it tries to move forward, as it seeks to propel itself into a second body, the body shimmering in the wake of speech—what Annette Stahmer calls the "voice body" and which assists us in *becoming*, in coming out.[1]

This *threshold of speech*, this *prior to*, is suggested in Christian Kesten's *zunge lösen* ("releasing the tongue"), a composition for the mouth staged by any number of performers.

The piece consists of the following elements:

- (Fine) Slaps of the tongue on the bottom of the mouth
- (Visible) Tongue movements

- Tongue movements, which articulate a (chance) text, based on a given material of phones, the atoms of language (syllables and smaller). Through breath, they are made audible from time to time (whispering). Tongue movements and breath function as independent layers which interact.

Lips and jaw don't move. They only open at the beginning to a relaxed position and close at the end.[2]

The work gives us the mouth exposed, opening and then closing, with its tongue a figure poking out, then slipping back, induced by "the atoms of language" that steer the mouth toward speech. In following these movements, we may hear not the voice, or any sound *per se*—maybe a whisper . . .—but rather an oral site always already preceding speech; a reverberating gap—this oral *cavity*—allowing for and conditioning what may appear: a syllable suddenly there on the tongue (Figure 9.1).

In focusing on this threshold of speech, the gap, and the cavity, I'm interested in considering the mouth as a vessel not filled with language, but more so, *haunted* or stammered by it. The hesitant moment of all such vocal pauses lead the way for considering the greater territories of lisping, stuttering, and finally aphasia. Might stuttering give us this gap, this hesitation, amplified and embodied, performed and tensed, to afford a glimpse onto the profound nature of the speaking mouth? And importantly,

FIGURE 9.1 *Christian Kesten,* zunge lösen, *1999. Performed by WE SPOKE: Serge Vuille and Guy-Loup Boisneau, 2011. Photo: Andreas Zihler.*

a view onto a subject under duress by the force of a linguistic order? A tensing of the body under the pull of voice? Within its tiny repetitions, its clicks and pops, its irregularities, might stuttering put on display this *prior to speech*, a speech caught in the mouth, this pause, or lag, of a body moved by and *moving into* speech? Or, expressed also in the lisp, as a softening of the articulated, a prolonged sibilance, where the mouth slips over words and letters? Kesten's composition gives entry into such openings, exposing not the grain of a voice, but its *material envelope*, allowing us to query the mouth as *rhythmed* by a certain linguistic friction.

Interrupt

The vocal lag or lisp interrupts the production of a proper speech, yet one that may supply it with added cultural breath, a friction that leads the way toward a poetics and politics of the oral imaginary. *The very discursive performative that drives this lexicon, and which sets its sights on capturing a horizon of expanded utterance*, which is equally an expanded sociality—for what or whom might be left out.

Stuttering may be understood as a form of *negotiation* played out in sudden rhythmical breaks, a sort of beating that catches the breath, the tongue, and the jaw; a voice that staggers over vocabularies, and against the contour of words—stuttering as a complex, somatic weave that holds the voice, stammers it. Yet, the interruption of proper speech is to be found already *in* the mouth: "The threat to coherence, to the established course, to smooth flow, proliferates in the mouth that utters . . ."[3] Christof Migone underscores speech as always already prone to erring. To open the mouth is to already open the way for mishap, salivation, excess—the mouth "cannot help but get confused, jumbled, mixed up."[4] For Migone, there is a primary tension found in the relation between the mouth and language, the buccal and the spoken, corporeality and linguistic grammar, that stuttering captures or makes explicit. The stutter breaks into language, into the scene of speech, to interrupt that steady stream of words with an unmistakable gyration. What comes forward, in this mouth movement, is not only the stigmatization often experienced by the stutterer, but also the subsequent appearance of something—*the thing . . .*—that haunts the dominant functionality of wording and the foundational narrative of proper speech.[5]

As Marc Shell outlines in his extremely poignant book, being a stutterer can lead to difficult experiences of ridicule: "Being teased in the schoolyard was not the only problem. One day, the school principal, Mr. Webster, asked me into his office. He explained to me that stuttering was a 'sure sign' of being mentally deficient, or 'retarded.' My failure to read aloud properly, said the principal, was not *my* 'fault.'"[6] Examining histories of stuttering individuals and related narratives, found in linguistic and religious traditions in particular, Shell also points to various "techniques" developed by a stutterer as means for negotiating these social tensions and the words or vocabularies that trip up one's speaking, for instance by changing one word for another in midsentence (intralinguistic synonymy). As Shell suggests, such techniques lead a stutterer to develop a "second language," one that shadows a primary language and that derives from a negotiation with all that bears down on the one who misspeaks.

Extra

Moments of fluid speech are actually quite rare. Rather, speech is most often punctuated by small interruptions and hesitations, notably pronounced in the micro-vocables *er*, *um*, and *uh*—those "additions" so annoying to the operations of broadcast media in particular. A series of vocables that take up residence within the flow of wording and that, rather than undermine speech, aid in the steady stream of thought by giving space, for an instant, so as to let what's next find their way. *Er*, *um*, and *uh* begin the process of voicing by bringing sound into the mouth, massaging lip and tongue into movement, and pushing air through the passages of the oral cavity, so as to stir it into motion, in preparation for the enunciative act. In preceding the spoken, these hesitations come to *assist* in the final delivery of words: they figure a *gap* in order to get the body going. Breaths that ease onto the plane of wording without fully arriving, and that no less register the intentionality of the speaker—they say: *I intend to speak more*. Or, *I can't find the words yet*.

As intervals, these *disfluencies* or *extra* phonemes are interruptions, yet one's that stave off any absolute break: they catch the mouth, letting it linger for an instant; we can almost hear the silent word taking shape here at the back of the mouth as one attempts to hold the conversation, and the interlocutor, within a flow of the spoken. Yet there is always a looming void just on the other side, an emptiness that infringes upon these small utterances and threatens to propel speech into full breakdown: if one hesitates too long, letting *er*, *um*, and *uh* take over, recovery may be difficult. In being drawn out, or held too long within the mouth, these spacings may also overtake us. In this regard, such breaks, like the stutter, interrupt our speaking. Yet, they do so by inflecting its rhythms; they expose the body, uncovering language as a material sculpted by the oral cavity.

Er, *um*, and *uh* thus reveal a body within the motion of speech, and a mouth in search of words—that is, a mouth in search of voice. Subsequently, speech can be appreciated as a dramatic movement, a choreography modulating all the intensities that pass between body and language, between emotional energy and semantic meaning, between memory and conversation. The gaps and spacings that do appear, here and there, only reinforce and remind of this primary action: that one is located within the flow of surrounding life, and wherein language is central. *Er, um,* and *uh* reveal a body tuning itself to the sociality of speech, of being in front of another, and navigating all the affective geographies encapsulating our individuality.

By hearing in the *stop* of speech a tussle between body and language, the mouth that trips or lags behind, *that shies away,* may also remind of hidden musicalities, of difficult silences, of the needed gaps by which we may find the means to progress, through any number of "second languages," slipping and sliding—a *lisping* . . . a mumbling—as well as a phonic profusion; tuning as well as detuning—that is, negotiation and *performance.* As an amplification of the inherent relational dynamic of the voice, stuttering raises this into a tension; it stammers speech with the somatic logic of the mouth to sound all the breaths and rhythms, punctuations, and hesitations that words come to impart.

Scratch/Delay

Shifting perspectives, these stammered poetics also find a certain musical expression or equivalent in the operations of backspinning and scratching within traditions of hip-hop and rap. The appropriation of turntables as instruments renders the vinyl record a potent surface, not only for sampling, but also for cutting, breaking, and scratching the *in-between,* an amplification of exactly that point of the stammer or the lisp.

"The Adventures of Grandmaster Flash on the Wheels of Steel" (1981) is a perfect rendering of early hip-hop, capturing the DJ aesthetic in which samples—and in this case, we cruise through a montage of familiar riffs, beats, and lyrics, from Blondie to Queen to Chic—all cut and scratched together, are performed with unexpected dexterity. These turntable musicalities accentuate precisely that point of capture, the gap between repeated samples, to produce a "stutter effect"[7]—one sample cut into another, further underscored in the scratch, where the record is pushed and pulled, back and forth, as an act of radical suspension: the beat is forced onto unsteady ground, in a dizzying spell of capture and release; we hang there, in this gap, the stammered and lisped dynamics agitate us for an instance, as a body, only to support a feverish audition.

Employing three turntables, this particular mix reworks existing matter to lead us directly into the center of a hybrid sonority, a "sonic fiction" drawing forward the beat over the melody, the break over the time signature. These breaks, of course, find expression in break dancing, and especially, in acts of popping. Quickly contracting and releasing muscles, popping creates jerky movements timed to the beats of the mix. All such jagged and exaggerated tensions move the body along in robotic fashion, though giving way to surprising fluidity; as in the sampled mix and related scratch, the particular vocabulary of the pop achieves great agility and elegance, giving deep suggestion for the stammer and the stutter, the lisp and the *disfluent*, as vehicles for cultural expression.

The aesthetics of the mix, and its expression of the stuttered, the stammered, the broken beat, finds a deeper and hallucinatory appearance in the legacies of reggae and dub music. Dub's absolute obsession with delay and echo leads the mix into greater uncertainty; the swaying rhythms of the dancehall, punctuated by the stylized syncopation or back beat expressed in the guitar's tinny chording, are suddenly thrown into disarray through delay's exaggerated repetitions. Such electronic repeats break into the mix to stagger the logic of duration, melody, and lyric. Dub deepens the space of the cut, locating the break, the gap, within a composition of repetition, bass grooves, percussive spread, and the stoney rhythms of delay.

Weak

The break, cut, scratch, dub, and delay all support a notion of the pause, the disfluent, and the stutter as cultural and linguistic platforms, narratives of what I'd like to refer to as "the weak." It is my view that interrupted speech supplies our oral imaginary with poetical matter; matter equally generative of an assemblage of bodily expressions founded on weakness. I'd like to suggest that interrupted speech may provide a vehicle for an agency of the weak-mouthed, the weak-footed, or the weak-minded, where "lackluster" vocability may in effect spirit another type of logic or epistemology.

To give greater focus onto this notion of the weak, I'd like to turn to the work of Gianni Vattimo, and in particular, his idea of "weak thought." Vattimo's philosophical project of weak thought, developed notably in the 1980s, specifically aims to challenge metaphysics, as the truth of Being, in support of an "anti-foundationalism." For Vattimo, metaphysics performs a primary suppression by limiting "the free play of dialogue and interpretation" and by "silencing those voices that are not appropriately related to the foundation" of Being.[8] In contrast, Vattimo understands Being not as a foundational narrative, but rather as "an event" located within a historical framework, and one passed down, as a type of echo, from being to being. As he states: "Being never really *is* but sends itself, is on the way, it transmits itself."[9] In this regard, the foundational narrative of metaphysics is overturned by a "positive nihilism" where the "occurrence of being is a background event."[10] Weak thought stakes out a position by which to unsettle "powerful thought" and the "violence" of metaphysics; weak thought is a project that ultimately opens a space for "the silenced" and in support of public life. "Instead, Being is dissolved in the history of interpretation, in which there are no facts, only more or less cogent interpretations."[11]

Read in an expanded way, weak thought is extremely suggestive for a model of subjectivity prone to digression, susceptible to dislocation and distraction, a horizontal perception aimed at interconnectivity, dialogue and even, slowness. In this regard, I find in weak thought support for the weakly spoken, and for weak bodies; lazy tongues, incredibly slow sentences, and prolonged repetitions manifest also in the slow learner. In short, weak thought as the basis for *delayed presence*.

"I think, however, and speaking in general, that the manner in which humanity can experience and live its human dimension in this postmodern world is by developing the positive potential of a 'declining' experience of values, one that is more diffuse and less intense."[12] Following Vattimo, we might learn from this "declining" and diffusion a form of weak speech tuned to the delicate and *interrupted* movements of the spoken, that is, language as it lives inside the mouth, and in particular, from the mouth that squirms in the midst of the stutter, with all the materiality of its animate force placed there on the lips, against the teeth, and on the sky of the mouth.

These weak poetics may spirit an interrogation of linguistic ordering, of the powerful and the proper, staged in the very gap or cut of disfluent hesitations. A gap in which power performs to shame the stutterer, according to a narrative of "foundational speech," but also where we might rescue the primary energies of the spoken, exemplified by way of a certain *noise*.

Significantly, Migone understands such noise as the appearance of "the foreign." Stuttering, in other words, may be heard as the articulation of radical porosity—an agitation precisely upon the lines of the delimited body, the one functioning under the orders of the proper and the powerful. "Most experts do agree, however, that somewhere along the line a stutterer has been bullied to be vocally clear."[13] If the stutter is to be understood as the result of external pressure, it might also be heard to *speak back* this pressure, returning it precisely in the form of the unclear, the improper, the tensed, and the pressured. It is above all the noise of a pressured mouth, whose lisped speech, as George Watsky eloquently demonstrates through a hyperbolic poetry focused upon the letter S—that very point upon which the lisp rests—may also cut into the principles of the proper.

My subtle lisp is not sinful. I'm not sorry Saturday,
I'm not sorry Sunday; I'm spiritual and when I speak I
celebrate the Sabbath seven days a week.
I've got special S sauce all smothered on my skull
walls like a tossed salad so silk screen the Sistine
ceiling on my soft pallet.
I sing along with super seensters reciting Sufjan
Stevens songs in skinny jeans.
Dance salsa with soccer moms sneaking out in skimpy
see-through sarongs.
I will answer your questions in stout with my sexy
subtly lisping sparkling incisor small.[14]

Watsky's litany of the S delivers the lisp as an attack on the law and order of the vocally clear; it returns to the "speech bullies" the very thing they abhor, to ultimately prolong the agitation, the vocally unsure, and in doing so, to harness the energy of the poetic, there in the logic of the weak mouth.

The poetics posited by Watsky—as that which hovers in a mouth navigating the territories of proper speech—finds an elaborated reference in the phenomenon of beatboxing. Stemming from hip-hop, as a vocal imitation of the first "beatbox" machines, the practice has developed significantly since the 1980s. Here the mouth is used as a percussive machine, capturing all the turntablism of the hip-hop mix there on the tongue, between the lips, to perform an extremely rich assemblage of multiple breaks, gaps, and rhythmical cuts. Beatboxing creates a sonic poetics precisely from the agitating stammers of the broken voice.

An inside contorted by an outside; a background coming forward; a voice pressed inward, or pressing back, *beating*, flushed or flummoxed, and whose sudden hesitation brings into relief these forceful tensions provoked at the very moment one opens the mouth. "If one conceives the body as porous, it becomes impossible to think of an individual without a collective, impossible to keep your distance, impossible to delimit the outside from the inside."[15] All such interrupted speech, disfluent articulations, lisped and stuttered words reveal these relational intensities, always already in the mouth and yet conditioned by the looming narrative of proper speech. Instead, the porosity Migone highlights may support the weak body, a body always already as an echo of another—being to being, and in the throes of so many exchanges.

This radical porosity is at play in Richard Serra's video work *Boomerang* (1974). Through the invasive dynamics of the echo, the work can be heard to capture this foreignness, of what has already been passed down, or what lurks within. In the video, the artist places a microphone in front of a woman (the artist Nancy Holt). The woman wears headphones and can hear her speaking voice, yet delayed—her voice comes back to her, slightly behind her own speaking. The woman speaks, talks about this experience—she refers to the situation, tries to describe what she is hearing, and how this echo disrupts her speech, her ability to control her own thinking. Something is always coming back to interrupt her:

Yes, I can hear my echo and the words are coming back on top of me
Uh, the words are spilling out of my head
    and then returning into my ear
It puts a distance between the words and their apprehension, or their
    comprehension
The words coming back seem slow, they don't seem to have the same
    forcefulness as when I speak them
I think it's also slowing me down

I think that it makes my thinking slower
I have a double-take on myself
I am once removed from myself
I am thinking and hearing and filling up a vocal void
I find that I have trouble making connections between thoughts
I think that the words forming in my mind are somewhat detached
    from my normal thinking process
I have a feeling that I am not where I am
I feel that this place is removed from reality . . .[16]

Serra's *Boomerang* stages the dynamics of echoing sound, and in doing so, captures a body tripping up, and an unsettled speech. As the woman states, it's as if she is absent from her own body, *evacuated*, to become stranger to herself, with her voice coming back to her as though from another reality— she is out-of-sync. The work operates as a sort of test, a laboratory aimed at this difference of oneself, and its ultimate amplification. The mouth, in this regard, is a definite echo chamber that may at times give way to this porosity of the body outlined by Migone—that it is susceptible to any number of intrusions.

Returning to Marc Shell's critical analysis of the ways in which stuttering performs as a sign of "deficiency," for Migone such a feature may in effect announce passage toward a productive undoing of the self held by the imperative of wording. Using stuttering as a metaphoric engine, Migone sets the scene for elaborating a vocal somatic whereby the voice is not captured by the foundational narrative of proper speech—of getting the words right. Rather, porosity introduces an instant of dynamic exchange in which voice is exposed to the confluences and contaminations at the heart of bodily life.

The weak thought of Vattimo is precisely a philosophy aimed at debunking pure narratives and symbolizations, and accordingly can be read to locate porosity and echoes within the powerful languages of philosophy to ultimately encourage a multiplicity of voices. The deficiency of the stutterer, and found in the echoes of *Boomerang*—this speech undoing itself, at odds with Being—introduces a vulnerable body. That is, a human body, and one open to the world.

Creole

To extend this examination, I'd like to consider the work of Édouard Glissant. Glissant's important analysis of colonialism triggers an extremely suggestive discourse, one sensitive to the complex productions of linguistic culture. Stemming from the discursive schools of the French Caribbean (e.g., found in the literary work of Aimé Césaire, and the theories of Frantz Fanon), Glissant strives to rescue what he sees as "the poetic vitality," or "relational exchange" at the center of postcolonial cultures. The "creolization" of the French language, for instance found in the Caribbean, signals a "complex mix" that, for Glissant, "brings into Relation but not to universalize," rather to underscore "our identities" in dialogue with the possible, with multiplicity.[17]

> We are not going to save one language or another here or there, while letting others perish. The floodtide of extinction, unstoppable in its power of contagion, will win out. It will leave a residue that is not one victorious language, or several, but one or more desolate codes that will take a long time to reconstitute the organic and unpredictable liveliness of a language. Linguistic multiplicity protects ways of speaking, from the most extensive to the most fragile. It is in the name of this total multiplicity and in function of it, rather than of any selective pseudo-solidarities, that each language must be defended.[18]

Glissant's analysis cuts against the "normalization" of language often prompted by nationalistic identification. Is not language often called upon to withstand the pressures of hybridity so as to embolden the pronouncements of a nation? To carry forth traditions, and to secure the limited identity of a culture? Glissant instead reminds of the vividness of language in its "minor" status. Against the "dictations and decrees" of a colonizing empire, such minor linguistics is an opening for identities caught below or outside the powerful dominance of one culture over another.

> Dictating, decreeing: both activities (in their secret complicity: a decree affixes laws to us, a dictation is from an edict now essential) attempt to form a dam against what makes languages fragile—contaminations, slovenliness, barbarism. But what you would call barbarism is the inexhaustible motion of the scintillations of languages, heaving dross and inventions, dominations and accords, deathly silences and irrepressible explosions, along with them.[19]

Accordingly, the languages that search for ways around the colonial project, and that fester and err through oralities here and there, in bodies contaminated by the mixing reality of modernity, carve out all sorts of energetic socialities expressed in what Glissant boldly calls "the poetics of relation." I understand such poetics as a key platform for contemporary voicing. Glissant's work locates a space from which to support the hybridity central to postcolonial culture, not to overlook barbarity, rather to nurture local culture as a sheer cascade of identity in the midst of multiple languages. A cultural project whose languages veer along their course to negotiate the force of decrees and dictates with their own "scintillations"—an "inexhaustible motion" whose poetics cultivates the "migrancy" of relation.

Minor

In considering interrupted speech, we enter into a politics of the mouth. By tripping over the word, stuttering evidences the deep performative drive of the mouth under the spell of the linguistic. It stumbles precisely over a syllable, a grammar, a phoneme; the mouth gasps along the fault lines of a given vocabulary, to lisp over words, and in doing so, raises the volume on the very question as to what constitutes "proper speech."

Is not interrupted speech revealing a body negotiating the "decrees" of proper speech to which all subjects must turn? Is not the stutterer subjected to the particular laws that place blame on "contaminations, slovenliness, barbarism" and whose stammer performs under such law? This "slovenly speech," a deficiency that Shell seeks to undercut and which Migone supports as the beginning of a "foreign body"—a hybridity Glissant further calls "creolization" and finally, "the poetic"—might this represent what Michel de Certeau further terms the "noises of otherness"?[20] "Bodily noises, quotations of delinquent sounds, and fragments of others' voices punctuate the order of sentences with breaks and surprises."[21] These noises suggested by Certeau are precisely what disrupt "the organizing system of meaning," surprising the narrative of proper speech not with aggression or violence, but with what he terms "fragility"—*a fragile speech from a fragile body*. A weakness. The porous body, the creole body, or a "minor body" with a foreign tongue, whose stammering "tattoos . . . the body of discourse."[22]

Questions of the "minor" are given fuller consideration by Deleuze and Guattari, particularly in their work on Kafka. In their examination of Kafka's use of Czech German in the 1920s, Deleuze and Guattari locate an operative tension: "Kafka deliberately kills metaphor, all symbolism, all signification, no less than all designation. Metamorphosis is the contrary to metaphor."[23] In this regard, language turns into a substance whose mutation in writing suspends the sensefulness of meaning, allowing Gregor to become a beetle, dogs to play music, a badger to reflect upon noises overheard. A becoming-difference. "Instead, it is now a question of a becoming that includes the maximum of difference as a difference of intensity, the crossing of a barrier, a rising or a falling, a bending or an erecting, an accent on the word." This "minor literature" exemplified in Kafka's work, for Deleuze and Guattari reveals the "internal tensions of a language"—"Language stops being representative in order to now move toward its extremities or its limits."[24]

The operations of the minor described by Deleuze and Guattari supply a dynamic perspective on the "tensions" inherent to language, found not only in the writings of Kafka, but also in the mouth movements tripped up by the grammar of a major language. While Kafka's animals speak toward a becoming of form, a becoming different, the dynamics of the minor can also be heard as that which mobilizes, if not incarnates, the flexing and lisping of the mouth in its *search for words*. Might we hear in the fragile noises that break onto the scene of proper speech that of a minor voice? A creolization unsettling any metaphysical notion of "origins"?

I'm interested to hear in the stutter (and all such related pauses and disfluencies) the production of an alternative: a negotiation that draws out the tensions of language, as that which captures the body and against which speech cuts, to materialize in a minor poetics and weak being. The "tensors" Deleuze and Guattari identify in Kafka's metamorphosing works, which express or amplify embedded tensions of a language, are additionally to be found in the stutter, the scratch, and break of rhythmed productions: jaw jittering, teeth clicking, throat stopped and tongue caught, each instant of these mouth movements draws out language's powerful capture, leading to the production of *tensed* and fragile speech.

Agency

In cataloging the movements of the mouth, I've been led into a space of animation, of exuberance and excess; even in the unvoiced hiss of the whisper, or the unsounded production of inner voice, there is still an energetic release, and a subsequent alteration of the formed and the fixed. The mouth is especially a vital organ, and a site of vitality. Yet surrounding all such animation there also appears a shutting down, a letting go, and a refusal; within the choreographies of mouth movements there exists the potentiality for keeping quiet, of silence, and of withdrawal. The pause and the gap central to the arena of stuttering and lisping have upon their horizon a prolonged silence.

To resist or to refuse the demands of speech, of "the forced narrative,"[25] leads us into a complicated territory, riddled with questions of citizens' rights, political representation, coercion, and torture, as well as the smaller currents flowing through relationships. To *not speak* is to draw into relief the embedded politics of voice in general, as that which always negotiates the operations of power and the obligations to *pronounce*.

> "Agency" would then be the double movement of being constituted in and by a signifier, where "to be constituted" means "to be compelled to cite or repeat or mime" the signifier itself. Enabled by the very signifier that depends for its continuation on the future of that citational chain, agency is the hiatus of iterability, the compulsion to install an identity through repetition, which requires the very contingency, the undetermined interval, that identity insistently seeks to foreclose.[26]

Judith Butler's argument here positions "agency" as a "citation" of an existing power discourse, and yet importantly, one whose realization necessitates a "disloyalty" to the signifier—a gap, a hesitation, a performative appropriation; a process of interruption, inciting a debate on what or who is excluded, and which may unsettle the dominion of the symbolic. "Agency" is a gap realized and eventually filled in by an identity *in search* of articulation.

Such views return us to the territory of interrupted speech, to give radical suggestion for appreciating the stutter, for example, as one such perturbation. Is not speaking a process of seeking out agency? Does not the voice search through any number of vocabularies for an opening, toward argument, intimacy, or the communicative? To open the mouth is to open a space of negotiation, wherein self and the symbolic meet, to formulate an unsteady weave of vocalizations. Voice must be emphasized less as an articulation of certainty, and more as a *performative attempt* at identity. One that no doubt fully integrates all such hesitations, pauses, distortions, and disfluencies—these are, in effect, the very indication of agency, as being under the pull of language.

I'd like to prolong the "hiatus" and the hesitation even farther, along with the gap of agency Butler details, also to register the voice that may never return—a loss of voice. A mouth movement expressed through an absence, a nonmovement, a full stop. Mute.

Aphasia

Amidst the refusal to speak, and the difficulties in finding the words—of being choked up, stammering, or hesitating—aphasia comes to perform. As with all types of speech impediments, aphasia is mostly the result of sustained trauma or illness. The loss of speech is founded on the diminishing of motor functions due to cerebral damage or injury (notably afflicting stroke patients), as well as experiences of psychological and emotional trauma. In these instances of trauma, voice is literally choked back, restricted as a defense mechanism. "Trauma can rupture the circuit that makes up the vocal process, disturbing the boundary between inside and outside. Making sounds is an act of trust: to allow the intake and expulsion of air you must open up the body. A traumatized person finds such openings too risky."[27] Mutism thus fully locates us, by way of an absence, within the territories of the voice *as* agency and its breakdown.

Uniterable

To be mute leads us into particular histories related to deafness and dumbness, as well as an overall theoretical perspective to query the socialization of subjectivity. As Jonathan Rée chronicles in *I See A Voice*, deafness and dumbness historically chart a particular tension around the topic of agency, and what may constitute individuality or citizenship, as deafness "entailed not just sensory deprivation, but exclusion from language as well, and hence from social and cultural achievement."[28] In both ancient Greece and Rome it was generally "permissible to kill deaf children up to the age of three," while other legal policies, for instance in Jewish traditions, "did not grant them the responsibilities or rights of adults—[the deaf and dumb] were neither liable to punishment, nor competent to own property, particularly buildings and land."[29] In this regard, deafness and dumbness brought forward challenges to legal as well as moral structures; the inability to fully hear or speak immediately placed one outside the normative lines of the social and political order, to force a tension with understandings of citizenship.

The mouth's ability to sound forth in speech is problematically placed at the center of what defines a subject, also leading to debates within the Christian churches whether "the deaf could ever be validly received into Christian communion, since they could neither show that they understood and accept the creed, nor confess their sins."[30] Such views no doubt carry forward into "pejorative attitudes enshrined in the very language of loss of voice"[31] captured in the psychological view of "the neurotic personality." (As I've tried to show, disfluence and speech impediments in general are also susceptible to such discriminations.)

Mutism though is often linked to trauma, fear, and anxiety, and is understood to express withdrawal, and a means for bypassing words and the inherent dangers found in speaking. "Losing one's voice can be a way of going on strike, a withdrawal from the social world . . ."[32] The difference between a lack of speech caused by deafness or illness, and that of aphasia forced by difficult experiences, is captured equally in terms of withdrawal, either from the point of view of a social or legal mechanism, which withdraws the subject, or by the personal conflict that silence may assist in alleviating. This double movement, or double withdrawal, captures the troubling perspective of how *exclusion* functions explicitly against the one who does not speak, or speaks with difficulty, to foreclose identity and participation.

Returning to Butler's outline of agency, as a "hiatus of iterability," we might wonder how the deaf and dumb figure? Metaphorically, many of Butler's terms—of iterability and enunciation—refer us to the domain of the spoken, of the speech act in general. In this way, mutism draws into the open the assumptions we make on what constitutes a "signifying practice." If one is *called* into being, traced out as a subject through the mechanics of *citation* and the signifier, what occurs when one cannot hear or speak? Of course, the force of inscription need not be only heard; surely, the order of power performs through multiple operations and means, locating us through familial and social bonds into the structures by which we gain identity. To be without voice though does make clear the degrees to which language itself radically operates within this overall process, and how law is fully operative through a linguistic and vocal imperative.

Imperial

I'd like to recall Adriana Cavarero's notion of the "uniqueness" rendered by voice and that comes to provide deep resonance and confirmation of individual being: "The voice, indeed, does not mask . . . It communicates the uniqueness of the one who emits it, and can be recognized by those to whom one speaks."[33] Such vocalized uniqueness, by functioning as the central point of the subject, also places great terror on those who cannot speak: "I felt as though helpless and I couldn't get out . . ."[34] In this regard, the voice and its loss delivers fundamental experiences of pain and fright; as stuttering, stammering, and lisping reveal, such uniqueness—that resonating glow of vocal communing—is often shaped or suppressed by the reign of proper speech, by what Patsy Rodenberg also terms "vocal imperialism": "As soon as we open our mouths and speak we are judged,"[35] judgments fueled by social structures that enable some to speak over others, and that carry forward through understandings of what constitutes the "right voice." In this way, the uniqueness of being so pronounced in voicing must be underscored as wielding a dramatic relation to power, to the ordering principles that may support, at times, but that may also certainly bully us into speech. Into being "properly unique."

With experiences of aphasia, such perspectives perform a definite capture onto individuals, especially for those whose loss of voice is the result of injury or trauma. To lose voice might be then to lose that uniqueness so precious to individuation, to the promise of social presence, and that afford routes toward participation. The loss of voice then is a loss of agency[36]; it is a prolonged hiatus that may never return the subject back into the iterability of identity. Or, by necessity, may also force open another route in and around the order of the sensible.

Touch

We might glimpse these powerful vocal operations more fully by considering the Jane Campion film, *The Piano* (1993). The film captures the experience of mutism through the main character of Ada, locating it as a psychosexual device central to the making of certain relationships. Here, mutism functions as the vehicle by which identities take shape, and are ultimately transformed. Developed against the backdrop of the colonial operations of the British in New Zealand in the late nineteenth century, Ada's story is one of a silence sounded by the haptic and the sensual, a silence that both opens onto a horizon of intimacy while shutting down her place within the social.

In the film we learn of Ada's sudden mutism at the age of 6 years, and of her subsequent obsession with her piano (though it remains unclear which came first, her mutism or her piano playing, the two entering her life approximately at the same age); we also discover her closeness with her daughter, who comes to act as Ada's voice, translating her signing to the community around her.

Arriving in New Zealand after being married off by her father to Stewart, a landowner in New Zealand, Ada appears as a reluctant partner, withstanding her husband's advances and remaining in her world of silence, as well as the enveloping sonorities of her piano. Her subsequent relationship with Baines, a worker for Stewart but who also lives with the native Maori, radically alters Ada's life. Baines and Ada come to occupy equally marginal positions within the community; while Baines is white, he understands Maori and is tattooed with Maori symbols. In addition, we learn of Baines' illiteracy, which immediately places him as an echo of Ada—her inability to speak is juxtaposed with his inability to read, coupled as negatives within the sphere of colonial power in which language wields great force.

Yet, what are so active in the film are the sonorous operations of the piano. As Naomi Segal outlines in her analysis of the film, the piano both stands in for the voice while also importantly extending notions of language, and speaking, to that of the skin, the hand, and especially, the caress.

Ada looked at her piano from where she sat in the kitchen breakfasting. A beam of morning light fell across the instrument, highlighting the polished sheen of the rosewood. She moved toward the piano, running a cloth across the top, then brushed the back of her hand along the keys in a familiar and intimate caress. It was as though the piano provided a repository for her emotions, she needed to touch it in order to know her own mind.[37]

The film develops through a series of tensions driven by silence: of the hidden, the unspoken, and the mute, an entire emotional landscape held in mist and uncertainty; a longing that is never articulated, but held and heard through the piano. The piano is, in fact, the only voice: against all the silences that circulate through the film, the piano sounds forth—unabashedly caressed, fondled, and cared for by Ada; it acts as the instrument that literally draws Ada out, unsettling Baines with sudden sensuality, and forcing the husband, Stewart, into jealousy.

I come to interpret Ada's mutism as an expression of hesitation, a refusal that subsequently draws out the barbarity of the system around her; her silence, in effect, triggers suspicion and gossip among the community, and finally, the hatred of her husband, who in a moment of rage brutally cuts off her finger with an axe.

In Ada we are given a mouth that distrusts the voice, that withdraws from the world of men and capital, to seek refuge in the plenitude of the piano's tonal body; a union in itself, between her body and its responsive soundings, and which refers us to an unspoken past: what was it that drove Ada into silence? The sensuality at the center of *The Piano* is one that shifts from the order of affiliation and matrimony, and of patriarchal sensibilities, to that of sensuality and sonority, and in doing so, extends the voice to that of the hands, and the skin, in the formation of alternative relationships. Ada finds voice not through language and speech, but through a haptic intensity and a weakness of the heart. Her hands form a direct link to an enveloping assurance, bypassing the order of words and colonial possession in favor of the touch and related soundings.

Tremble

The weak, as I've been following here, is central to relocating "the right to speak" from the narrative of "proper voice" and toward the "creolization" suggested by Glissant; a move that may also include, in its supplemental vocabulary, a radical sensuality, where the lisp, the stutter, and the caress may perform as practices of unexpected agency, to support new modes of wording as well as being together. Here, the weak-mouthed may in fact provide the order of language with a raw poetics, explicitly allowing us to dialogue through an orality full of trembling and shivering dynamics.

These questions of the proper and improper, major and minor, underscore the difficulties the voice often negotiates. In this regard, I would underscore the voice precisely as a *search* for individuation. The voice is never fully given; rather, it demands investment and investigation, work and care. It supports our need for intimacy and sharing, as well as functioning within the greater territories of the political: to enable, empower, to challenge, as well as to refuse. The voice is rather unstable; instead, it continually brushes against so many relations and offices, histories and languages; it probes for openings and strives to reinforce existing exchanges, friendships, or traditions. It is endlessly shaped by movements in and through the mouth, and the overall structure of the senses. The voice is pressed out of us—to support us by literally taking away our breath. In this way, speaking also fundamentally weakens us, which might be one of its essential lessons.

10

Murmur, Whisper

In focusing on the mouth, it is my interest to consider the *substance* of speech, and how it is stretched and tensed by an array of micro-oralities. If the voice is deeply connected to the ways in which we become subjects, and by which we circulate through the world, the mouth plays a pivotal role as that particular organ whose surfaces and movements craft a multitude of vocalities, some heard and others silently performing.

As I've tried to show, the mouth is a highly dynamic assemblage, expanding in acts of shouting and screaming, while contracting, for instance, in mumbling and murmuring, *whispering*. In quieting one's speech, whispering brings breath and word closer together, to rest one on top of the other. Physiologically, whispering constricts the vibration of the vocal cords while, at the same time, releasing a continuous flow of breath. In this way, the whisper *pulls back* vocal extension, and that sense of outward reach so defining the voice. Yet, paradoxically, such acts of hushed speech come to greatly broaden voice's capacity for contact, communication, and influence. Although whispering may function as such an intimate, and at times, intimidating vocality, it also draws into its thin circumference a high degree of cultural and metaphysical presence. I'm interested in whispering as a modality of voice specifically aimed at communing with the haunted zones of the inhuman, or the *all too human*.

Meta-voice

In John Laver's *Principles of Phonetics*, whispering is catalogued as an "unvoiced" action. In contrast to "voicing," whispering "injects a continuous acoustic input into the vocal tract" without producing the muscular and aerodynamic movements found in voiced phonation.[1] With whispering the "airflow through the glottis is turbulent," thereby "giving a characteristic 'hissing' quality . . ."[2] As Xinghua Li further elucidates in her insightful essay, in whispering "voiced fricatives and stops lose their voicing. Nasals become faint. Regular tonalities of the speech mostly disappear," thereby making it difficult to detect the particular features of the speaker, such as age and ethnicity.[3] In this way, to whisper is to shift the articulated presence of the self, specifically constricting the communicative and informative thrust of the voice.

While voicing is often understood as an expressive movement that exits the body, and extends into greater audibility, as a step into conversation, the whisper, while being expressive, reduces its reach; it hovers at the edge of the audible spectrum as a subtracted orality that subsequently aims for those who are nearby (or for oneself only). It is to speak so not everyone will hear, enveloping conversation in secrecy, intimacy, and confidentiality. To whisper, in short, is often to *conspire*.

As a particular orality, the whisper defines this space of proximity, immediately drawing speaker and listener into radical meeting; the whisper might be appreciated as a *voice-event* seeking to redefine relationships, to resituate the space between two bodies, and to ignite, through such soft hissing, the possible. We whisper, in other words, to drop below the line of sociability, to speak what must be spoken, yet what also should not be overheard.

As numerous fictions and tales attest, the whisper is often *haunted*— the phonetic notion of the unvoiced is coincidentally also the voice of the undead, of ghosts, and sinister beings, of an identity touched by the supernatural, or by powers from the beyond. The manifestation of the whisper used to express horror, suspense, and uncertainty—and not to mention, pure evil—is testament to this deep mythology and vocalic power. Whispering performs precisely where the body is most exaggerated; in those moments of erotic becoming and dissolution, emptied out as well as full-blooded, or fully embodied—ghostly, or paradoxically, deeply physical. As Ying Yang Twins' "Wait (Whisper Song)" expresses, the whispered voice is also explicitly sexual: through its unvoiced articulations, these whispered lyrics speak what in more open circles may be unspeakable.

Hey how you doin lil mama lemme whisper in your ear
Tell you sumthing that you might like to hear
You got a sexy ass body and your ass look soft
Mind if I touch it . . .[4]

To follow the whisper is to enter into a space of intensity, of profound enclosure as well as sudden expansion—to slip underneath the sociality of speaking in search of alternative communication. If the power of voice is understood to modulate the state of subjectivity, with the whisper such modulation aims precisely to find contact with the supernatural, the occult, magic, and the erotic power of the intimate. The whisper, in other words, invites *someone* or *something* to come close, whether in the flows of sexual desire, in the logic of spirit contact, or in the desire for self-transformation. The unvoiced articulations thus carry the intensities of an enraptured body, one in search of or touched by another presence, connected to the ethereal, the immaterial, and the ghostly, or the erotic, the sexual, and the passionate. It is to bring the mouth up close, as a charged orality; when someone whispers to us, we feel the breath against our ear; we are drawn in, full of anticipation: *what does this voice want of me?* In this way, the whisper may threaten and endanger; it may excite or intimidate, but above all, the whisper is a voice used for secrets. Subsequently, while physiologically whispering may be defined as "unvoiced," from a cultural perspective it might be understood more as a "meta-voice," that is, a voicing that explicitly migrates away from semantics and toward secret words and incantations, animal contact and spirit communion, threat and enticement. Or that hovers below the line of clarity so as to capture the fragility of certain visions. The meta-voice moves language toward the peripheries of conventional discourse and human reasoning, to locate us upon a horizon of uncertainty as well as vocalic promise.

Animal

Such transformative voicing (or unvoicing) at the center of the whisper is found in a particular legacy of narratives that bypass the order of the civilized, recuperating instead a heightened relation with animals as well as the force of nature. "I know nature speaks to us if we listen. Every animal has a story to tell. Every flower blossoms with reminders to be creative, and every tree whispers with its rustling leaves the secrets of life."[5]

Ted Andrews's work on communing with nature locates the whisper precisely as a channel offering access to the world of natural secrets. The secret, in fact, appears as central to natural phenomena, as that particular energy that courses through trees, and also animals, giving power or spirit to all life forms, and which Andrews reminds is key to "animal-speak," a speech by which "you begin to learn the language of nature and open yourself to her secrets."[6] His journeys through the natural world are an education on how to listen to the natural signs and signals around us, which may tell us not only of immediate dangers, but also about our life and its circumstances. Learning the language of animals, in particular, can help tune us more deeply to the very world in which our body dwells, in all its animistic force. Animal-speak though is a process of observation and attention, of listening and honoring the "spirit guides." In other words, it is a continual exchange across the senses with all of nature's expressions, leading us into an active process of interpretation—of attuning to the natural world through its whispering presence.

The unvoiced nature of the whisper performs as a vital channel for narratives of human–animal contact, fueling the oral imaginary with metaphysical potential and materiality: of absolute *animation*, over and beyond the logic of capital and its languages of economic value (a language at odds with the speech of nature). The whisper may be what passes between the earth and the sky, as well as across species and natures, to deliver urgent messages. In this way, the closeness of the whisper, the hushed collapse of voice, and the unvoiced condition of the whispering body paradoxically carries across great distances; it bypasses the order of reasoned language, of social structures, even of the physical body, to open up an altogether different communion. A meta-voice for meta-physical relations.

This finds more popular presentation in the novel, and subsequent film, *The Horse Whisperer*. Written by Nicholas Evans, *The Horse Whisperer* recounts the story of a girl, Grace, who experiences a traumatic accident while riding her horse Pilgrim. Resulting in the death of her friend, and the loss of her leg, the event acts as a dramatic catalyst for the girl and her parents, Robert and Annie. In particular, the story of the survival of the horse Pilgrim, who is brutally injured and traumatized by the accident, opens up the rather difficult relationship between mother and daughter. Their already stressed relationship is pushed to its limit as Annie attempts to help her daughter, and Grace experiences the challenges of returning to school, as well as feeling guilty for her friend's death and Pilgrim's suffering.

The story eventually leads Annie to discover the phenomenon of "the horse whisperer"—men who through the ages have known the secrets of horses: "They could see into the creature's soul and soothe the wounds they found there. Often they were seen as witches and perhaps they were. Some wrought their magic with the bleached bones of toads, plucked from moonlit streams. Others, it was said, could with but a glance root the hooves of a working team to the earth they plowed . . . For secrets uttered softly into pricked and troubled ears, these men were known as Whisperers."[7] The whispers passing between horse and men return us to Andrews's theory of animal-speak, and provides a narrative of its performance.

Having discovered the Whisperers, Annie brings Grace and Pilgrim out to Montana, to visit the legendary Tom Booker, a rancher with the "gift." While relationships develop, between Tom and Annie, as well as Grace and Tom, and as Tom slowly begins his work with Pilgrim, a range of emotional intensities unfold. From such a narrative, the notion of whispering appears not only as a direct communicational link between Tom and the horse, but more, as a symbol for the pastoral beauty of the wilderness and the land, of the natural, as well as Tom's grounded philosophy: of family and animal life, of tradition, location, honest work, and above all, natural rhythm (against which Annie, as a professional editor from New York City, firmly contrasts). The dichotomy of rural landscape and urban professionalism— of animal magic and capital gain—ultimately stands as the gap in which

Grace and Pilgrim fall: their accident can be read as the expression of the family's primary imbalance, of lives whose secrets are so firmly buried and unspoken. The novel emphasizes the whisper as a means for mending the break, healing the wounds and returning the family to the purer rhythms expressed by animal spirit, and empathy.

Empathy

The whisper, as I'm proposing here, is a meta-voice fully tied to elemental forces and expressed through the sensitive channel of deep empathy.

> Animals do think, you know. This is probably the best part of being an *empath*, the ability to feel the profundity of nature to the nth degree. . . . I believe our purpose for being here is to be the keepers of nature, the gardens of our mother. No matter however brief our time is here, if a person has nursed one flower to full bloom in our mother's garden, that is a manifestation of the heart that will never be forgotten. We are given these wonderful gifts and opportunity and privilege to contribute our part in caring for our mother.[8]

The text above, written by Cyn, an empath, is but one example found in numerous websites and online forums dedicated to "animal whispering" and "silent communications." Her understanding of these whispered relations supports the "healing" and "restoring" potential unlocked by animal-speak. With Tom Booker this takes shape as a process of transformation; his practice might be understood as a radical form of empathy, where human and animal souls find connection. As the narrative indicates, Tom's power to assuage the inner wounds of the animal finds strength in his ability to feel the animal's pain.

> And now at last he understood what he'd been seeing all this time in Pilgrim's eyes. It was a total breakdown. The animal's confidence, in himself and all around him, had been shattered. . . .
>
> Maybe Pilgrim even blamed himself for what happened. For why should humans think they had a monopoly on guilt? So often Tom had seen horses protect their riders, children especially, from the dangers that inexperience led them into. Pilgrim had let Grace down. And when he'd tried to protect her . . . all he'd gotten in return was pain and punishment. . . .
>
> Later, as he lay sleepless with the light out and the house long fallen quiet, Tom felt something float heavily within him and settle on his heart. He now had the picture he'd wanted or as much of it as he was likely to get and it was a picture as dark and devoid of hope as he'd ever known.[9]

Although such anthropomorphic perspectives may center on certain projections onto animal life, they nonetheless tune themselves to a force of potential contact, indicating that the healing enacted is also one that goes from the powers of the horse and toward that of the human.

The Horse Whisperer supplies us with a vocabulary of the whisper, of hushed speech, ultimately highlighting its relational proximity to the metaphysical, the animal spirit, to transformation as well as that of secrets and trauma.

Darkness

Following the work of John Mowitt in his essay "Like a Whisper," whispering can be heard to interlock with the intensities of trauma, as indicated in Evans's book.[10] As Mowitt also suggests in a reading of *The Horse Whisperer*, that Tom comes to heal by bridging all the traumatic breaks within the stricken family (even between Annie and her husband Robert) bespeaks the power of whispering to give voice, by being unvoiced, to the terrors of experienced trauma, of breakage, while also operating to ease such pains. The whisper performs across this dark terrain, between trauma and desire, terror and sensuality, pain and pleasure. It is precisely unvoiced so as to occupy such a fragile territory, full of extreme emotion and psychological vulnerability, of social or familial collapse.

The whisper is also exploited to great lengths in Joseph Conrad's *Heart of Darkness*. Marlowe's narrative of his journey through the Congo in search of Kurtz, the mysterious and complicated figure around which the tale circulates, continually falls back upon the haunting sonority of the whisper.

> "Who was not his friend who had heard him speak once?" she was saying. "He drew men towards him by what was best in them." She looked at me with intensity. "It is the gift of the great," she went on, and the sound of her low voice seemed to have the accompaniment of all the other sounds, full of mystery, desolation, and sorrow, I had ever heard—the ripple of the river, the soughing of the trees swayed by the wind, the murmurs of the crowds, the faint ring of incomprehensible words cried from afar, the whisper of a voice speaking from beyond the threshold of an eternal darkness.[11]

Kurtz's wife's description of her deceased husband draws Marlowe into a mesmerizing constellation of the auditive—all the sounds that have previously circulated throughout his tale are gathered together here, to refer us back to the ultimate whisper, that of Kurtz's final breath: "He cried in a whisper at some image, at some vision—he cried out twice, a cry that was no more than a breath—'The horror! The horror!'"[12]

Kurtz's last words, whispered and cried at one and the same moment—
which fully captures the inherent ambiguity and metaphysical nature of the
whisper—come to embody the entire narrative and that "eternal heart of
darkness" that serves as the central destination of Marlowe's journey. Lost
in the jungle's inexplicable vertigo, Kurtz comes to symbolize the maddening
drive of European colonialism and its capitalist logic as it winds its way
deeper into itself and beyond all reason. The final whisper appears on Kurtz's
lips as the ultimate expression of this madness, a lost attempt at escape,
as well as description. In fact, as Marlowe recounts, the entire situation
is so disarrayed until finally there is nothing but voices, all confused and
displaced by the system to which everyone is painfully bound.

> Oh yes, I heard him more than enough. And I was right too. A voice. He
> was very little more than a voice. And I heard—him—it—this voice—other
> voices—all of them were so little more than voices—and the memory
> of that time itself lingers around me, impalpable, like a dying vibration
> of one immense jabber, silly, atrocious, sordid, savage, or simply mean,
> without any kind of sense.[13]

Marlowe's loss of perspective aptly describes the heart of darkness that was
to consume Kurtz and the enterprise of the ivory trade, driving him and
others toward the "horror"—one that can only, and finally, be spoken of
through a whisper.

That this horror, and the depths of the jungle, was to find expression
in a haunting sonority suggests that sound is precisely a medium for the
ineffable. The horror, spoken of through such an unforgettable whisper
indicates how the unvoiced—that voice held back in the throat—performs
explicitly to approach what cannot be spoken of otherwise. It's as if the
whisper is a voice barely able to touch its topic; a voice that hesitates to even
dare to utter. In this regard, I might posit the whisper as a center around
which all sonic (and existential) energies might be said to rotate: a central
axis of the unsounded, and the unnameable, to which sound and speech are
forever linked.

The whisper carries within it that primary acoustical feature, that of
ambiguity and uncertainty, of striking proximity as well as mysterious
propagation, echoing Paul Carter's explication of what he calls sound's
"erotic power of ambiguity."[14] Sound as the ultimate channel for bridging
the often-unsurpassable divide between the rational and the irrational.
Following such perspectives, the whisper fundamentally occupies a space of
darkness, of the unseen and unspoken, where, for instance, the living and
the dead may commune. Such is the voice that drives so many narratives of
ghosts and haunted houses, spirited fictions promulgated by a whisper—a
vocalization that *transgresses*. It is so fundamental to the haunted form,
performing an explicit break onto the orders that keep the living and the

dead apart. The mouth that whispers is one that conspires with spirits; it stages an orality full of ghostly want or possession.

Undead

In the TV series, *The Ghost Whisperer*, whispering appears as a means by which the dead and the living may correspond. Launched in 2008, the series centers on the character of Melinda Gordon, the ghost whisperer, and her husband, Jim Clancy, who happens to be a paramedic. Consequently, the couple's lives are unquestionably bound to the traumas of injury and death. In Melinda's case, this unfolds through numerous contacts with the undead: those souls who have not yet passed into the light, but remain on the plane of the terrestrial. Walking the earth, the ghosts are searching, for lost loves, for forgotten dreams, and mostly, for resolution. Throughout the series, each episode places Melinda in contact with a particular ghost or ghosts, locating her within various encounters and conversations, all of which ultimately lead to a successful moment, where the errant ghost finds its way into the light, and toward resolution. Troubled relationships are healed, and lives are allowed to move forward.

Whispering here appears not so much in any single acoustical moment, or in any specific speech act. Rather, it functions as the very conduit that allows communications with the undead; an occult (and hushed) epistemology Melinda and the ghost are empowered to speak, and by which the uncertain passage from life to death is conducted. Whispering, in other words, is not any specific sound or voice, but an alternative paradigm that allows previously unheard voices to be heard, ghosted conversations to ensue, metaphysical knowledge to be reshaped, and relationships to take an alternative course.

The Ghost Whisperer plays out the fundamental conditions of whispering, one that causes us to pause, to wonder, and to ask: *did I hear something?* To, in effect, consider what lies in the dark, which in this case may also appear in full daylight. The power of auditory ambiguity is thus an opening for other kinds of conversations and contact, specifically tuning us to the spectral, the silent, and the unspoken. Such whispering also appears throughout various cultural expressions of electronic phenomena, in which voices seem to hover in the static. From playing records backwards to electronic voice phenomena, electronics and whispering, transmission and murmuring have an intimate relationship. This is given as narrative in another example, that of the film *Poltergeist* (1982). Set in a suburban home in Southern California, the story unfolds around the youngest in the family, the 7-year-old girl Samantha. As the family falls asleep with the television on, in the absence of late-night broadcasting the subsequent static begins to *speak* to Samantha. To call for her. She awakens and starts to converse with these hidden, invisible voices.

The film develops into a haunted house scenario, leading eventually to the appearance of ghosts in the home, and the capture of Samantha by the "voices in the television." She is literally held in the TV, in the noise and murmuring static of this electronic region, which hovers vaguely between earth and sky, the rational and the irrational. *Poltergeist* thus gives contemporary rendering of a greater mythology, one that places emphasis on electronic media and its links to the supernatural.[15] The voices in the static perform within a repertoire of whispers, accentuating the unvoiced murmur as full of ghostly being.

Here we encounter the whisper also as a subliminal force: the static in *Poltergeist* comes to suggest the delivery of particular messages that only Samantha hears. In addition, the absence of any actual whisper in *The Horse Whisperer* conveys the inability to capture its secret passing: it performs undercover. Such covert communications articulate the whisper as a mouthing whose energies may also duck under the line of the spoken, to capture the subliminal ear of the other. The whisper finds its way in, pass the gates of conscious thought, trespassing the borders that maintain the discursive orders of the rational.

Close

Whispering is especially ambiguous. As I've tried to show, it hovers on the line between human and inhuman, supporting the uncertain movements of interspecies or spectral contact. Whispering, in other words, nurtures the forces of rupture and of haunting, as well as that of natural energies and healing. As a particular form of voicing, whispering travels far and wide, to ultimately support the potential transcendence of certain limits.

The whisper subsequently leads us to another perspective onto the mouth; the mouth's capacity to support free and open speech, as that very emblem of democratic society, of full communication, is shadowed by whispering, and the constriction of the vocal mechanism. That the mouth and throat conspire in the form of a whisper, to push back articulation while extending so many communicative possibilities, highlights a radical sensitivity found there on the tongue. Such a view reminds us of how all lingual matters are flushed with an oral ontology, an oral imaginary, that in this case, renders murmuring a means for conducting a different form of public enactment, one tuned to the greater forces of nature.

Hildegard Westerkamp's "whisper composition" from the late 1970s renders the deep performances enacted by the whisper. As a composer and soundscape practitioner, Westerkamp's work continually focuses on the details of the auricular, and experiences of listening that *bring us closer*, into the body of sound and the potent dreamspace of the ear. In her *Whisper Study* (1975–1979), we hear her voice—she whispers: "when there is no sound, hearing is most alert." In following her soft speech, repeated and multiplied over a soft movement of tones and frequencies, we are invited into a soundscape full of imagination, distant soundings, wind and forests, which find their evocative power through the whisper. Her whisper calls us into this sounded silence—that is, a soundscape of deep echoes, made from electronic treatments of the voice. The work delicately balances itself between sound and voice, silence and speech, to accentuate the whisper as deeply bound to the promises and evocations found in listening.

> *When there is no sound*
> *hearing is most alert*
> there are places in the imagination
> where the sound folds into itself
> like freezing
> where the soft crackle of ions
> moves into the air on snow-feet
> made of fine wire
> suddenly you are there
> from behind a boulder
> where you have been watching the moss begin
> and it's as if someone were filling a strangely-shaped cup
> with water from a creek
> somewhere close to your ear.[16]

Integrating the poem by Norbert Ruebsaat into its final section, *Whisper Study* searches for that moment of resonance passing between the real and the imaginary—the shudder between oneself and greater energies, and which hearing may tune us to. It is a soundscape harnessing the spirit of transformation, and transmutation, wherein the materiality of the body, its sensual assemblage, is captured in a greater flow of the otherworldly and the silence full of reverberation. The whispered voice inculcates such an exchange, making palpable this metaphysics at the base of audition through such soft means. Is not the power and paradox of the whisper found in its ability to reduce the audible reach of the voice and the spoken so as to expand our listening? Does not the whisper remind us of such shimmering acoustics, and the ways in which sonority is just such a channel for passage and for contact, for moving deeper into the animate world while connecting to its otherworldly echoes? Is not the whisper a voice transcending itself, an evocation of metaphysical movement, a body already leaving for elsewhere?

The whisper connects us to such supernatural instances, whether in the form of animal-speak, or through sudden contact with spirits; as a mouth movement, a micro-orality, it creates a mysterious geography between presence and absence, embodied articulation and airy ambiguity, evoking a sudden sensuality that pulls us close, into the transformative sphere of the unvoiced. As Edmond Jabès proposes, "Love speaks in whispers."[17]

Politics

"Unlike the coercive shouts, yells or screams, the ruling whisper wields a hegemonic, soft power and sneaks into our social unconscious without being questioned."[18] The movements of ideology, according to Xinghua Li, touch us precisely through a dynamic set of undercover energies, explicitly increasing the volume on power's grip. In this sense, the whisper is precisely a field upon which our attention may find alternative resonance or resistance—in order to "save this privileged means of communication for the disenfranchised and the marginalized."[19] For Li, the whisper may provide us with an extremely important means—a particular modality of speech—not only for overcoming our existential conditions, but also for thwarting the ever-deepening reach of "the ideological apparatus" at the center of the global landscape.

Li's examination of the "politics of whispering"—along with Westerkamp's sonic poem—may serve as a tender map of the transformative potential of the whisper I've been pursuing here. A speech that fuels the imagination with superstition, magic, divine contact, and telepathy, and with intimacy, the whisper may in fact speak for those *without voice*. In this way, the whisper may carve out an empty space, a quiet zone within the order of language and power, to charge the social and political structures with uncertainty, and promise: with all that seems to be relegated to the periphery. *To speak the unspeakable.*

The whisper trembles in front of full disclosure; it barely speaks up because it fears being caught, arrested, and interpellated. (Melinda Gordon has to hide her communications with ghosts; and we never witness Tom Booker actually speaking to horses. In fact, the animal and natural world may speak in whispers as means for avoiding logical arrest. Or as a way to avoid institutionalization.) Such fearful hesitation no doubt performs to quell the voice, to silence speech and to reduce conversation to a whisper. This takes exaggerated form in the operations of whisper jokes. Known primarily within Germany during the Nazi period, as well as under the East German governments, whisper jokes explicitly attack or criticize the totalitarian regime; their whispered passing were thus an undercover speech whose contents circulated through social environments, mirroring the degrees to which eavesdropping and surveillance pervaded society. (These movements of the whisper find additional expression in the "Ford whisper"—workers at the Ford factories whose strict regulations against speaking notoriously resulted in the propagation of whispered speech.)

That one had to keep one's voice down prompted not only a general air of secrecy, but also the rise of certain humor and gossip.

Other

The whisper specifically speaks what others should not hear, or what others might not understand; the whispering mouth is precisely a mouth shielded from the social field. Such secrecy locates us upon a transformative geography—a territory between, *ambiguous*—which incites a different listening, a different inhabitation, one outside the territories of reasoned debate and discourse. The whisper, in other words, incites the making of alternative worlds, whether in gossip and the reverberations within the whispering galleries, or poignantly in moments of silent prayer. It is this "special form of communication" caught in Westerkamp's study, and expressed through legacies of supernatural contact, spirit communications, and animistic communing—all such whispering may give radical suggestion for secret relations and societies. Might the whisper itself point to a legacy of alternative knowledge whose presence must remain silent? If the whisper is the medium by which to trespass and transverse the arena of reason and the reasonable, of capitalistic logic, it may be heard to point toward all that has been repressed by the powers of the outspoken. In other words, at which point did we start to whisper?

Might the alternative utterances of whispering lead the way also for alternative communing, in the making of underground societies, invisible territories, and imaginary nations? The unvoice might be heard as the very channel by which to support unexpected gatherings: the circulation of information, the gossiping of neighbors, whistleblowing, and tattling, all such whispered reports that occupy precisely the background—might these give suggestion for an alternative form of association and affiliation? I understand the whisper then as an orality aimed at all that lies behind the scenes; an undercover agency promoting official and unofficial movements alike—supernatural powers, secret police, resistance groups, love. A voice whose deep and intimate murmurings come to unsettle, and at times repair life with others.

11

Recite, Repeat, Vow

The movements of the mouth are inextricably tied to the plays of power—movements that, in making possible a statement of the self are fully informed by what has come before: histories, traditions, and institutions that perpetuate types of articulation through incorporation on the part of the subject. Language is certainly a dominating force by which such performative dynamics take place, to embed themselves onto the individual voice. The voice is circumscribed by this linguistic structure, empowered by the enabling support of language, while at the same time tensing what counts as proper speech.

The socializing force of language operates not only through vocalization, but also through what I may call "a figuring of the body." A certain repertoire of gestures and behaviors adopted, or *recited* to inform the "appearance" of subjectivity, influencing and effecting the presentation of the self. The mouth, in fact, shows us precisely how our physical form is susceptible to a type of education, one based on conforming to an existing system. Is not learning how to talk equally a shaping of the body, a contouring of our physical form so as to accommodate words and their grammatical organization? The way in which a language requires particular movements that extend across the body, from rhythms of breathing to the shaping of the mouth, and that also fully integrate hand gestures and facial expressions, lead to a complex configuration—a weave of established values and their individuation. Steven Pinker points to this physiological–linguistic relation in *The Language Instinct*, highlighting how "speech sound is not a single gesture by a single organ." Rather, "every speech sound is a *combination* of gestures, each exerting its own pattern of sculpting of the sound wave, all executed more and less simultaneously."[1]

The acquisition of language as an education on developing bodily skills (motoric, posture, spans of attention, etc.) evidences a pronounced interplay between speech and behavior, words and bodily expression. The anthropologist Edward Sapir highlights this interplay in his ground-breaking study of phonology. What is significant in Sapir's work is the degree to which he understands the voice as part of a greater "system of communication" that includes the micro-structures of speech, such as rhythm and intonation, along with bodily positioning and gesture. For Sapir, the voice participates within a larger gestural vocabulary tuned to social interaction and the dynamics of subjectification. As he famously stated: "In spite of . . . difficulties in conscious analysis, we respond to gestures with an extreme alertness and, one might almost say, in accordance with an elaborate code that is written nowhere, known by none, and understood by all."[2]

I'm interested in the ways in which the voice performs in this expanded sense, as a gestural articulation of not simply language, but language infused with affective patterning, with the stuff of the body and the shimmering tensions that occupy our words with so much memory and personality, with that which has come before.

Prior

Following the work of Judith Butler, the ability to "have a say" is first and foremost predicated on a prior announcement, a previous exercise of power always already in the voice, and inside the mouth. For Butler, to appear as a subject, an "I" within the sphere of social life, is to also hold, as a type of potentiality, the force to name again.

> Where there is an "I" who utters or speaks and thereby produces an effect in discourse, there is first a discourse which precedes and enables that "I" and forms in language the constraining trajectory of its will.. . . Indeed, I can only say "I" to the extent that I have first been addressed, and that address has mobilized my place in speech.[3]

To be "in speech" is to participate within the performative dynamics of naming—to *stand up* within language. The name, which is placed over a body and subsequently draws that body forward as an identity, also enables further naming—it gives to the one who is named the potentiality of naming again, of addressing the world around and, in doing so, to conjure, capture, or pronounce; to command, resist, or appeal. It produces a futurity by which power relations and discourses are fundamentally sustained, and also challenged. This *bequeathment* though is never a given. Rather, it functions as a "citational chain," a lineage—an ethos—that places demand upon the subject (to repeat, restate, reiterate), while suggesting a horizon of possible modulation—repetition or recitation is never a perfect copy, rather it necessarily falters, struggles to fit, or to search for a way through. *We must try identity on.* It may be a process by which we find ourselves, already waiting.

These citations passing through the name opens up a perspective that recognizes the *coming into being* as an appropriation of what has been given; what precedes my name is the force of a normative (linguistic) order, which once placed over my body enfolds me in its grip while also demanding an individuation of its terms. I enter the name given to me, yet only in so far as I'm able to express its embedded meaning; I may live up to its expectations, to this body, or I may also fall short.

To return to the work of Sapir, and the subsequent development of kinesics as a branch of study on learned, patterned body-motion behavior (pioneered by Ray Birdwhistell), the performances that come to direct our social interactions are fully conditioned by an array of micro-exchanges that pass across the social field. Each situational instance is determined by not only what we bring forward to that moment, openly, but also how we come to interpret the setting, and our place within it. In this regard, "the body" is not only defined by the linguistic enactment of the name, but importantly, the paralinguistic and kinesic repertoire of behavioral patterns and gestures that come to occupy and animate the social field.

Importantly, for Butler, this "enactment" is also never fully certain: "the impossibility of . . . fully inhabiting the name by which one's social identity is inaugurated and mobilized, implies the instability and incompleteness of subject-formation."[4] The "instability" of this subject-formation is precisely the point at which the citation that is oneself takes on modulation, animation, discovery; a respeaking that is also a *mouthing the words* by which we come to *inhabit* language, by which we bring it into the body, and elaborate it through gesturing and figuring, as well as there between the lips.

Accent

The performativity intrinsic to one's identity finds expression in *and* upon the voice. Butler's work supplies us with so many stimulating points of entry onto the subject of speech, and from my perspective, gives suggestive force for probing the mouth as the *site* of citation; again, not as a privileged dominion of authentic self, but a performative cavity that labors precisely on this territory of naming, iterability, and modulation; of trying on, failing, and finding again. We may enter the field of language, to recite an existing form, but it is within the mouth that such speech takes shape, to exit from a body inscribed within a certain setting, and within a certain lineage.

Speech is deeply marked by the particulars of place, as a looming backdrop to what is inherited. In short, Butler's notion of reciting can be found exactly on the tongue, in the form of dialect and accent. These language behaviors, which blend numerous specificities, of class and ethnicity in particular, come to intersect with locale to produce an identifiable voice, a familial voice, or a voice of the neighborhood. Accent and dialect might be said to class the voice and texture the tongue with history. Such particular inflections imprint onto the sonority of speech, sculpting and conditioning the mouth with specific movements and behaviors, words and their meaning. All these conditions, in sounding forth come back to mark the body as being *from* certain places.

In her project, *Topography of a Voice,* the artist Imogen Stidworthy explores these dynamics of accent. Here the accent is literally captured as a topographical image, an inflection that presses and sculpts the voice, in this case, by following *Scouse,* that particular accent spoken in Liverpool, England. The project consists of interviewing different residents in the city as well as recording them speaking the single phrase, "Get Here!" (meaning, "come here" and spoken mostly by women calling their errant children, as the artist suggests). The audio recordings are then digitally visualized as waterfall plots—graphic representations that show decibel levels, wavelength, and duration. Appearing as a three-dimensional mass, the plots render the voice not only as an individualized sound, but one figured by the particulars of the city, even by particular streets. For instance, in the neighborhood of Everton "you learn that back of the throat tension— the back of the throat is really quite active in sounds like 'wachh'. You haven't got that Western 'drive' but here, you could say, people almost have a slightly harder skin at the back of their tongues because it's in use all the time."[5] In contrast, in Toxteth "your tongue hits the roof of the mouth, the alveolar ridge."[6] Between north and south Liverpool the tongue is pushed back or upward, hitting the back of the throat or the roof of the mouth. Scouse then is not only an overarching accent, but one further demarcated by neighborhood, even by street, and crafted according to labor and class histories, ethnic backgrounds, and the particulars of slang that easily mutate across generations (Figure 11.1).

I consider the accented voice so as to identify this moment of recital as one fully inflected by particularities that are both superstructural, as the passing down of the name, and importantly, on the street, in the micro-politics and community dynamics at play in the weave of place and speech. William Labov also points to the interplay of voice and place in his large-scale study of speech in New York City. Through this study Labov ultimately showed that the linguistic variations of individual speakers, while unpredictable on a certain level, could be referred back to community speech patterns.[7]

We can appreciate this further by placing the "Get Here!" of Liverpool alongside Althusser's voice of ideology sounding out in the phrase, "Hey, You There!"—a voice that captures us from behind and which we unconsciously anticipate. Each phrase performs to call us into a certain structure, whether in the form of familial bonds, or according to the strictures of the state. Through such calling, the subject is literally named (and for Althusser, captured by ideology): whether in the form of the family name, or as "You"

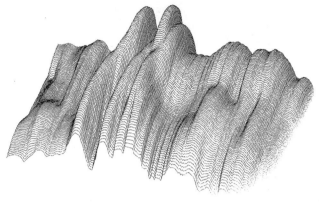

Toxteth

ˈɡɛr ↘ɪə

"'b's and 'd's and t's can be dentalised - if you go 'd-d-d-d-d'
your tongue hits the roof of the mouth, the alveolar ridge.
Here, rather than hitting against the roof of the
mouth - which is quite an effort - it just bangs against the top
teeth, so you get that slight hissiness. Almost like
the tongue's too big for the mouth space.

'I SAY "GET HERE"... VERY SLOW AND CAREFUL.' EDGE HILL 'I KNEW YOU WERE

FIGURE 11.1 *Imogen Stidworthy, from* Topography of a Voice *(2008–2009),*
a print series that attempts to describe the accent of Scouse. Recordings of
Scouse spoken by different people and taken through forms of transcription/
translation: phonetics, waterfall plots, comments and reflections about the accent,
and an analysis of its production by a voice trainer and dialect specialist. Media:
copperplate and offset print on six sheets 510 × 320 mm and one sheet 255 ×
320 mm.

which is already enough to identify, or *arrest*. "Get Here!" grounds, in its
specificity, the more general "Hey, You There!" Yet Stidworthy's work also
shows the performative dynamics by which speech operates in the reciting
moment to redirect the power of such naming. Are not accent and slang
vehicles by which to recite *and* resist, repeat *and* modulate the citational
chain of identity? A reciting that traces over the inheritance passed down
through language, and often through family, yet one that may also seek to
blur the delineations and demarcations—Labov additionally points to this

in terms of how second-generation immigrants often alter speech patterns to overcome being identified as "foreign."[8]

Speech and place intertwine, unfolding as an auditory geography that often pits the desire to speak up with the pressures of finding commonality, of public space against expressions of public life. The inheritance of language, and the name, is carried forward in the dramas of place, neighborhood life, and the social circle. Finding one's voice is equally finding one's place.

State

Judith Butler's notion of reciting, of speaking *through* what is given, connects us back to what has already come; to particular histories, the speeches of others, and words that may have been forgotten, and yet which come back into the present *through* another body, respoken by another mouth. "Reciting" is literally to perform a certain script, to play out an existing text, sounding out its monologues and dialogues, reverberating it against the acoustics of a certain place. In doing so, the script or text is given new life—it speaks through us, to occupy the body, and to find place within the present. This scene of recital may also give way to buried histories, repressed languages, or disappeared bodies. Reciting, in other words, may also be a restaging, or a reenactment aimed at dramatizing the very relationship we have to history, to the citational chain embedded in bodies and names, and in the places wherein such histories take root (or are erased).

There is an extremely strong and pertinent body of artistic works that reenact, replay, and recite, and from which historical consciousness, political critique, and public empowerment find form. From such works we learn of the embedded energies and struggles found in the name—the politics of representation—as well as the importance of the particular: that every name is an inheritance that may at times go missing, to seethe from underneath, and that may also supply us with a source for new vitality.

Here I'd like to turn to the work of artist Sharon Hayes. Hayes's projects are often based on a performative respeaking of an existing text, letter, or speech, mostly drawn from political histories. These often play out specific tensions between the personal and the political, and utilize her presence as a specific body (gendered, classed, cultured, etc.) within a particular place. The intersections between past and present, original and restaged, history and memory are mobilized to create extremely considered works. For example, her project *My Fellow Americans 1981–1988* is a 10-hour performance in which the artist reads aloud all of Ronald Reagan's official "address to the nation" speeches. Performed in 2004, Hayes re-presents to us this particular "voice," inviting us to consider a number of aspects, such as the mode of presidential address—the languages at play in addressing the nation—as well as the actual content, which returns us to this period in American (and global) history. The content refers us to certain events and issues, and yet such critical respeak also makes us wonder as to what is missing, and what might have been (intentionally) left out or glossed over. Yet something additional is happening in this performance, something that can only be found or heard *in the voice*. The work performs an act of reversed ventriloquism—the mouth that moves, pronounces, and addresses, conjures forth the figure of Reagan, as that which is behind the scenes. Hayes opens her mouth and, in doing so, calls forth what is *prior* to her body, to her voice, and to this moment. The words may not fit her mouth or her body, her image, yet in finding their way onto her tongue they reappear to reveal disjunctions and discrepancies, as well as connections and linkages. In respeaking, the work performs a type of archaeology, researching the materiality of what is buried to discover what we have forgotten, or what continues to ghost the present, and the nation, as well as the body of a citizen.

Acts of respeaking open up this haunted space; a voice captured by the words of another, or prolonging, as a mysterious echo, their reverberations. It's as if Hayes is entranced or arrested by particular voices and events, histories and politics, which have come before. In such instances of recital, the speaking body is a sort of conduit giving way to the pressures of the past, or the forgotten, and the remembered. The mouth that moves may also be driven by uncertainty, as a channeling that unsteadily maps the politics of speech. A forced ventriloquism that, in throwing a voice forward, reveals its own distant and problematic origins.

Nevin Aladag's performance works also often operate through a mechanism of recital, focusing precisely on this instant of uncertainty. Someone appears before an audience and speaks, telling a story or narrative, and yet the voice itself is played back from a loudspeaker off-stage or out of sight. What we witness then is a moment of lip-syncing, a mouthing of words that unsettles the relation between what we see and what we hear, this body and its voice. The performer's mouth is filled with another's voice; it tries to shape itself according to the words, mimicking the rhythms of speech, to carry it across the face, flexing the muscles here and there and articulating the lips in time to the flow of sound. This appears, for example, in her work, *Hochparterre Wien (Mezzanine Vienna)* (2010). In this case, a sofa is placed on a street, turning the sidewalk into a stage, a zone of performance. A woman suddenly appears in a window on the first floor, pulling back the curtains to address the crowd. She "tells" stories, each originally recorded as part of interviews with residents of the apartments within, and amplified from behind the scenes. In this way, the woman literally *stands in* for the residents, miming their expressions and vocal identities, and assembling them together within a single body.

Aladag's performances of lip-syncing are extremely suggestive of the modality of reciting I'm exploring here. They put on display the performativity central to speech, as that which moves *through* us, cast from another, and from which we define our own. Her works draw this out, as an enactment that is always already reenactment. The voice that comes from outside the scene is in actuality fundamental to this moment of presence, to appearing before, as a subject with a voice. Aladag's work traces this movement, to materialize it as a bodily experience, a process of *trying on* that voice which surrounds us and which we have heard before. In doing so, the work underscores the degree to which the voice draws us forward, into a sense of agency, yet one which is already influenced by *someone else*.

Oath

The performative dynamics of reciting are openly expressed in moments of oath taking. *Repeat after me* . . . The ceremonies that require one to repeat the words of another (which are always already no one's, but fundamentally that of an institution) make palpable the ways in which repetition and recital are intrinsic to truth telling. The oath taken refers us to a greater tradition whose futurity is guaranteed in the voice that repeats, in this body that follows a given script. To *take* the oath—already this suggests the oath is something we must *perform* . . .—is to announce not only one's promise, or adherence, but to solidify the sanctity of the thing spoken, the lineage behind the words. The marriage vow, for instance, expresses one's dedication to the particular marriage, yet it also sustains the institution of marriage as being central to a particular society. In repeating the vow, history and tradition come flooding into my mouth.

I announce myself as a subject beholden to the powers that have come before; I participate in a lineage greater than myself. In short, *I swear*. Yet the oath must also be heard; there must be others who witness its speaking. The marriage vow can only be guaranteed if someone—a friend, a family member, even a stranger . . .—hears its voicing.[9] The oath is ultimately administered.

The voice is precisely what is called upon to guarantee participation, in social circles and familial bonds as well as in the lineages at the center of our institutions. To "repeat after me" immediately calls the subject into a particular order; it sustains the citational imprint that makes voice possible in the first place.

The dynamics of oath-taking, as a politics of repetition, finds poignant expression in the recent debates over the Supreme Court Justice Salim Jourban's refusal to sing the Israel national anthem during a recent retirement ceremony. Although the Arab judge offered no specific explanation, it is clear that for Arabs the national anthem is a sign of Israeli nationalism. The Justice's refusal subsequently prompted many Israeli judges to call for his resignation, and one Jewish leader has gone so far as to demand the Justice's Israeli identification card be revoked.[10]

In this regard, recital clearly carries powerful meanings whose performance not only brings one forward into a clearly defined public realm, but does so by reinforcing the authority of the state. To recite is to subscribe to the symbolic message that locates one firmly within traditions of power, the very lineage announced in speaking the words, or challenged by refusing them.

Public

The operations of reciting carry within its soundings the messages over and above the coordinates of daily life; to import the gravity of tradition onto the spaces of such life, so as to remind of greater legacies, and greater narratives. As in the traditions of prayer, and the religious service, to recite an existing text is never only about words. Rather, the respeaking of such texts solidifies, through its collective reverberations, a metaphysical, and institutional, bond: that my voice is but a modest carrier that joins in assembly with a particular set of beliefs. Here the citational chain performs explicitly to embed us within its historical reach, though one aimed toward the transcendental and the divine, and their institutional traditions. To pray is to affirm a particular constellation—of text and word, voice and subject, of spirit and faith. We might ask, how many voices have gone before to trace over this text, along this citational pathway? I understand such recitals as a central act for the establishment of belief systems; to believe is already to recite, to subscribe to the citation itself, as one that possesses me, channels itself through my voice, and to which I am fully beholden.

To repeat the words is thus to support the formation of a public. Or more precisely, recital is a process by which a public is brought forward (even across history), managed as well as contested—where the powers of voicing and naming are tried on, turned over, and reshaped. This can be appreciated by considering another artistic work, that of Tania Bruguera's *Tatlin Whisper #6 (Havana version)* (2009). On the basis of the first speech delivered by Fidel Castro in 1959 following the Cuban revolution, Bruguera set up a podium with a live microphone in the central courtyard of the Havana Biennial, and invited audience members to freely speak for 1 minute. Integrating two persons dressed in military uniform, a white dove (referencing the legendary moment when a white dove landed on Castro's shoulder during his speech), and loudspeakers placed inside and outside the courtyard, people were allowed to say freely what they wanted, including reflections and opinions on the Cuban political system. Delivering praise as well as criticism, this arena of free speech explicitly challenged policies of national censorship, bringing into question the "revolution" as a defining historical image. In this regard, the work creates a situation of recital, quoting the image of Castro and the emergence of "freedom" contained therein while allowing for new voices to come forward and reanimate this mythical event. These voices come to *possess* the image of national history, filling it with a contemporary language of hope as well as anger that gains in poignancy through a discrepancy with current state policy. Bruguera's performance ultimately captures the spirit of citizenry, as the continual (re)enactment of public freedoms (Figure 11.2).

FIGURE 11.2 *Tania Bruguera,* Tatlin Whisper #6 (Havana version), *2009. Performance at Central Patio of the Wifredo Lam Contemporary Art Center. Tenth Havana Biennial. Havana, Cuba. Courtesy of Studio Bruguera.*

The public speech is an appeal to public life, to the social and collective body, and we might say, to the legacies of public institutions. From sermons to testimonies, anthems to oaths, soapbox rants to demonstrations, public speech finds its resonating energy by occupying given modalities of voicing, and their traditions, tuning the private individual toward the greater sphere of civic culture and empowerment, while testing the limits of what a certain body can say.

Echo

Following these examples, I understand the operations of recital and reenactment as wielding a complicated relation to the "original." While the voice may reinforce an existing tradition, it does so by introducing a potentiality for resistance, and for delirium, found in the utterance of words, and their respeak—as Jean-Jacques Lecercle suggests, language contains within itself an element of madness.[11] When fitting the words into my mouth, I may also contour and test, inflect, and even accent their given meanings. Reciting thus supports a greater value system into which an individual is called, while also unsettling this system with that potentiality found in personal expression—in language itself.

Returning to Butler, to recite is to repeat, and also to *supplement*; it is to prolong the reverberations that have come before, and in doing so to tease their stability with a certain proliferation. Being drawn into subjectivity is to playback, in modified form, the force of what or who has preceded our presence. In doing so, it is essentially to introduce an *echo*.

Fundamentally, the echo provides a means for orientation: the auditory reflections that surround us at all times capture a given sound, to return it, bringing it back into the environment. In this regard, it teaches us the dimensions of our surroundings—we gauge the material envelope of place through these reflections of sound. Echo thus locates us precisely through a reverberation, a type of repetition that we might also hear as a recital. Is not the echo a "citation" of a given sound, refigured, or restaged? In this way, we come to orient ourselves explicitly by way of *reflection*. I would highlight this "reflection" as both physical and cognitive, underscoring the echo also as a metaphor for understanding these operations by which voices circulate—a circulation that allows for formations of individuation and agency, and that may also perform to appropriate voice.

The echo may provide us with a vocabulary for exposing, and also performing, the inherent supplementality found within the citational chain. As Butler suggests, identity is always already a quotation, yet one that requires appropriation, *performance*. I would suggest that the echo is one expression of such performativity: it takes the moment of a sound and repeats it, expanding beyond the original event, and yet also returning it, as *other* to itself. The echo explicitly unsettles singularity and the foundational narrative of the "original," connecting one instead to a greater public arena—a multiplicity that is equally *wild*. In other words, the echo is expressive as well as potentially monstrous—sounding through its trajectory a hybridity of voices; the echo always threatens to exceed into noise.

Doubling

The echo is a reflection arising as a sound or a voice, an animate, mysterious energy that, in coming back to us appears *as if* from another body. How many times the echo, in all its reverberating energies, becomes *other* to its own origin, to return as a friend, or a monster? What returns to us might take shape as a reassuring reflection, by which we find ourselves, yet it may also appear as a voice in the dark, to startle us so we pause, to wonder: *who is there?*

I want to underscore the echo then as a replay, an iteration whose reverberations expand to pry open a space between the "original" and its rearticulation, and one that wields a particular ambiguity: to put into motion an uncertain trajectory, where orientation may also tend toward disorientation; where singularity may give way to multiplicity. The echo widens that space—between a source and its meaning—to support forms of expressivity that inherently confuse the structures that hold us in place, under a certain name. The echo is a citation that retains the promise of always leaving behind the fidelity of proper articulation: a repetition that wraps the words with *too much* voice, and which may inspire the imagination: to double, repeat, and spin out of control. In this regard, the echo is extremely generative of understanding orientation and the name as containing their own proliferation or multiplicity, yet one that may also radically assist us in finding ourselves. Is a name then casting one adrift into the sea of language, supporting articulations that must, on some level, err? The name, in other words, must come to life. To be called out, so as to echo back.

Echoing is a practice aligned with mimicry, doubling, mirroring, and shadowing—a repertoire of performative strategies for figuring this body—which afford opportunities for navigating through and around the limits of the name. Yet the echo might also surprise us, to appear without our knowing; it may take us over, suddenly, from under our skin, or within our voice to lead us elsewhere. The echo has its own life, always already within the replay that is identity—within those gaps between the source and its recital. In other words, identity may also will itself into other forms, to sabotage the body, trespass our vocabularies, and ultimately frighten or delight us.

Repeat

The uncanny behavior of the echo I'm mapping here can be appreciated as a fundamental condition of sound in general. Is not sound performing as a vital animation of things and bodies, objects and materials, extending their limits toward a distance? By unfurling their embedded features, orienting and disorienting at one and the same time? Sounds, in a sense, are *stretching* the identity of a thing, elaborating its material body through a force of vibration and propagation, a friction that always moves away to activate and conjoin the acoustics of so many situations, and their echoes. This acoustic property extends to that of speech and the voice, to refer us back to Butler's work, and what she further identifies as the gap, or "hiatus" from which agency finds expression. As Butler states: "agency is the hiatus of iterability, the compulsion to an identity through repetition, which requires the very contingency, the undetermined interval, that identity insistently seeks to foreclose."[12] The echoes that continually depart from a single event, from that name called from over there, might be heard to give way to a productive ambiguity by which we learn to use our voice. A contingent space opened up between the body that speaks and the echo that returns, and within which identity resides. If the voice extends my limits, in this moment I also listen: to myself, as a body in the making, as a figure on an expanding ground, empowered through a repetition that is never the same twice. We trace over the words and, in doing so, their repetitions open a channel by which to negotiate what has come before—a literal gap within which identity announces itself by amplifying the skin, performing gender, responding to what is so present, and mouthing new words. *I am always already in this gap.*

Speaking is thus a project founded upon acts of recital that are equally individuated, playing back certain grammars and voices, beliefs and expressions of a greater system *through* this body; one fits these into the mouth, as a process from which we gain appearance within the social field. The sheer expressivity of the mouth, as an organ conditioned by so many actions and matters, drives and words, dreams and memories greatly assists in negotiating the pressures of such systems: how narratives of the normative embed themselves onto this body, and how they may also be reimagined, rejected, and reworded. Repetitions and echoes are prone to surprising interference, recitals that may suddenly fixate on certain syllables, drawing upon histories of dissidence to deliver anew the resistant energies of particular speeches.

12

Whistle

The paralinguistic forms and oral modalities I've been studying here can be appreciated as lending, if not fully animating, much of speech's communicative aim. Is not spitting, for instance, an action whose force finds its way into speech, affording one a gestural education on how to "spit out one's words"? Or might we understand instances where we "belt out" a sudden demand as being shaped by crying and its emotional energies? Or when the mouth grows tired, and we pause, to suddenly understand what it means to listen? Not to mention the "sighs of relief" by which we learn to let go the pressure of finding the right words? In other words, this lexicon of the mouth is equally a proposition for a more integrated, inclusive, and radical linguistic perspective, one that fully appreciates the dynamic range of our oral expressiveness and that aims to support those marginalized by the pressures of the linguistically proper. Part of this perspective has as a feature an alignment between language and poetics, and an understanding of words as material. That this material can be sculpted, crafted, bent, and produced, as an aesthetical or expressive project, is certainly a key aspect to paralinguistics and an understanding of the oral imaginary. This finds further expression in whistling, which draws us closer to the musicality of speech, and what Allen S. Weiss terms "audio mimesis."

Weiss develops the notion of audio mimesis as a way to argue for a more expansive understanding of the relation between language and its sounding. Drawing on the work of Roman Jakobson in particular, Weiss spirits a phonic perspective onto what constitutes language's meaningfulness, drawing a link between words and the world through the figure of onomatopoeia. On a phonic level, words retain a profound connection to their referent, drawing forward correspondences that too often are subsumed by the theory of the arbitrariness of the signifier to the signified. For Weiss, language is fundamentally "expressive *and* referential, sensual *and* significative, mimetic *and* conventional."[1]

As I've been arguing, the range of oral expressions and mouth productions greatly expand and extend our linguistic capabilities, supplying vocality with imagination, as well as material input. With whistling this takes us into a musical territory that is equally communicative: whistling performs as a sonorous, aesthetical, and emotional project as well as a semantic construction. It links together the sensuality of the oral with the practicalities of communicating, facilitating while also compounding this relation.

Language

At times, as breath blown out from puckered lips, or even back in, to brush past the mouth's narrow passage; elaborated through the use of the fingers, sometimes with index and thumb pressed down onto the bottom lip, or also only with a single finger stuck between—whistling pierces the soundscape to capture attention.

Whistled languages found on the Canary Islands, Turkey, Cuba, and France craft the whistle into a linguistic articulation. As R. G. Bursnel describes, whistled languages essentially "replace the cord-tone of everyday phonation by a whistle, that is to say, in the case of a steady note, practically a sine wave."[2] These whistled languages are found mostly within highland regions, where shepherds and farmers live across valleys that often make it difficult to communicate. Interestingly, a Turkish village where whistling is to be found is called Kusköy, meaning "village of the birds." Here, "whistling is used by the whole population of highlanders which is dispersed into no less than 35 villages . . ."[3] Living in the midst of steep hills that rise between 800 and 1200 meters, with no central trading center, the villagers use whistling to communicate and exchange information.[4]

With the development of mobile phone technologies, whistled languages are increasingly rare. Although surprisingly, much of the culture remains, with whistling still prevalent in the Canary Islands, as well as Turkey. In some cases, whistled language has come to act as a "secret code" for countering the police or other officials (in particular on the Canary Islands, during the dictatorship of Franco), or as in the case of Cuba, as part of the secret society known as the Abakuá. Stemming from African traditions found in Nigeria and the Congo, the Abakuá are an extremely hermetic fraternity originating in Cuba (since the early nineteenth century) and often appear during carnival as dancers clothed in ceremonial dress—a multicolored checkerboard costume topped with a conical headpiece. The Abakuá are also known for their secret whistled language, which they use in oaths, as well as in their music and dance practices (which deeply influenced the emergence of the Cuban rumba).

Musicality

I'm interested in how whistling enables communication for specifically negotiating the challenges of geography, as well as that of an authoritarian regime. A type of secret code bonding particular groups, whistled languages spirit such negotiations and navigations by drawing a link between speech and musicality, crafting it as a type of cultural practice.

This relation is brought forward in a work by artist Alessandro Bosetti who recorded the whistled language found on the Canary Islands. Appearing on his CD *Zwölfzungen* (2010), track three of the collection, "Advertencia," is based on the recording of a woman whose whistling Bosetti recorded outside the village of Chipude, on La Gomera, as he hiked around in search of the Silbo speakers.[5] Her whistling rises and falls, as an oscillating sonority around which the artist has added small tonalities; a composition, as with all the works on *Zwölfzungen*, that emphasizes the melodic and punctuated movements of "spoken" language.

Bosetti presents us with a catalogue of languages from around the globe by focusing on their tonalities, their sonorities, their dialects and accents, each recorded and further composed within a larger arrangement. The work explores the phonic expressivity that hovers in and around language, and speech in particular, accentuating the way in which voice draws us into that doubleness suggested by Weiss—language as both "expressive *and* referential."

The musicality of languages certainly leads us to the heart of audio mimesis mapped by Weiss, and that whistling evidences with such beauty. In many of the examples and accounts that follow in Weiss's *Varieties of Audio Mimesis*, the question of birdsong features prominently, revealing a level of poetical material that gains much of its playfulness and performativity through a mimetic mirroring of winged creatures.

One important and prominent example Weiss presents is that of the music of composer Olivier Messiaen. In particular, Messiaen's *Catalogue d'oiseaux* (1956–1958) provides us with a musical translation of birdsong that, as Weiss suggests, unfolds the vibrant energy of the mimetic to support new and unexpected expressions.

Messiaen's fascination with birdsong gives articulation to the composer's deep belief in the power and exuberance of nature. As he states: "An inexhaustible treasure of sounds and colors, shapes and rhythms; a peerless model of total evolution and endless variety. Nature is the supreme resource."[6] For Messiaen, drawing from nature in the form of birdsong opens up a channel by which his musical activities could find ready alignment with the dynamics of the natural world. Thus his *Catalogue d'oiseaux* leads us to the whistle as a conduit of exchange between human and animal, where the small yet no less dramatic sonorities of the nightingale or the robin may inspire corresponding vocalities, as well as compositions. (Here, I might also point to the object of the "bird whistle" further enabling this potential exchange across species.)

For Weiss, birdsong and music, as a connective site for such sonorous exchanges, also elaborates a deeper point, that of the mimetic faculty within language (as he developes through an analysis of onomatopoeia). Audio mimesis is precisely that point where sound and sense interweave, supporting synesthetic correspondences and phantasmic shimmerings, where the borders separating words as signifying entities and their sounds dissipate to inspire a true poetics.

These correspondences again appear prominently within David Rothenberg's *Why Birds Sing*, which can be read as a diary of one man's attempt to speak with birds. Exploring a variety of scientific and naturalist accounts of birdsong, Rothenberg leads us into a primary appreciation for the "wonders" of the rich musicality of birds. Importantly, for Rothenberg, this musicality provides an opportunity for engaging in more direct contact and conversation. His joy of birdsong is founded on his own work as a musician, brought forward in the desire to also share in a musical exchange across the human/animal divide. Bringing his clarinet into the National Aviary in Pittsburgh, or out into breeding grounds in Australia, for example, Rothenberg tunes into an array of birdsong; playing in response to birds, he enters into an exchange of melodic expressions, tonal bursts, an enrapturing sonority that also leads to dancing.

> The song continues, I try to place my clarinet in and around the breaks. I am dancing in the underbrush, crackling branches underfoot, leaping up and down, curving my shoulders in imitation of those long delicate feathers I'll never swing. The resonance of the clarinet in the forest is full and clear, as if the wood that made the horn has somehow returned to its place.[7]

The enchanting presence of the bird captures the musician, nurturing an intensity of exchange, a "becoming-bird" that also, upon his return home, haunts his musical consciousness: "Back home I try to listen again to human music, but it doesn't seem right. I've spent too long with the lyrebirds, and I've begun to hear music their way."[8]

I might read Rothenberg's account, in the light of Weiss's essay, as an attempt to bridge the gap between sound and meaning, musicality and the languages that so define our understandings of the world. The clarinet is a literal vehicle for crafting another form of tonality, another form of speaking, one guided by the bird and its festival of whistled sonorities—a festival that equally affords new appreciation for our own auditory capabilities.

> Why do birds sing? For the same reasons we sing—because we can. Because we love to inhabit the pure realms of sound. Because we must

sing—it's the way we have been designed to tap into the pure shapes of sound. We celebrate this ability in our greatest tasks, defining ourselves, defending our places, calling out to the ones we love. But form remains far more than function. We spend lifetimes immersed in the richness of these creations.[9]

I'm interested in Rothenberg's attempts to capture the musicality of birdsong, and how this gives expression to the oral imaginary—the materialization of an extended orality and one aligned with a reshaping of the body and its figuring. Although his clarinet is an instrument well beyond human whistling, it greatly supports the mimetic exchange whistling is often called upon to perform. Whistling is our fundamental means for mimicking birdsong, and Rothenberg's example highlights this also as a greater move toward *echoing* the world around.

Pleasures

Here I want to follow Rothenberg's desire for the rich arena of birdsong, as a plenitude of musicality, and to hear in this another instant of the oral imaginary. As with other modalities of mouthing, whistling tunes us to the sensual delights as well as difficulties of corporeality, reminding of the intensities that surround us, and that may lead to certain oral performances. As Peter Ostwald suggests, the sensual dynamics of whistling can be understood to reconnect us to a state of physical comfort, originating from early experiences of "oral gratification."

> Since oral gratification, at least in those people who were mothered during infancy, involved the simultaneous satisfaction of other needs besides hunger—closeness, warmth, protection, etc.—whistling may call forth a more general hedonic state . . .[10]

Whistling is an oral activity that, like chewing, licking, or kissing, to name a few, gives pleasure by explicitly aligning the movements of the respiratory system with the vocal cords, tongue, and lips, and bringing them into a unified action that sends light vibrations through the mouth and facial muscles. Importantly, such sensations, as well as their related sonorities, recall early experiences as a child when the difference between our bodies and the world was less sharp or distinct. Instead, the sounds we made, particularly those generated by the mouth, were heard to interweave with the worldly sounds around us, giving way to a sense for synchronization, immersion, and sensual enfoldment (from which speech also arises; here we should not overlook humming, as that primary vocal vibration discovered while breast-feeding: the hum easily leads to a repertoire of sonorous mouthings, including whistling). In this intermingling, the child may come to hear in his or her whistle a meaningful link to outside phenomena, not only to those close by, but importantly to wind in the trees (captured in the corresponding phrase "the whistling wind"), the cries and purring of animals, and even the sounds of vehicles, such as cars or trains (and their horns or "whistles"). To whistle in relation to events and things around us creates a channel by which to participate—or imagine a relation—and influence surrounding environments. These primary sensations (and expressions) of the trill and the tweet, the warble and the chirp, find a prolonged reference in birdsong, generating mimetic play that locates the whistle, and its referents, close to the animal kingdom; a sonority that we also learn as means for testing out and mapping reverberant chambers and surfaces, or for musicalizing our environment.

These experiences imbue whistling with affective force and lend to our ability for interacting with the world, highlighting the whistle as a fundamental communicative vocality. We use the whistle to state intentions, or warn of danger, to play and create special imaginary and musical communications, to call animals and birds, and to gauge the world through its reverberations. Whistling thus functions within our oral imaginary by affording a relational play full of great performativity or musicality, and whose grammars are given an elaborate education by the birds.

Wings

Might we hear in the whistle a narrative of primary pleasures, a sonority that sends its energies out into the world, with the intention of spiriting an echo in return? As Rothenberg demonstrates, to commune with nature features as an inherent longing, and the whistle may operate as a path for such deep interactions. Messaien's bird-music is not only a catalogue of compositions finding inspiration in birdsong, but a means for the composer to enjoy the pleasures of being *in* nature, in returning via a whistled sonority to the voluptuous fullness of natural landscapes.

Such narratives express a deep human enthusiasm and fascination for what Bachelard calls the "poetics of wings" wherein birds lend imaginary energy. For Bachelard, "The bird is an uplifting force that wakes all of nature."[11] In the bird we come to identify the very promise of flight, of boundlessness, and the positive forcefulness of the imagination itself, which gains continual input from that expanse of sky above and those seemingly limitless creatures that find residence in the air. Birds readily invade our poetical and oneiric fantasies, our mythologies and legends, to flit through dreams and nightmares, emanations and projections, supplying raw material for our aerial desires or terrors.[12]

To have wings is already to enter a space beyond the earth; it is to have
access to the kingdom of spirits, the ghostly, and of breath itself. (The poetics
of wings no doubt finds further embodiment in the figure of the angel, where
wings allow passage through the heavens.) The bird may open our eyes to
the sky itself, as a space for possible occupation—and to the whistling song
as an articulation full of delight and fantasy, as well as transformative power.
The rich musicality of birdsong reveals the whistle as a sonorous potential
for the elaboration of language, whose poetics may also give pleasure by
aligning human perception with greater natural forces—that of birds, yes,
as well as that of the imagination.

We might recall the expression "whistle while you work" and its lyrical
rendering. Originally featured in Disney's 1937 animation *Snow White and
the Seven Dwarves*, the lyric functions to lend amiable support to Snow
White as she cleans the house of the dwarves. Curiously, Snow White's
melodic lyric is answered, if not led by the whistling of birds, creating a
dialogue that places her firmly within an imagined natural order, and which
also renders that particular fantasy of the animal as a speaking subject.
In fact, her whistling not only incites the response of birds, but the entire
animal kingdom also comes out to assist Snow White in her chores. From
deer to squirrels to turtles, each lends a hand, or a tail, to sweeping,
washing, and stacking various household items. Whistling, in this way, is
called upon again to bridge the human/animal divide, echoing back and
forth between species as a flexible linguistic device. Whistling specifically
opens up a communicative channel that, in this instance, brings into play an
anthropomorphic dynamic.

Snow White sets the scene for aligning the whistle with expenditures and
labors of the body, its relation to the animal as well as to the dramas of
life's archetypal negotiations. The fantasy at the center of this narrative is
certainly one of an imaginary innocence, where the "good, domestic" young
woman overcomes the evil wicked queen full of vanity. The whistle, in this
regard, gives expression to an idea of innocence, functioning to tune Snow
White's labors to the "natural" and the domestic.

Two things stand out in this scene, and can be heard to echo within
our cultural landscape. Does not whistling often become a tool for feigned
innocence? Do we not whistle in moments of distraction, or to distract
others from the truth of a certain action? In addition, isn't whistling often
performed during moments of labor? During particular chores or errands?
Both of these instances return us to Peter Ostwald's proposal, of whistling as
a recall of primary sensations, of communion with a natural order, as means
for overcoming separation and absence, or embarrassment. As Rothenberg's
work shows, whistling enfolds the moment with melody to assuage feelings
of alienation.

To further capture this understanding of the whistle, I'd like to recall the
work of Fred Lowery (1909–1984), the blind whistler whose experiences of

whistling enabled him to overcome much of the difficulties of growing up without sight. Born into a family of tenant farmers in East Texas, Lowery early on struggled to fit in. Left behind by his father, he grew up with his grandmother, and learned how to pick cotton, though not without difficulty. It was by chance that Lowery was taken to a school for the blind by his uncle, where he stayed until he was 20 years old, learning music, though eventually it was his whistling that would catapult him into stardom.

Discovered by a piano teacher at the school, Lowery was recognized as an extremely gifted whistler. He could follow along to classical works and popular songs, accompanying instruments with his agile and adept whistling. One of his early hits was a rendition of the "William Tell Overture," which he continued to perform well after becoming a performer on numerous radio programs in Chicago and New York City. His musical talents eventually landed him work with various big bands, notably the Vincent Lopez band, resulting in extensive touring across the country, as well as regular appearances on radio throughout the 1930s and 1940s, alongside Bing Crosby and Bob Hope.[13]

Lowery's famous whistle stands out as a marginal vocality that took center stage, figuring amidst classical orchestras and big bands, and capturing the devotion of numerous fans. (His version of "Indian Love Call," released in 1939, sold over 2 million copies.) I take such cultural expression as indicating a further dimension to the whistle. As Lowery states in his autobiography, his whistling journey was a process of "finding the light" out of the dark tunnel of blindness, and to escape from the brutal hardships of childhood, and importantly, from feelings of being ostracized. For Lowery, whistling turned his life into a great adventure, leading to journeys on and off the stage. Whistling became precisely a productive labor connected to the pleasures of musicality, figuring him into the fold of a social life rife with friendship. In fact, he would not only find the light, but occupy the spotlight time and again.

The whistle may be a sound that leads us forward, to spirit an echo and to locate ourselves; and which aids in carving a space in moments of darkness, labor, and uncertainty—how often the whistle appears on the lips when we know not what to say, or how to respond, in the face of embarrassing knowledge or errant judgment.

Whistling's ability to ease discomfort applies not only to acts of labor, but also to that of waiting. "Whistle while you wait" is an additional refrain that highlights the whistle as a guard or countermeasure against distress. Importantly, it seems whistling functions precisely in moments where we may not be in control of our emotions or of a certain situation, helping to bring forward a sense of self-direction, protection, and calm—*to find our way*. Whistling returns us to a pleasure of being a body in the world, full of vitality and animation. This again appears in another example, found in those particular whistles aimed at a beautiful woman (or man!) and stereotypically heard at the construction site, where workers interrupt their labor by gaping at women that walk by. Immediately, this locates us back at the place of work, at the site of a laboring body whose sonorous outpourings aim for renewed "natural" pleasures against the hard edges of industrial production. Coincidentally, such whistling is referred to as "wolf-whistling," accentuating further the links between whistling *and* the animal.

Might Lowery's whistle, or even that of Snow White, or the construction worker on site, be heard as a spirited vocality aimed precisely at a horizon beyond the ordering principles of language, industrial production, and the social mechanisms that place emphasis on the reasonable (and the sighted)? Like interrupted speech, or laughter, the whistle supplements our talking with not only punctuations and hesitations, but in this case, with musicality and a mimetic tuning to the world, a musicality that might also produce an alternative sense of belonging.

Yet this correspondence of the wolf-whistle also brings us to another level of the whistle that I would like to turn, that is, the disciplinary ordering of the military. Originating from military training, the wolf-whistle is characterized by a two-tone sonority, for instance "whip-woo," and was originally produced by a boatswain's pipe to call for attention aboard a naval vessel. It was then purportedly used more generally by sailors while in port to draw each other's attention to a particular object or event, for instance, a beautiful woman passing by. The "whip-woo" then morphed into "whip-wooah" and often replaced the pipe with various finger techniques so as to produce a more penetrating tone. In this regard, a device of military ordering—which already appropriates the act of whistling into a structure of training—is reappropriated and brought back onto land and within the dynamics of longing and pleasure.

Instrument

The agency performed by whistling is extended here to draw forth childhood fantasies of projecting oneself into the world, of conjuring responses or directing the movements of things. As with all whistles, the wolf-whistle breaks into the existing soundscape with its tonalities to gain attention, and to seek to influence what is surrounding—fantasies of sexual conquest?

Whistling may float along in the ether, or demand someone's attention; it may follow along with certain melodies, or accentuate the figure of a particular body. From birds to wolves, labor to waiting, music to sex, whistling extends, like most paralinguistic expressions, the reach of the individual and the orders of language.

While whistling may delight us, to send one skipping or feeling free, to ease or fill us with joy, it is also dramatically utilized in contrast to such poetical occupations. In fact, the whistle can perform precisely to set straight what is out of line. In this case, the whistle, as that particular object appearing on the lips of policemen, referees, commanders, and other judges, acts as a communicative device to control groups of people, to signal precisely when something or someone must halt, or jump forward in a certain direction. The whistle, in other words, exercises a certain power, there on the lips, in support of disciplinary order.

In the early part of the nineteenth century, for example, the whistle (as an instrument) was incorporated into the Metropolitan police in England to aid a cop on his beat: the whistle could alert crowds of danger, to command a person to stop, to direct traffic, and generally perform an ordering effect onto moments of disorder or panic. This no doubt paralleled the whistle as it came to be used for military maneuvers, allowing commanders to signal troops in formation, or call to attention as in the wolf-whistle.

As Michel Foucault examines in *Discipline and Punish*, the emergence of modern disciplinary culture in the eighteenth century wielded much of its power through formulating methods for shaping and controlling the new modern subject. From the school to the prison, the military to industrial labor, strategies were developed for directing, or rather as Foucault states, "coercing" the body into "a precise system of command." "All the activity of the disciplined individual must be punctuated and sustained by injunctions whose efficacity rests on brevity and clarity; the order does not need to be explained or formulated; it must trigger off the required behaviour and that is enough."[14] In this regard, such a system operated not through debate and discussion, but through efforts of training and "signalization"—a "world of little signals" by which individuals are brought into a structure radically shaped by military tactics. The military, and all its strategies of training and signalization, was to significantly lend to instituting a greater structure for the management of modern industrialized society, and all the bodies therein.

The whistle comes to participate within these strategies of signalization, and can be seen in operation within the mechanics of the workplace, the school, the prison, and the sporting arena, central to dynamic spaces where bodies labor, compete, and train.

Blow

Whistling within such structures of law and order also lends to the phrase "whistleblower"—that is, an individual who informs of illegal activity to a particular authority. To "blow the whistle" on someone is to reveal their illicit or criminal activities. It is to provide information: to break the silence or interrupt the flows of certain dark movements in favor of the proper and the moral. Whistling as a primary, pleasuring sonority that supports feelings of comfort and assurance thus also aids in keeping the social order in proper balance; it returns the social body to a certain alignment. The supple delight in one's individual whistle, as it sends air through the mouth and across the lips, to connect across species and nature, in turn becomes a powerful sound for the creation of lawfulness and judgment, moral integrity and regulation.

Subsequently, we can appreciate whistling as a sonority that assists in maintaining equilibrium. From the organic rhythms of sensual warmth and musical playfulness to the maintenance of particular rhythms and rules, the significance of the whistle is found in its ability to call forth the powers of a sound in service of an imaginary or original order. The gesture of the whistle brings us closer to a natural order, while its appropriation and incorporation into the mechanics of capital and law lead us firmly into a social order defined by rules and regulations.

Kaw!

It is clear that the whistle supports a variety of articulations, extending the mouth and its oral expressiveness into a surprising array of musical, linguistic, and ideological territories. In this way, whistling holds a special place within the spectrum of paralinguistic behavior, for it both presents particular soundings that move in and around the spoken, supplying pathways for mimetic correspondence, while also acting as a dynamic communicative vocality, as linguistic grammar. It moves from our own lips to that of an instrument, weaving together the poetics of wings with tactics of coercion and lawfulness. As I've tried to show, whistling may establish a platform by which linguistic orders interweave with the powers of nature, the life of birds, and the recessed phantoms of memory to ultimately give important entry onto the poignancy of the poetical, as well as the necessities of connecting geographic distances and bodies in distress. I take the whistle then, following other paralinguistic expressions, as a vocality in and around words that nonetheless fully communicates. Yet in such a way as to finally conclude this lexicon with a sense for the correspondences passing between semantics and soundings, voices and the mouth. A channel that spirits numerous linkages and conduits between interior life and social experience, across geographies and politics, and that may also lead us into journeys with animals and winged creatures—which is certainly a central coordinate within our oral imagination.

Conclusion: Dirty

In writing *Lexicon of the Mouth*, I've been led to think about the futurity of the voice—what an expanded perspective on our vocal behaviors and oral imagination might suggest in terms of a future voice, a voice yet to come. The study of the mouth movements and productions I've sought to examine here ultimately aspires to support not only an oral exuberance, but also forms of bodily figuring; it aims to give view onto linguistic performances, vocal soundings, and oral gestures as a greater question of embodiment, as well as an assemblage that might connect us to other forms and formulations of the animate and inanimate, the expressed and the shared. In doing so, I have wanted to avoid an oversimplified dichotomy that places the voice on one side, and the mouth on the other, language here and body there; instead, *Lexicon of the Mouth* seeks a more complex and dirty interweave so as to consider the ways in which the voice and the mouth are fundamentally nested one in the other.

What strikes me about this assemblage is a particular tension or restlessness—a series of endless events: *poetics . . .*—that enfolds and links the uttered, the viscous, the voiced, the respired, and the unsounded, and that fully supports the emergent, the *not yet* known, or the *not yet* spoken; of what might appear in a word and through gestures of mouthing, to find animation in unexpected glossolalia, or in a creole utterance traversing national borders. Or, that might also remain as pure imagination, pure drive.

Already the movements of speech locate us in a multitude of relations, we are enmeshed in a web of exchanges to which speech performs a dramatic role. To utter is to immediately participate, to be enclosed within structures that bind us to others and to which we are held accountable; to modulate these structures, to press in on them as one is impressed, imprinted, enfolded within and against others and the logic of relations (however illogical or unreasonable these might be . . .). Such performative movements, as I've tried to show, generate a multiplicity of oral gestures constituting the greater force of an affective pressure and poetics always already passing from mouth to body, body to language, language to skin, skin to sense, sense to nonsense, etc. The "granularity" of the voice is just such an expanded production, etched with psychoemotional drives, a history of the heart found in speech, along with the respirations and vibrations that pass across the lips, all of which participate in our attempts to be someone, or to undo who we are.

That I *speak to you* is already a sign, an indication, the making of a scene by which a range of experiences are to be found—a primary scene of *figuring* oneself, as a type of labor, a type of outpouring; to literally find a body for oneself, or for each other, even one always already unfulfilled or incomplete. The voice is a search for vocabulary, for a grammar of the moment; it is the tensing of the body within a network of relations. It is a modulation of that plateau of oral rhythms. Yet speech is also a movement that comes to stand within space; it enters and creates a room around itself; it gathers into momentary form the ongoing narratives of social life; it twists and turns, samples and plays back—every choreography is fundamentally spatial.

One such form I'd like to point to by way of conclusion is found at the base of speech, hovering in the flesh of the mouth, upon its buccal stage, and which can be named as that instance by which I confide in you. To literally *tell*—something, for someone.

Telling is immediately a *giving of narrative*, a crafting of the story, as well as a caring for what it purports or reveals. In the telling I also stand behind the words—I give myself over to not only the particular narrative, but also the dialogical arena this telling uncovers. An arena that swells with the weight of voice, with the tussle that is speech; it is always in motion, this arena. The telling and the narrative form a couple, one that has been tracked here as a complex *linguistic embodiment*—an oral assemblage— and that, following the work of Nick Couldry, may function as a type of resistance within today's intensely privatized neoliberal world.[1] To locate new forms of cooperation by *giving narrative*, especially in support of sustained dialogue.

It has been my interest to further this telling—to support its grammars and its obsessions: *to open the mouth*—by extending and complicating what a voice can be and how narrating may actually be performed—especially for those who might not have a voice, but who may certainly have a mouth. The mouth assembles together what may appear external and separate from the body; it produces links and connections, across material and immaterial states; it choreographs numerous exchanges, and it breaks off and cuts into; it sustains, regulates, and nurtures; it sounds and signifies—it "interrupts and connects," to proliferate the rhythms passing across the "saying and the said." That is to say, it is my hope that *Lexicon of the Mouth* can provide a route for spiriting a diverse range of tellings, for a diverse range of bodies within a diverse set of circumstances. For it is clear that if the voice has been so central to giving narrative, to representing, relating, and lending agency, then such a voice requires an expansion of platforms and horizons, modalities and means, *embodiments*—an expansion of what constitutes voice and body, as well as that imaginary listener: *the listener is always there*

. . .—in order to negotiate the intensities, and the narratives, that define our contemporary global moment.

As Frank Farmer has sought to tell in his book *After the Public Turn*, what constitutes "a public" can be found not only in the spaces in which bodies gather openly, but also in the marks we put to paper, and circulate through any number of possible channels.[2] While I may "speak" of the voice and the mouth, it is through writing that I lay out such thoughts, and so it is through writing that I exercise my mouth, as well as my right to speech: to tune my voice to the cultures around me, and to explore how this voice can take shape through not only the seriousness of discourse, but also laughter's hilarity, whisper's ghostly manners, the yawn's contagion, the unpredictability of the stutter, the animality of the grunt, or the breathlessness of a sudden kiss—in short, the erotic, palpitating force of an oral poetics, which interrupts and flavors our language with possibility. The mouth and all its oral productions may provide a feverish view—an opening, a horizon, an elaborated sensuality—for the imagination of a future voice, one that may ultimately surprise us with stammering, singing, biting its lip, or speaking an unforgettable sound.

Etc.

It seems important to append to this study of the mouth, and all its movements, a page dedicated to everything that cannot be cataloged: even in the midst of such defined features as the chew, the kiss, the laugh and the stutter, there exists expressions that fall to the side; those that hover in and around such movements, and that signal (once again) the incredible range of animation the mouth enacts. While I've sought to capture this diversity, still, I have done so by naming: a lexicon is precisely a list, a catalog whose entries delineate a certain territory in order to expand in detail that which is captured. Yet, in doing so, a lexicon necessarily falls short; in setting out to draw critical attention to the oral cavity, as a resonant chamber full of food and politics, sociality and emotional energy, fantasy and longing, my list inevitably must contain, at least as a sort of phantom limb (or phantom mouth), that which is lost or left out (and what might even be unwittingly excluded). I can only point toward such gaping emptiness through this postface—a page that I will leave empty henceforward so as to incite the drama of the mouth as always already greater than the word.

NOTES

Preface: Associative

1 Édouard Glissant, *The Poetics of Relation* (Ann Arbor, MI: University of Michigan Press, 1997).
2 David Michael Levin, *The Listening Self: Personal Growth, Social Change and the Closure of Metaphysics* (London: Routledge, 1989).
3 Gemma Corradi Fiumara, *The Other Side of Language: A Philosophy of Listening* (London: Routledge, 1990), 51.

Introduction

1 Mladen Dolar, *A Voice and Nothing More* (Cambridge, MA: MIT Press, 2006), 73.
2 See Judith Butler, *Bodies That Matter: On the Discursive Limits of "Sex"* (New York: Routledge, 1993). I expand upon the issue of "citation" in chapter 11.
3 "Through the mouth that I fill with words instead of my mother whom I miss from now on more than ever, I elaborate that want, and the aggressivity that accompanies it, by *saying*." Julia Kristeva, *Powers of Horror: An Essay on Abjection* (New York: Columbia University Press, 1982), 41.
4 See Walter J. Ong, *The Barbarian Within and Other Fugitive Essays and Studies* (New York: Macmillan Company, 1962).
5 Dolar, *A Voice and Nothing More*, 70.
6 Ibid., 60.
7 Fred Moten, *In the Break: The Aesthetics of the Black Radical Tradition* (Minneapolis, MN: University of Minnesota Press, 2003), 14.
8 Dolar, *A Voice and Nothing More*, 73.
9 Moten, 213.
10 "Perhaps the voice is identified principally as a mode of extended reach, as a way of stretching towards what one cannot physically reach." Steven Connor, "The strains of the voice," *Parole #1: The Body of the Voice* (Cologne: Salon Verlag, 2009), 9.
11 See Roland Barthes, "The grain of the voice," *Image/Music/Text* (London: Fontana Press, 1977).
12 See Samuel Beckett, *Not I* (London: Faber & Faber, 1973). Also, Samuel Beckett, *Krapp's Last Tape and Other Shorter Plays* (London: Faber & Faber, 2009).

13 John Laver, "Voice quality and indexical information," *Communication in Face to Face Interaction* (Middlesex: Penguin Books, 1972), 189–203.

14 A view supported by way of Artaud's corporeal poetics, as well as Burroughs' viral theories, both of which figure language as an *invasion* onto the body.

15 See William Labov, *The Social Stratification of English in New York City*, 2nd edition (Cambridge: Cambridge University Press, 2006).

16 I'm thinking of the work of Adriana Cavarero and Gemma Corradi Fiumara. Both provide an extremely important critique of Western philosophy, and how a logic of semantics has overshadowed the voice and vocality, as well as our ability to truly listen. In doing so, their works open an important pathway for deepening understanding of voice's corporeal dimension. Yet in their works the voice is often presented as conveying an inherent "truthfulness" to selfhood, one based upon a recuperated bodily vocal pleasure (escaping the semantic) and leading to a scene of "resonance," or a plurality of singular voices. In this regard, I often miss a greater tussle with the very question of *how* to have voice, and how voice is not always intrinsically revealing of oneself, especially in a pleasurable way. In fact, voice more often than not is cause for anxiety, and can be even more so when it is called upon to be authentically pleasurable. We must ask the brutal question: does the voice "naturally" tune itself toward truthfulness and the resonating glow of genuine communion? See Adriana Cavarero, *For More Than One Voice: Toward a Philosophy of Vocal Expression* (Stanford, CA: Stanford University Press, 2009), and Gemma Corradi Fiumara, *The Other Side of Language: A Philosophy of Listening* (London: Routledge, 1990).

17 In this regard, the work of Steven Connor, Allen S. Weiss, and Christof Migone provide notable exceptions as much of their research on voice and vocality integrates a profound understanding and engagement with questions of corporeality and the paralinguistic. See bibliography for a list of related publications.

18 Maria Rhode, "Developmental and autistic aspects of vocalization," *Signs of Autism in Infants. Recognition of Early Intervention* (London: Karnac, 2007), 230.

19 René Spitz, "The primal cavity—A contribution to the genesis of perception and its role for psychoanalytic theory," *The Psychoanalytic Study of the Child*, 10 (1955): 215–240.

Chapter 1

1 Georges Bataille, *Encyclopedia Acephalica* (London: Atlas Press, 1995), 79.

2 Bataille examines the dynamics of seduction, seeking out the baseness of the erotic as figured in the big toe—this part of the body that exemplifies a certain animality and abjectness. See Georges Bataille, *Visions of Excess: Selected Writings, 1927–1939* (Minneapolis, MN: University of Minnesota Press, 1985).

3 John Berger, *Why Look at Animals?* (London: Penguin Books, 2009), 62–63.

4 Ibid.

5 Mary Douglas, *Purity and Danger: An Analysis of Concepts of Pollution and Taboo* (London: Routledge, 2002), 150.

6 Comments from various witnesses, found in Gabriel Baumgaertner, "An oral history: Tyson–Holyfield bite fight," *Sports Illustrated* online (June 29, 2012),

http://sportsillustrated.cnn.com/2012/writers/the_bonus/06/28/tyson-holyfield-oral-history/1.html (accessed April 2013).

7   See Judith Butler, *Gender Trouble: Feminism and the Subversion of Identity* (London: Routledge, 2006).

8   Melanie Klein, *Love, Guilt and Reparation and Other Works 1921–1945* (London: Vintage, 1998), 97.

9   Vito Acconci, quoted in Kathy O'Dell, *Contract with the Skin: Masochism, Performance Art and the 1970s* (Minneapolis, MN: University of Minnesota Press, 1998).

10 O'Dell, *Contract with the Skin*, 17–31.

11 See Oswald de Andrade, *The Manifesto Antropófago* (Cannibal Manifesto, 1928), http://events.ccc.de/congress/2009/Fahrplan/attachments/1386_cannibalmanifesto1928.pdf (accessed January 2013).

12 Ibid.

13 Michael Taussig, *Mimesis and Alterity: A Particular History of the Senses* (London: Routledge, 1993), 241–242.

14 Homi Bhabha, *The Location of Culture* (London: Routledge, 2004), 128–129. I also want to refer my own reading to the article by James G. Ferguson, "Of mimicry and membership: Africans and the 'New World Society'," *Cultural Anthropology*, 17(4) (2012): 551–569. Ferguson makes an extremely important critique of the ways in which mimicry is called upon to perform within cultural accounts of colonialism. He seeks to remind that Western understandings of mimicry, as forms of resistance, often overlook the political and economic forces that play out between the West and Africa in particular. Mimicry, in other words, often has real stakes in forging institutional channels for empowering citizens of African nations and redressing the colonial project.

15 Steve Pile, *Real Cities: Modernity, Space and the Phantasmagorias of City Life* (London: Sage Publications, 2005), 97.

16 Ibid.

17 Ibid., 107.

18 Ibid., 109.

19 The logic of the bat finds additional expression in the figure of Batman (a figure that already makes a reference to Dracula, with his dark stare . . .); Batman's uncertain position between law and criminality indicates the dynamics of Dracula I'm mapping here, as one of radical ambiguity. For more on this ambiguity and ambivalence, see the important work by Mario Vrbančić, *The Lacanian Thing: Psychoanalysis, Postmodern Culture, and Cinema* (Amherst, MA: Cambria Press, 2011).

20 Susie Orbach, *On Eating: Change Your Eating, Change Your Life* (London: Penguin Books, 2002), 103.

21 Ibid., 104.

22 Jean-Jacques Lecercle, *Philosophy through the Looking Glass* (La Salle, IL: Open Court, 1985), 29. See also Louis Wolfson, *Le Schizo et les langues* (Paris: Éditions Gallimard, 1970).

23 Jean Genet, quoted in Allen S. Weiss, *Feast and Folly: Cuisine, Intoxication, and the Poetics of the Sublime* (Albany, NY: State University of New York Press, 2002), 63.

24 Weiss, *Feast and Folly*, 63.

25 See Georg Nussbaumer, "Big Red Arias," *Parole #1: The Body of the Voice*, ed. Annette Stahmer (Cologne: Salon Verlag, 2009).

26 Jane Bennett, *Vibrant Matter: The Politic Ecology of Things* (Durham, NC: Duke University Press, 2010), 49.

Chapter 2

1   Robert Horvitz, "Chris Burden," *Artforum*, XIV(9) (May 1976): 24–31.

2   Susie Orbach, *Bodies* (London: Profile Books, 2010), 25–26.

3   Mary Cappello, *Swallow: Foreign Bodies, Their Ingestion, Inspiration, and the Curious Doctor Who Extracted Them* (New York: The New Press, 2011), 83.

4   Ibid., 66.

5   From an informal conversation with the author, 2013.

6   Ibid., 68–69.

7   Antonin Artaud, *Watchfiends & Rack Screams: Works from the Final Period* (Boston, MA: Exact Change, 1995), 243.

8   James P. Hansen, "Sick shit happens: Everyday histories in Martin Creed's Body docs," *Jump Cut: A Review of Contemporary Media*, No. 52 (summer 2010). This can also be appreciated in the related *Work No. 660 (Shit Film)* (2006). http://www.ejumpcut.org/archive/jc52.2010/hansen-bodydocs/index.html (accessed January 2013).

9   See Melanie Klein, on the topic of weaning, in *Love, Guilt and Reparation and Other Works 1921–1945* (London: Vintage, 1998), 294.

10 Allen S. Weiss, *Perverse Desire and the Ambiguous Icon* (Albany, NY: State University of New York Press, 1994), 27.

11 Jean-François Lyotard, *Libidinal Economy* (London: Continuum, 2004), 67.

12 For an in-depth analysis of these spit operations, see Christof Migone, *Sonic Somatic: Performances of the Unsound Body* (Berlin: Errant Bodies Press, 2012), in particular Chapter 2, Section 3.

13 Migone's investigations of spit also led to his own sonic work, in collaboration with Alexandre St-Onge (working under the name "undo"), which takes as its starting point Acconci's *Waterways*. Undo's version, titled *Vito Acconci's Undoing* (2001), reworks *Waterways* by "undoing" Acconci's original; the direct relation between body and sound (and image) in the original video works is eclipsed, to give way to an expanse of prolonged agitations, textured patterns, and electronic murmurings. The saliva studies appear in condensed form, containing the original as a ghost lodged within undo's own sonic iteration. See undo, *Vito Acconci—Waterways: Four Saliva Studies* (Montréal, Canada: Squint Fucker Press, 2001).

14 Migone, *Sonic Somatic*, 108.

15 For more see: http://worldburpingfederation.com/

16 Julia Kristeva, *Powers of Horror: An Essay on Abjection* (New York: Columbia University Press, 1982), 11.

17 Sigmund Freud, quoted in Norman O. Brown, *Life Against Death: The Psychoanalytical Meaning of History* (London: Sphere Books, 1970), 126.

18 Kristeva, *Powers of Horror*, 12.

19 Brown, *Life Against Death*, 132.

Chapter 3

1 Emily Cockayne, *Hubbub: Filth, Noise and Stench in England, 1600–1770* (New Haven, CT: Yale University Press, 2008), 107.

2 Peter Linebaugh, *The London Hanged: Crime and Civil Society in the Eighteenth Century* (London: Penguin Books, 1991), 144–145.

3 Quoted in Cockayne, *Hubbub*, 107.

4 A competition of town criers is regularly held in Kingston, Ontario, bringing together criers from around Europe and North America.

5 David Mitchell, *For Crying Out Loud: The Story of the Town Crier and Bellman, Past and Present* (Seaford, NY: Avenue Books, 2010), 37.

6 Quoted in ibid., 77.

7 Ibid., 79.

8 Michel Chion, *The Voice in Cinema* (New York: Columbia University Press, 1999), 49.

9 For an analysis of hate speech, see Judith Butler, *Excitable Speech: A Politics of the Performative* (New York: Routledge, 1997).

10 Fred Alan Wolf, *The Eagle's Quest: A Physicist Finds Scientific Truth at the Heart of the Shamanic World* (New York: Touchstone, 1991), 49.

11 Ibid.

12 Ibid., 59.

13 See Adriana Cavarero, *For More Than One Voice: Toward a Philosophy of Vocal Expression* (Stanford, CA: Stanford University Press, 2009). I return to this question of "vocal uniqueness" formulated by Cavarero throughout *Lexicon*, notably in chapter 4 on the topic of gibberish.

14 Ibid., 182.

15 Ruth Murray Underhill, *Singing for Power: The Song Magic of the Papago Indians of Southern Arizona* (Tucson, AZ: The University of Arizona Press, 1993), 6.

16 Bruce Chatwin, *The Songlines* (New York: Vintage, 1998), 72–73.

17 Ibid., 73.

18 Quoted in Emma Hurd, "Unholy Row in Jerusalem over status of women," *Sky News* (December 18, 2011), http://news.sky.com/story/910145/unholy-row-in-jerusalem-over-status-of-women (accessed April 2012).

19 A further example of the politics of song appears also in the recent debates over the Arab Supreme Court Justice Salim Jourban's refusal to sing to the Israel national anthem during a retirement ceremony. While the judge offered no particular explanation, it is clear that for Arabs the national anthem is a sign of Israeli nationalism. The Justice's refusal has prompted many Israeli judges to call for his resignation; one Jewish leader has gone so far as to demand the Justice's Israeli identification card be revoked. See Barak Ravid, "Arab justice's refusal to sing Israel's national anthem sparks furor among right-wing MKs," *Haaretz* (February 29, 2012), http://www.haaretz.com/news/national/arab-justice-s-refusal-to-sing-israel-s-national-anthem-sparks-furor-among-right-wing-mks-1.415560 (accessed July 2012).

20 Cavarero, *For More Than One Voice*, 106.

21 Mark Holloway, *Heavens on Earth: Utopian Communities in America 1680–1880* (New York: Dover Publications, 1966), 75.

22 James Baldwin, *Go Tell It On The Mountain* (New York: Bantam Dell, 1981), 167–168.

23 Judith Butler cites a compelling example of how singing may perform in relation to state power, referring to a demonstration by illegal immigrants in Los Angeles in 2006, who gathered to openly sing the national anthems of the United States and Mexico, in English and in Spanish. Such a demonstration brought forward questions of citizenship, and who is defined as having the right to stay, by explicitly staging an intersection of language, the body of the immigrant, and song. See Judith Butler, "Performativity, precarity and sexual politics," *AIBR. Revista de Antropología Iberoamericana*, 4(3) (2009): i–xiii.

24 See the documentary film, *The Singing Revolution*, directed by Maureen and James Tusty (Sky Films, 2006).

25 The artist Susan Philipsz has developed numerous works using her own singing voice as the main material. Her installations, which mostly appear within public spaces in cities around the world, draw upon existing songs that she records herself singing *A capella*. Her recorded voice is located within particular sites, often drawing parallels between the lyrical content and its location. Her voice appears in this conjuring manner, as a sort of ghostly overlay whose rather "amateurish" quality may not necessarily tempt but certainly disquiets our listening presence, as a body within a particular building, or on the street. I understand Philipsz' work as a celebration of the power of song, but one that may also refer us to histories of voice and music, folk culture and narrative, social ceremony and ritual. This singing that weaves its way under bridges, across rivers, inside shopping malls, or museums operates as a rather poetical enchantment of place. Yet, Philipsz' works are intensely lonely; she mostly sings alone, "appearing" as an invisible body whose lingering harmonies reverberate with absence, laced with great pathos, and in search of community.

26 See Louis Althusser, *On Ideology* (London: Verso, 2008).

27 Stephen Dowling, "St. Paul's Cathedral protest camp deadline passes," *BBC News* (November 17, 2011), http://www.bbc.co.uk/news/uk-england-london-15769999 (accessed December 2011).

28 Mladen Dolar, *A Voice and Nothing More* (Cambridge, MA: MIT Press, 2006), 27.

Chapter 4

1 Jean-Jacques Lecercle, *Philosophy through the Looking Glass* (La Salle, IL: Open Court, 1985), 8.

2 Adriana Cavarero, *For More Than One Voice: Toward a Philosophy of Vocal Expression* (Stanford, CA: Stanford University Press, 2009), 35.

3 Ibid.

4 Ibid., 182.

5 Ibid., 24.

6 Velimir Khlebnikov, "On poetry," *The King of Time: Selected Writings of the Russian Futurism* (Cambridge, MA: Harvard University Press, 1985), 152–153.

7   Kurt Schwitters, "Sonate in Urlauten," *Futura* CD (Milano: Cramps Records, 1978).

8   Renato Barilli, in ibid., 9.

9   Michel de Certeau, "Vocal Utopias: Glossolalias," *Representations*, (56) (Autumn, 1996): 33.

10 For more on the history of sound poetry, see Steve McCaffrey, "From phonic to sonic: The emergence of the audio-poem," *Sound States: Innovative Poetics and Acoustical Technologies*, ed. Adelaide Morris (Chapel Hill, NC: University of North Carolina Press, 1997), and Brandon LaBelle, "Raw orality: Sound poetry and live bodies," *Voice: Vocal Aesthetics in Digital Arts and Media*, eds. Norie Neumark, Ross Gibson, and Theo van Leeuwen (Cambridge, MA: MIT Press, 2010).

11 Certeau, "Vocal Utopias: Glossolalias," 34.

12 Such works operate within modernism's avant-garde, aligned with groups such as Dada, to rupture traditional mechanisms and equations of representation, formulating instead ecstatic and transgressive depictions that, while symbolic, sought more direct and penetrative expressions. In addition, these actions locate themselves as vehicles toward a rebirthing of signification, according to esoteric, metaphysical, and idiosyncratic imaginings that, for Schwitters, stood often in contrast with the stylized reductions of many of his peers (such as Mondrian). As Rudi Fuchs suggests, "Modernism's insistence on abstraction and on the way to arrive at it, by stripping the medium of its unnecessary or impure elements, had to result in a very rarefied idea of an artwork as a thing of extreme clarity, physical elegance, balance, intelligence, and perfection." In contrast, Schwitters' projects are attempts to relocate a primary ground of human experience and expression aligned with the fragmentation of modern life. Rudi Fuchs, *Schwitters: Ich ist Stil* (Amsterdam: Stedelijk Museum, 2000), 6.

13 See Julia Kristeva, *Revolution in Poetic Language* (New York: Columbia University Press, 1984).

14 François Dufrêne, "Pragmatic of Crirythme," *OU—Cinquième Saison*, CD box set, ed. Emanuele Carcano (Milan: Alga Marghen, 2002), 47.

15 Gaston Bachelard, *Air and Dreams: An Essay on the Imagination of Movement* (Dallas, TX: Dallas Institute Publications, 1988), 239.

16 See Michel Serres, *Genesis* (Ann Arbor, MI: University of Michigan Press, 1997).

17 Charlie Chaplin, *The Great Dictator* (1940).

18 See Jacques Lacan, *Écrits* (New York: W. W. Norton & Company, 2007).

19 Rudolph Herzog, *Dead Funny: Telling Jokes in Hitler's Germany* (Brooklyn, NY: Melville House Publishing, 2012), 32.

20 For more on the dynamics of hate speech, see Judith Butler, *Excitable Speech: A Politics of the Performative* (New York: Routledge, 1997).

21 See Judith Butler, "Performativity, precarity and sexual politics," *AIBR. Revista de Antropología Iberoamericana*, 4(3) (2009): i–xiii.

22 Judith Halberstam addresses the figure or persona of the "stupid male" as it appears throughout popular culture; she takes a critical view onto this, suggesting that stupidity performs to reinstate patriarchal order rather than overturn or subvert it. Often in the narratives in which male stupidity is mobilized, related female characters, in their sympathetic appreciation for the stupid

male, inadvertently subscribe to the dominate male order, allowing their own subjectivity to be encircled by the stupid male's ultimate "heroic" end. While I take this as an important perspective, I see the figure of the clown as a "stupid male" designed to gain sympathy, for sure, yet also one that offers a possible route in and around the dominating vocabulary of male performance: rather than aim for the logic of mastery, the clown cultivates and enjoys failure, which may supplement the orders of the male body with a grammar of alternative movements. Here I might refer to aspects within punk performance, in which male stupidity and the attributes of clowning are incorporated into a position of resistance—for instance, Iggy Pop as an emblematic fool. See Judith Halberstam, *The Queer Art of Failure* (Durham, NC: Duke University Press, 2011).

23 Butler, "Performativity, precarity and sexual politics," iii.
24 Henri Chopin, quoted in Teddy Hultberg, "A few points of departure," *Literally Speaking: Sound Poetry and Text–Sound Composition* (Göteborg: Bo Ejeby Editions, 1993), 10.
25 McCaffery, "From sonic to phonic," 159.
26 Barilli, *Futura: Poesia Sonora*, 155.
27 Mel Blanc, *That's Not All Folks: My Life in the Golden Age of Cartoons and Radio* (New York: Warner Books, 1988), 5.
28 In his article Certeau loops the movements of glossolalia back onto the quotidian space of common speech, identifying where it "pushes up through the cracks of ordinary conversation: bodily noises, quotations of delinquent sounds, and fragments of others' voices punctuate the order of sentences with breaks and surprises." Certeau, "Vocal Utopias: Glossolalias," 29.
29 Lecercle, *Philosophy through the Looking Glass*, 16.

Chapter 5

1 See Mark Hodgkinson, "Wimbledon 2011: The strangest behavior," *Telegraph* (June 18, 2011), http://www.telegraph.co.uk/sport/tennis/wimbledon/8582419/Wimbledon-2011-the-strangest-behaviour.html (accessed April 2012).
2 Runhild Gammelsæter, *Amplicon* CD (Milwaukee, WI: Utech Records, 2008).
3 Raquel Stolf, from an informal correspondence with the author, 2012.
4 Robert R. Provine, *Curious Behavior: Yawning, Laughing, Hiccupping, and Beyond* (Cambridge, MA: Belknap Press, 2012), 18.
5 Charles Babbage, quoted in Allan Conrad Christensen, *Nineteenth-Century Narratives of Contagion: "Our Feverish Contact"* (Oxon: Routledge, 2005), 249.
6 Morgan Kelly, "More than a sign of sleepiness, yawning may cool the brain," *Science Daily* (September 19, 2011), http://www.sciencedaily.com/releases/2011/09/110919171340.htm (accessed April 2012).
7 Paul Ekman, *Emotions Revealed: Understanding Faces and Feelings* (London: Phoenix, 2004).
8 Naomi Segal, *Consensuality: Didier Anzieu, Gender and the Sense of Touch* (Amsterdam: Rodopi, 2009), 212.
9 Ibid., 228.

Chapter 6

1   Steven Connor, "Writing the white voice," a talk given at the *Sound, Silence and the Arts Symposium*, Nanyang Technological University, Singapore, 2009. Found on the author's website, http://www.stevenconnor.com (accessed May 2013).

2   Ibid.

3   Denise Riley, "'A voice without a mouth': Inner speech," *Qui Parle*, 14(2) (Spring/Summer 2004), 61.

4   Ibid., 67.

5   Ibid., 73.

6   See Jean-Luc Nancy, *Listening* (New York: Fordham University Press, 2007).

7   Chuck Jorgensen, quoted in Michael Braukus and John Bluck, "NASA develops system to computerize silent, 'subvocal speech'," NASA website (March 17, 2004), http://www.nasa.gov/home/hqnews/2004/mar/HQ_04093_subvocal_speech.html (accessed April 2012).

8   Jean-Jacques Lecercle, *Philosophy through the Looking Glass* (La Salle, IL: Open Court, 1985), 41.

9   Hearing voices also humorously appears in the film *What Women Want* (2000) starring Mel Gibson. Gibson, who appears as a "man about town," is suddenly able to hear the inner thoughts of women. The film plays out the inner voice in a startlingly suggestive way, leading ultimately to a number of role reversals, and transforming Gibson into a more "sensitive male."

10 See Michel Foucault, *Care of the Self: History of Sexuality Vol. 3* (New York: Vintage Books, 1988).

11 Paul Dickinson, *Sleep Talk Recordings Vol. 1: 1986–2000* CD (Chicago: Gosh Yes, 2000).

12 Paul Dickinson, "Sleep talk," *Parole #2: Phonetic Skin*, ed. Annette Stahmer (Cologne: Salon Verlag, 2012), 15.

13 Erving Goffman, *Forms of Talk* (Philadelphia, PA: University of Pennsylvania Press, 1981), 87.

14 Ibid., 82–83 (my emphasis).

15 See Faye Stanley, "Vygotsky—From public to private: Learning from personal speech," *Making Sense of Theory and Practice in Early Childhood*, eds. Tim Waller, Judy Whitmarsh, and Karen Clarke (Berkshire, UK: Open University Press, 2011).

16 Quoted in ibid., 12.

17 Quoted in ibid., 13.

18 Robert Clowes, "The problem of inner speech and its relation to the organization of conscious experience: A self-regulation model," *Proceedings of AISB06 Symposium on Integrative Approaches to Machine Consciousness*, eds. R. W. Clowes, S. Torrance, and R. Chrisley (London, 2006), 122. Found on the author's website, http://www.sussex.ac.uk/Users/robertc/Papers/IntegrativeApproachesToMachineConsciousnessAISB06.pdf (accessed December 2012).

19 David Stoop, *You Are What You Think* (Grand Rapids, MI: Revell, 1996), 50.

20 Ibid., 184.

21 For more on Inner Talk: http://www.innertalk.com
22 Ibid.
23 Found in "Audio guide to self regulation through private speech—Improve your life." This audio guide is available through Amazon, and yet no information exists on the author or the publisher. Having received the work in the mail (2012), it appears completely unauthored. The package includes an extensive pdf of all the texts spoken on the CD. I quote here from this pdf.
24 Ibid.
25 Robert Ashley, *Automatic Writing* CD (New York: Lovely Music, 1996).
26 Robert Ashley, *Outside of Time: Ideas about Music* (Cologne: MusikTexte, 2009), 590.
27 See Gilles Deleuze and Félix Guattari, *Anti-Oedipus: Capitalism and Schizophrenia* (Minneapolis, MN: University of Minnesota Press, 1990).
28 See Adriana Cavarero, *For More Than One Voice: Toward a Philosophy of Vocal Expression* (Stanford, CA: Stanford University Press, 2009).
29 See Steven Connor, "The strains of the voice," *Parole #1: Body of the Voice*, ed. Annette Stahmer (Cologne: Salon Verlag, 2010).

Chapter 7

1   William Cane, *The Art of Kissing* (New York: St. Martin's Griffin, 2005), 25.
2   Adam Phillips, *On Kissing, Tickling and Being Bored: Psychoanalytic Essays on the Unexamined Life* (Cambridge, MA: Harvard University Press, 1994), 96.
3   Ibid., 100.
4   For a highly engaging work on this question see Kaja Silverman, *World Spectators* (Stanford, CA: Stanford University Press, 2000).
5   Alice Lagaay, "Between sound and silence: Voice in the history of psychoanalysis," *e-pisteme*, 1(1) (2008), 60.
6   Catherine Clement, *Syncope: The Philosophy of Rapture* (Minneapolis, MN: University of Minnesota Press, 1994), 81.
7   Ibid., 256.
8   Holland Cotter, "In the naked museum: Talking, thinking, encountering," *The New York Times* (January 31, 2010), http://www.nytimes.com/2010/02/01/arts/design/01tino.html?pagewanted=all (accessed January 2013).
9   Franco Berardi Bifo, *Skizo-Mails* (Berlin: Errant Bodies Press, 2012), 89.
10 Ibid., 91.
11 Loretta Napoleoni makes an extremely important examination of the emergence of new sex trade following the collapse of the Soviet Union, highlighting the relation between global economy and the body as a commodity. See Loretta Napoleoni, *Rogue Economics* (New York: Seven Stories Press, 2008).
12 See Abbie Hoffman, *Steal This Book* (New York: Four Walls Eight Windows, 2002).
13 See report "Kiss Protest held at Turkey subway station," *Al Jazeera* online (May 25, 2013), http://www.aljazeera.com/news/europe/2013/05/2013525191210116123.html (accessed June 2013).

14 D. W. Winnicott, quoted in Josephine Klein, *Our Need for Others and Its Roots in Infancy* (London: Routledge, 1987), 77.
15 Melanie Klein, *Envy and Gratitude and Other Works 1946–1963* (London: Vintage, 1997), 63.
16 René Spitz, "The primal cavity—A contribution to the genesis of perception and its role for psychoanalytic theory," *The Psychoanalytic Study of the Child*, 10 (1955), 220.
17 Ibid., 221.
18 Melanie Klein, *Envy and Gratitude and Other Works 1946–1963*, 71.
19 For more on the "mirror stage" see Jacques Lacan, "The mirror stage as formative of the function of the *I* as revealed in psychoanalytic experience," *Écrits* (New York: W. W. Norton & Company, 2007), 75–81.
20 Eric Rhode, "The boy who had dreams in his mouth," found on the author's website: http://www.ericrhode.co.uk/ (accessed July 2013).
21 Monique Witting, *The Lesbian Body* (Boston, MA: Beacon Press, 1975), 68. While I am relating Wittig to Cixous, I also understand that there existed a critical tension between the two, and their theoretical positions. While Cixous proposed a notion of "women's writing," Wittig challenged the idea that the very category of "woman" was already decided upon by a patriarchal logic.
22 Julia Kristeva, *The Powers of Horror: An Essay in Abjection* (New York: Columbia University Press, 1982), 41.

Chapter 8

1 Sam Taylor-Johnson's close up view onto laughter finds its partner in another artistic work, that of Phil Collins's film *He Who Laughs Last Laughs Longest* (2006). The work captures a live competition organized by the artist in which the person who laughs longest wins. Here, laughter's contagious potential is given a heightened rendering.
2 Luce Irigaray, *This Sex Which Is Not One* (Ithaca, NY: Cornell University Press, 1985), 25–26.
3 Jacqueline Rose, *Sexuality in the Field of Vision* (London: Verso, 2005), 232.
4 See Paul Carter, "Ambiguous traces, mishearing, and auditory space," *Hearing Cultures*, ed. Veit Erlmann (Oxford: Berg, 2004).
5 As Griselda Pollock has stressed in her seminal *Vision and Difference*, "Conventional feminist theorization has stressed the possessive look of the presumed masculine spectator *at* the objectified female form." Griselda Pollock, *Vision and Difference* (London: Routledge, 1988), 134.
6 Julia Kristeva, *Revolution in Poetic Language* (New York: Columbia University Press, 1984), 65.
7 Hélène Cixous, *Coming to Writing and Other Essays* (Cambridge, MA: Harvard University Press, 1991), 53.
8 Lefebvre states: "Wherever there is illusion, the optical and visual world plays an integral and integrative, active and passive, part in it. It fetishizes abstraction and imposes it as the norm." Henri Lefebvre, *The Production of Space* (Oxford: Blackwell, 2000), 97.

9   Henri Lefebvre, *Rhythmanalysis* (London: Continuum, 2004), 67.
10 See Edmund Carpenter and Marshall McLuhan, "Acoustic space,"
    Explorations in Communication, eds. Edmund Carpenter and Marshall
    McLuhan (Boston, MA: Beacon Press, 1960).
11 Irigaray, *This Sex Which Is Not One*, 163.
12 Sigmund Freud, *The Joke and Its Relation to the Unconscious* (London:
    Penguin Books, 2002), 144.
13 Moshe Halevi Spero, "The joke envelope: A neglected precursor of the psychic
    envelope concept in Freud's writing," *Psychoanalytic Study of the Child*, 64
    (2009), 204.
14 Ibid., 195.
15 Ibid., 207–208.
16 Christie Davies, "Jokes as the truth about Soviet Socialism," *Folklore*, 46 (2010).
17 Ibid., 10.
18 One incident detailed by Rudolph Herzog tells of a cabaret performer, Fritz
    Grünbaum, who made a comical jab at the Nazi's during a black out at the
    Simpl Theater in Vienna. After attempting to escape across the Czech border,
    Grünbaum was captured and sent to Dachau. Rudolph Herzog, *Dead Funny:
    Telling Jokes in Hitler's Germany* (Brooklyn, NY: Melville House Publishing,
    2012), 30–31.
19 Hélène Cixous, *The Newly Born Woman* (Minneapolis, MN: University of
    Minnesota Press, 1991), 33.
20 Andrew Stott, *Comedy* (London: Routledge, 2005), 34.
21 Georges Bataille, *The Unfinished System of Nonknowledge* (Minneapolis, MN:
    University of Minnesota Press, 2001), 144.
22 Ibid., 90.
23 Ibid., 97.
24 Henri Bergson, *On Laughter* (Mineola: Dover Publications, 2005), 3.
25 Ibid., 4.
26 Ibid., 10.
27 Robert Provine, *Laughter: A Scientific Inquiry* (New York: Viking, 2000), 37.
28 Ibid., 37.
29 Richard Schechner, *Performance Theory* (London: Routledge, 2003), 281.
30 Carter, "Ambiguous traces, mishearing, and auditory space."
31 Alenka Zupančič, *The Odd One In: On Comedy* (Cambridge, MA: MIT Press,
    2008), 49.
32 See Hélène Cixous, "The laugh of the Medusa," *New French Feminisms*, eds.
    Elaine Marks and Isabelle de Courtivron (New York: Schocken Books, 1981).
33 Janet Beizer, *Ventriloquized Bodies: Narratives of Hysteria in Nineteenth-
    Century France* (Ithaca, NY: Cornell University Press, 1994), 44.
34 Irigaray, *This Sex Which Is Not One*, 163.

Chapter 9

1   See the Parole series edited by Annette Stahmer: *Parole #1: The Body of the
    Voice*, and *Parole #2: Phonetic Skin*, both published by Salon Verlag, Cologne.
2   Found on the artist's website: www.christiankesten.de (accessed January 2013).

3   Christof Migone, *Sonic Somatic: Performances of the Unsound Body* (Berlin: Errant Bodies Press, 2012), 4.

4   Ibid., 113.

5   Erving Goffman, in his book *Stigma*, quotes a stutterer: "We who stutter speak only when we must. We hide our defect, often so successfully that our intimates are surprised when in an unguarded moment, a word suddenly runs away with our tongues and we blurt and blat and grimace and choke until finally the spasm is over and we open our eyes to view the wreckage." Erving Goffman, *Stigma: Notes on the Management of Spoiled Identity* (New York: Touchstone, 1986), 84.

6   Marc Shell, *Stutter* (Cambridge, MA: Harvard University Press, 2005), 19.

7   Tricia Rose, *Black Noise: Rap Music and Black Culture in Contemporary America* (Hanover, NH: Wesleyan University Press, 1994), 53.

8   Ashley Woodward, "Weak thought and its discontents: Engaging the philosophy of Gianni Vattimo," *Colloquy: Text, Theory, Critique*, 15 (2008), 80.

9   Gianni Vattimo, quoted in Woodward, "Weak thought and its discontents," 78.

10 Gianni Vattimo, *The End of Modernity: Nihilism and Hermeneutics in Postmodern Culture* (Baltimore, MD: John Hopkins University Press, 1991), 86–87.

11 Woodward, "Weak thought and its discontents," 182.

12 Gianni Vattimo, "Bottles, nets, revolution, and the tasks of philosophy," *Cultural Studies*, 2(2) (May 1988), 146.

13 Patsy Rodenburg, *The Right to Speak: Working with the Voice* (London: Methuem, 1992), 43.

14 George Watsky, performed at the 2010 Collegiate National Poetry Slam, Boston. Found on youtube: www.youtube.com/watch?v=6GvTLfV8fls (accessed April 2013).

15 Migone, *Sonic Somatic*, 10.

16 Quote from the video, *Boomerang*, by Richard Serra.

17 Édouard Glissant, *The Poetics of Relation* (Ann Arbor, MA: The University of Michigan Press, 1997), 89.

18 Ibid., 96.

19 Ibid., 101.

20 Michel de Certeau, "Vocal Utopias: Glossolalias," *Representations*, (56) (Autumn 1996), 30.

21 Certeau, "Vocal Utopias: Glossolalias," 29.

22 Ibid.

23 Gilles Deleuze and Félix Guattari, *Kafka: Toward a Minor Literature* (Minneapolis, MN: University of Minnesota Press, 1993), 22.

24 Ibid., 23.

25 Judith Butler, *Excitable Speech: A Politics of the Performative* (New York: Routledge, 1997), 137.

26 Judith Butler, *Bodies that Matter: On the Discursive Limits of "Sex"* (New York: Routledge, 1993), 220.

27 Anne Karpf, *The Human Voice: The Story of a Remarkable Talent* (London: Bloomsbury, 2006), 127.

28 Jonathan Rée, *I See a Voice: Deafness, Language and the Senses—A Philosophical Inquiry* (New York: Metropolitan Books, 1999), 94.

29 Ibid., 95.
30 Ibid.
31 Karpf, *The Human Voice*, 126.
32 Ibid., 127.
33 Adriana Cavarero, *For More Than One Voice: Toward a Philosophy of Vocal Expression* (Stanford, CA: Stanford University Press, 2009), 24.
34 Susie Parr, Sally Byng, and Sue Gilpin, *Talking about Aphasia: Living with Loss of Language after Stroke* (Maidenhead: Open University Press, 2003), 9.
35 Ibid., 4.
36 This is not to suggest that the one who does not speak is not without "communicative" or meaningful exchange, social presence, and modes of agency. On the contrary, rather, following Butler, it is to appreciate the *performative* dynamics by which "losing voice" gains signifying momentum by unsettling what we mean by "speech" itself.
37 Jane Campion and Kate Pullinger, *The Piano: A Novel* (London: Bloomsbury, 1994), 146.

Chapter 10

1 John Laver, *Principles of Phonetics* (Cambridge: Cambridge University Press, 1994), 191.
2 Ibid., 190.
3 Xinghua Li, "Whispering: The murmur of power in a lo-fi world," *Media, Culture and Society*, 33(1) (2011): 21.
4 Ying Yang Twins, "Wait (The Whisper Song)", from the album *U.S.A. (United State of Atlanta)* (New York: TVT Records, 2005).
5 Ted Andrews, *Animal Speak: The Spiritual & Magical Powers of Creatures Great & Small* (St. Paul, MN: Llewellyn Publications, 2003), ix.
6 Ibid., 8.
7 Nicholas Evans, *The Horse Whisperer* (London: Sphere, 2010), 98.
8 Found at: http://indigosociety.com/showthread.php?25233-Animal-Whispering-Silent-Comunications (accessed May 2013).
9 Evans, *The Horse Whisperer*, 236–237.
10 John Mowitt, "Like a whisper," *Differences: A Journal of Feminist Cultural Studies*, 22(2 and 5) (2011): 178–179.
11 Joseph Conrad, *Heart of Darkness* (London: Penguin Books, 1989), 119.
12 Ibid., 111.
13 Ibid., 84.
14 See Paul Carter, "Ambiguous traces, mishearing, and auditory space," in *Hearing Cultures Essays on Sound, Listening and Modernity*, ed. Veit Erlmann (Oxford: Berg, 2004).
15 For more on the relation of electronic media and the supernatural, see John Durham Peters, *Speaking into the Air: A History of the Idea of Communication* (Chicago, IL: University of Chicago Press, 2000).
16 From the poem "When there is no sound" by Norbert Ruebsaat, recited in Hildegard Westerkamp's "Whisper study" (1975–1979). The poem was published in *Soundscape Newsletter*, No. 7 (January 1994): 17–18.

17 Edmond Jabès, *A Foreigner Carrying in the Crook of His Arm a Tiny Book* (Hanover, NH: Wesleyan University Press, 1993), 27.

18 Li, "Whispering: The murmur of power in a lo-fi world," 32.

19 Ibid.

Chapter 11

1 Steven Pinker, *The Language Instinct: The New Science of Language and Mind* (London: Penguin Books, 1994), 170.

2 Edward Sapir, quoted in R. L. Birdwhistell, "Paralanguage twenty-five years after Sapir," in *Communication in Face to Face Interaction*, eds. John Laver and Sandy Hutcheson (Middlesex, UK: Penguin Books, 1972), 88. Sapir's work led to the emergence of paralanguage as a field of study, and can be further glimpsed in the work of Erving Goffman, for instance, in so far as the question of social interaction is brought forward.

3 Judith Butler, *Bodies That Matter: On the Discursive Limits of "Sex"* (New York: Routledge, 1993), 225.

4 Butler, *Bodies That Matter*, 226.

5 Imogen Stidworthy, "Topography of the voice," *Parole #2: Phonetic Skin*, ed. Annette Stahmer (Cologne: Salon Verlag, 2012), 20.

6 Ibid., 19.

7 See William Labov, *The Social Stratification of English in New York City*, 2nd edition (Cambridge: Cambridge University Press, 2006).

8 For more on this see Peter Trudgill, *Sociolinguistics: An Introduction to Language and Society* (London: Penguin Books, 2000).

9 Jacques Derrida considers the question of the oath, and more generally the issue of "iterability" in his essay "Signature event context." He underscores writing itself as a system that fully relies upon its ability to be repeated, beyond the presence of an actual "receiver." "The possibility of repeating and thus of identifying the marks is implicit in every code, making it into a network that is communicable, transmittable, decipherable, iterable for a third, and hence for every possible user in general" (p. 8). Derrida extends this view beyond the specifics of writing, to claim that all "marks" including that of oral expression, as well as "presence" in general, exist "cut off" from its site of "production" or "origin." Further in this essay, Derrida also uses the example of the wedding vow, highlighting how this "performative utterance" fulfills the basic claim of "iterability" as always already housed within a code available for repetition. Jacques Derrida, "Signature event context," in *Limited, Inc.* (Evanston, IL: Northwestern University Press, 1988).

10 See Barak Ravid, "Arab justice's refusal to sing Israel's national anthem sparks furor among right-wing MKs," *Haaretz* (February 29, 2012), http://www. haaretz.com/news/national/arab-justice-s-refusal-to-sing-israel-s-national-anthem-sparks-furor-among-right-wing-mks-1.415560 (accessed July 2012).

11 See Jean-Jacques Lecercle, *Philosophy through the Looking Glass* (La Salle, IL: Open Court, 1985).

12 Butler, *Bodies That Matter*, 220.

Chapter 12

1 Allen S. Weiss, *Varieties of Audio Mimesis: Musical Evocations of Landscape* (Berlin: Errant Bodies Press, 2007), 14.

2 R. G. Bursnel and A. Classe, *Whistled Languages* (Berlin: Springer-Verlag, 1976), 2.

3 Ibid., 20.

4 The Austrian artist Heimo Lattner has developed work on the whistled language of La Gomera. For Lattner, the language points toward the dynamics of a culture under pressure, a political sphere that both supports the language while also forcing it into particular meanings. The ways in which the whistled language of La Gomera has been propped up as a touristic attraction—a sign of authenticity—while receiving little support in terms of research and study, for Lattner, highlights the degrees to which the language operates within a greater ideological tension. See *Heimo Lattner—A Voice That Once Was in One's Mouth* (Berlin: Errant Bodies Press, 2013).

5 Alessandro Bosetti, *Zwölfzungen* CD (Pioneer Valley, MA: Sedimental Records, 2010).

6 Olivier Messiaen, liner notes to the CD, *Catalogue d'oiseaux* (Hongkong: Naxos, 1997), 3.

7 David Rothenberg, *Why Birds Sing: A Journey into the Mystery of Bird Song* (New York: Basic Books, 2005), 226.

8 Ibid., 227.

9 Ibid., 228–229.

10 Peter F. Ostwald, *The Semiotics of Human Sound* (The Hauge: Mouton & Co., 1973), 60.

11 Gaston Bachelard, *Air and Dreams: An Essay on the Imagination of Movement* (Dallas: Dallas Institute Publications, 1988), 70.

12 The ability to understand the language of birds appears throughout numerous mythological tales and legends, and often performs to provide key information to humans. For instance, in the Saga of the Volsungs, the slayer of the dragon Fanfir, Sigurd, is granted the ability to communicate with birds once he tastes the blood of the dragon. The birds subsequently come to impart to Sigurd his imminent betrayal by that of Regin, affording Sigurd the opportunity to escape. See *The Saga of the Volsungs* (London: Penguin Books, 1999).

13 See Fred Lowery, *Whistling in the Dark* (Gretna: Pelican Publishing Company, 1983).

14 Michel Foucault, *Discipline and Punish: The Birth of the Prison* (New York: Vintage Books, 1979), 166.

Chapter 13

1 Nick Couldry, *Why Voice Matters: Culture and Politics after Neoliberalism* (London: Sage Publications, 2010).

2 Frank Farmer, *After the Public Turn: Composition, Counterpublics, and the Citizen Bricoleur* (Salt Lake City, UT: Utah State University Press, 2013).

BIBLIOGRAPHY

Althusser, Louis. *On Ideology*. London: Verso, 2008.

Andrade, Oswald de. *The Manifesto Antropófago* (Cannibal Manifesto) (accessed online January 2013).

Andrews, Ted. *Animal Speak: The Spiritual & Magical Powers of Creatures Great & Small*. St. Paul, MN: Llewellyn Publications, 2003.

Artaud, Antonin. *Watchfiends & Rack Screams: Works from the Final Period*. Boston, MA: Exact Change, 1995.

Ashley, Robert. *Automatic Writing* CD. New York: Lovely Music, 1996.

—. *Outside of Time: Ideas about Music*. Cologne: MusikTexte, 2009.

Bachelard, Gaston. *Air and Dreams: An Essay on the Imagination of Movement*. Dallas, TX: Dallas Institute Publications, 1988.

Baldwin, James. *Go Tell It on The Mountain*. New York: Bantam Dell, 1981.

Barilli, Renato. *Futura* CD. Milano: Cramps Records, 1978.

Barthes, Roland. "The grain of the voice." In *Image/Music/Text*, 179–189. London: Fontana Press, 1977.

Bataille, Georges. *Encyclopedia Acephalica*. London: Atlas Press, 1995.

—. *The Unfinished System of Nonknowledge*. Minneapolis, MN: University of Minnesota Press, 2001.

—. *Visions of Excess: Selected Writings, 1927–1939*. Minneapolis, MN: University of Minnesota Press, 1985.

Baumgaertner, Gabriel. "An oral history: Tyson–Holyfield bite fight." *Sports Illustrated* online, June 29, 2012 (accessed April 2013).

Beckett, Samuel. *Not I*. London: Faber & Faber, 1973.

Beizer, Janet. *Ventriloquized Bodies: Narratives of Hysteria in Nineteenth-Century France*. Ithaca, NY: Cornell University Press, 1994.

Bennett, Jane. *Vibrant Matter: The Politic Ecology of Things*. Durham, NC: Duke University Press, 2010.

Berger, John. *Why Look at Animals?* London: Penguin Books, 2009.

Bergson, Henri. *Laughter: An Essay on the Meaning of the Comic*. Mineola, NY: Dover Publications, 2005.

Bhabha, Homi K. *The Location of Culture*. London: Routledge, 2004.

Bifo, Franco Berardi. *Skizo-Mails*. Berlin: Errant Bodies Press, 2012.

Birdwhistell, Ray L. *Kinesics and Context: Essays on Body Motion Communication*. Philadelphia, PA: University of Pennsylvania Press, 1970.

Birdwhistell, R. L. "Paralanguage twenty-five years after Sapir." In *Communication in Face to Face Interaction*, edited by John Laver and Sandy Hutcheson, 82–100. Middlesex: Penguin Books, 1972.

Blanc, Mel. *That's Not All Folks: My Life in the Golden Age of Cartoons and Radio*. New York: Warner Books, 1988.

Bosetti, Alessandro. *Zwölfzungen* CD. Pioneer Valley, MA: Sedimental Records, 2010.

Braukus, Michael and John Bluck. "NASA develops system to computerize silent, 'subvocal speech'." Found on NASA website, March 17, 2004 (accessed April 2012).

Brown, Norman O. *Life against Death: The Psychoanalytical Meaning of History*. London: Sphere Books, 1970.

Bursnel, René-Guy and André Classe *Whistled Languages*. Berlin: Springer-Verlag, 1976.

Butler, Judith. *Bodies That Matter: On the Discursive Limits of "Sex"*. New York: Routledge, 1993.

—. *Excitable Speech: A Politics of the Performative*. New York: Routledge, 1997.

—. *Gender Trouble: Feminism and the Subversion of Identity*. London: Routledge, 2006.

—. "Performativity, precarity and sexual politics." *AIBR. Revista de Antropología Iberoamericana*, 4(3) (2009): i–xiii.

Campion, Jane and Kate Pullinger. *The Piano: A Novel*. London: Bloomsbury, 1994.

Cane, William. *The Art of Kissing*. New York: St. Martin's Griffin, 2005.

Cappello, Mary. *Swallow: Foreign Bodies, Their Ingestion, Inspiration, and the Curious Doctor Who Extracted Them*. New York: New Press, 2011.

Carpenter, Edmund and Marshall McLuhan. "Acoustic space." In *Explorations in Communication*, edited by Edmund Carpenter and Marshall McLuhan, 65–70. Boston, MA: Beacon Press, 1960.

Carter, Paul. "Ambiguous traces, mishearing, and auditory space." In *Hearing Cultures: Essays on Sound, Listening and Modernity*, edited by Veit Erlmann, 43–63. Oxford: Berg, 2004.

Cavarero, Adriana. *For More Than One Voice: Toward a Philosophy of Vocal Expression*. Stanford, CA: Stanford University Press, 2009.

Certeau, Michel de. "Vocal Utopias: Glossolalias." *Representations*, (56) (1996): 29–47.

Chion, Michel. *The Voice in Cinema*. New York: Columbia University Press, 1999.

Christensen, Allan Conrad. *Nineteenth-Century Narratives of Contagion: "Our Feverish Contact."* Oxon: Routledge, 2005.

Cixous, Hélène. *Coming to Writing and Other Essays*. Cambridge, MA: Harvard University Press, 1991.

—. "The laugh of the Medusa." In *New French Feminisms*, edited by Elaine Marks and Isabelle de Courtivron, 245–264. New York: Schocken Books, 1981.

Cixous, Hélène and Catherine Clement. *The Newly Born Woman*. Minneapolis, MN: University of Minnesota Press, 1991.

Clement, Catherine. *Syncope: The Philosophy of Rapture*. Minneapolis, MN: University of Minnesota Press, 1994.

Clowes, Robert. "The problem of inner speech and its relation to the organization of conscious experience: A self-regulation model." In *Proceedings of AISB06 Symposium on Integrative Approaches to Machine Consciousness*, edited by R. W. Clowes, S. Torrance, and R. Chrisley. London, 2006. Found on the author's website (accessed December 2012).

Cockayne, Emily. *Hubbub: Filth, Noise and Stench in England, 1600–1770*. New Haven, CT: Yale University Press, 2008.

Connor, Steven. *Beyond Words: Sobs, Hums, Stutters and Other Vocalizations*. London: Reaktion Books, 2014.

—. *Dumbstruck: A Cultural History of Ventriloquism*. Oxford: Oxford University Press, 2000.

—. "The strains of the voice." In *Parole #1: The Body of the Voice*, edited by Annette Stahmer, 6–12. Cologne: Salon Verlag, 2010.

—. "Writing the White Voice." A talk given at the Sound, Silence and the Arts symposium, Nanyang Technological University, Singapore, 2009. Found on author's website (accessed May 2013).

Conrad, Joseph. *Heart of Darkness*. London: Penguin Books, 1989.

Cotter, Holland. "In the naked museum: Talking, thinking, encountering." *The New York Times* online, January 31, 2010 (accessed January 2013).

Couldry, Nick. *Why Voice Matters: Culture and Politics after Neoliberalism*. London: Sage Publications, 2010.

Davies, Christie. "Jokes as the truth about Soviet socialism." *Folklore*, 46 (2010): 9–32.

Deleuze, Gilles and Félix Guattari. *Anti-Oedipus: Capitalism and Schizophrenia*. Minneapolis, MN: University of Minnesota Press, 1990.

—. *Kafka: Toward a Minor Literature*. Minneapolis, MN: University of Minnesota Press, 1993.

DeNora, Tia. *Music in Everyday Life*. Cambridge: Cambridge University Press, 2000.

Derrida, Jacques. "Signature event context." In *Limited, Inc.*, 1–23. Evanston, IL: Northwestern University Press, 1988.

Dickinson, Paul. *Sleep Talk Recordings Vol. 1: 1986–2000* CD. Chicago: Gosh Yes, 2000.

—. "Sleep talk." In *Parole #2: Phonetic Skin*, edited by Annette Stahmer, 15–17. Cologne: Salon Verlag, 2012.

Dolar, Mladen. *A Voice and Nothing More*. Cambridge, MA: MIT Press, 2006.

Douglas, Mary. *Purity and Danger: An Analysis of Concepts of Pollution and Taboo*. London: Routledge, 2002.

Dowling, Stephen. "St. Paul's Cathedral protest camp deadline passes." *BBC News* online, November 17, 2011 (accessed December 2011).

Dufrêne, François. "Pragmatic of Crirythme." In *OU—Cinquième Saison*, CD box set, edited by Emanuele Carcano. Milan: Alga Marghen, 2002.

Ekman, Paul. *Emotions Revealed: Understanding Faces and Feelings*. London: Phoenix, 2004.

Evans, Nicholas. *The Horse Whisperer*. London: Sphere, 2010.

Farmer, Frank. *After the Public Turn: Composition, Counterpublics, and the Citizen Bricoleur*. Salt Lake City, UT: Utah State University Press, 2013.

Ferguson, James G. "Of mimicry and membership: Africans and the 'New World Society'." *Cultural Anthropology*, 17(4) (2002): 551–569.

Fiumara, Gemma Corradi. *The Other Side of Language: A Philosophy of Listening*. London: Routledge, 1990.

Foucault, Michel. *Discipline and Punish: The Birth of the Prison*. New York: Vintage Books, 1979.

—. *The Care of the Self: Volume 3 of The History of Sexuality.* New York: Vintage Books, 1986.

Freud, Sigmund. *The Joke and Its Relation to the Unconscious.* London: Penguin Books, 2002.

Fuchs, Rudi. *Schwitters: Ich ist Stil.* Amsterdam: Stedelijk Museum, 2000.

Gammelsæter, Runhild. *Amplicon CD.* Milwaukee, WI: Utech Records, 2008.

Glissant, Édouard. *The Poetics of Relation.* Ann Arbor, MI: University of Michigan Press, 1997.

Goffman, Erving. *Forms of Talk.* Philadelphia, PA: University of Pennsylvania Press, 1981.

—. *Stigma: Notes on the Management of Spoiled Identity.* New York: Touchstone, 1986.

Halberstam, Judith. *The Queer Art of Failure.* Durham, NC: Duke University Press, 2011.

Hansen, James P. "Sick shit happens: Everyday histories in Martin Creed's Body docs." *Jump Cut: A Review of Contemporary Media*, No. 52 (summer 2010) (accessed January 2013).

Herzog, Rudolph. *Dead Funny: Telling Jokes in Hitler's Germany.* Brooklyn, NY: Melville House Publishing, 2012.

Hodgkinson, Mark. "Wimbledon 2011: The strangest behavior." *Telegraph* online, June 18, 2011 (accessed April 2012).

Hoffman, Abbie. *Steal This Book.* New York: Four Walls Eight Windows, 2002.

Holloway, Mark. *Heavens on Earth: Utopian Communities in America 1680–1880.* New York: Dover Publications, 1966.

Horvitz, Robert. "Chris Burden." *Artforum*, XIV(9) (May 1976): 24–31.

Hultberg, Teddy. "A few points of departure." In *Literally Speaking: Sound Poetry and Text-Sound Composition*, 7–15. Göteborg: Bo Ejeby Editions, 1993.

Hurd, Emma. "Unholy Row in Jerusalem over status of women." *Sky News*, December 18, 2011 (accessed April 2012).

Irigaray, Luce. *This Sex Which Is Not One.* Ithaca, NY: Cornell University Press, 1985.

Jabès, Edmond. *A Foreigner Carrying in the Crook of His Arm a Tiny Book.* Hanover, NH: Wesleyan University Press, 1993.

Karpf, Anne. *The Human Voice: The Story of a Remarkable Talent.* London: Bloomsbury, 2006.

Kelly, Morgan. "More than a sign of sleepiness, yawning may cool the brain." *Science Daily* online, September 19, 2011 (accessed April 2012).

Khlebnikov, Velimir. *The King of Time: Selected Writings of the Russian Futurism.* Cambridge, MA: Harvard University Press, 1985.

Klein, Josephine. *Our Need for Others and Its Roots in Infancy.* London: Routledge, 1987.

Klein, Melanie. *Envy and Gratitude and Other Works 1946–1963.* London: Vintage, 1997.

—. *Love, Guilt and Reparation and Other Works 1921–1945.* London: Vintage, 1998.

Kristeva, Julia. *Powers of Horror: An Essay on Abjection.* New York: Columbia University Press, 1982.

—. *Revolution in Poetic Language.* New York: Columbia University Press, 1984.

LaBelle, Brandon. "Raw orality: Sound poetry and live bodies." In *Voice: Vocal Aesthetics in Digital Arts and Media*, edited by Norie Neumark, Ross Gibson, and Theo van Leeuwen, 147–171. Cambridge, MA: MIT Press, 2010.

Labov, William. *The Social Stratification of English in New York City*, 2nd edition. Cambridge: Cambridge University Press, 2006.

Lacan, Jacques. *Écrits*. New York: W. W. Norton & Company, 2007.

—. "The mirror stage as formative of the function of the *I* as revealed in psychoanalytic experience." In *Écrits*, 75–81. New York: W. W. Norton & Company, 2007.

Lagaay, Alice. "Between sound and silence: Voice in the history of psychoanalysis." *e-pisteme*, 1(1) (2008): 53–62.

Lattner, Heimo, *A Voice That Once Was In One's Mouth*. Berlin: Errant Bodies Press, 2013.

Laver, John. *Principles of Phonetics*. Cambridge: Cambridge University Press, 1994.

—. "Voice quality and indexical information." In *Communication in Face to Face Interaction*, edited by John Laver and Sandy Hutcheson, 189–203. Middlesex: Penguin Books, 1972.

Lecercle, Jean-Jacques. *Philosophy through the Looking Glass*. La Salle, IL: Open Court, 1985.

Lefebvre, Henri. *Rhythmanalysis*. London: Continuum, 2004.

—. *The Production of Space*. Oxford: Blackwell, 2000.

Levin, David Michael. *The Listening Self: Personal Growth, Social Change and the Closure of Metaphysics*. London: Routledge, 1989.

Li, Xinghua. "Whispering: The murmur of power in a lo-fi world." *Media, Culture and Society*, 33(1) (2011): 19–34.

Linebaugh, Peter. *The London Hanged: Crime and Civil Society in the Eighteenth Century*. London: Penguin Books, 1991.

Lowery, Fred. *Whistling in the Dark*. Gretna: Pelican Publishing Company, 1983.

Lyotard, Jean-François. *Libidinal Economy*. London: Continuum, 2004.

McCaffrey, Steve. "From phonic to sonic: The emergence of the audio-poem." In *Sound States: Innovative Poetics and Acoustical Technologies*, edited by Adelaide Morris, 149–168. Chapel Hill, NC: University of North Carolina Press, 1997.

Messiaen, Olivier. *Catalogue d'oiseaux* CD. Hong Kong: Naxos, 1997.

Migone, Christof. *Sonic Somatic: Performances of the Unsound Body*. Berlin: Errant Bodies Press, 2012.

Mitchell, David. *For Crying Out Loud: The Story of the Town Crier and Bellman, Past and Present*. Seaford, NY: Avenue Books, 2010.

Moten, Fred. *In the Break: The Aesthetics of the Black Radical Tradition*. Minneapolis, MN: University of Minnesota Press, 2003.

Mowitt, John. "Like a whisper." *Differences: A Journal of Feminist Cultural Studies*, 22(2 & 5) (2011): 168–189.

Nancy, Jean-Luc. *Listening*. New York: Fordham University Press, 2007.

Napoleoni, Loretta. *Rogue Economics*. New York: Seven Stories Press, 2008.

Nussbaumer, Georg. "Big Red Arias." In *Parole #1: The Body of the Voice*, edited by Annette Stahmer, 48–53. Cologne: Salon Verlag, 2009.

O'Dell, Kathy. *Contract with the Skin: Masochism, Performance Art and the 1970s*. Minneapolis, MN: University of Minnesota Press, 1998.

Ong, Walter J. *The Barbarian Within and Other Fugitive Essays and Studies*. New York: Macmillan Company, 1962.

Orbach, Susie. *Bodies*. London: Profile Books, 2010.

—. *On Eating: Change Your Eating, Change Your Life*. London: Penguin Books, 2002.

Ostwald, Peter F. *The Semiotics of Human Sound*. The Hague: Mouton & Co., 1973.

Parr, Susie, Sally Byng, and Sue Gilpin. *Talking about Aphasia: Living with Loss of Language after Stroke*. Maidenhead: Open University Press, 2003.

Peters, John Durham. *Speaking Into the Air: A History of the Idea of Communication*. Chicago: University of Chicago Press, 2000.

Phillips, Adam. *On Kissing, Tickling and Being Bored: Psychoanalytic Essays on the Unexamined Life*. Cambridge, MA: Harvard University Press, 1994.

Pile, Steve. *Real Cities: Modernity, Space and the Phantasmagorias of City Life*. London: Sage Publications, 2005.

Pinker, Steven. *The Language Instinct: The New Science of Language and Mind*. London: Penguin Books, 1994.

Pollock, Griselda. *Vision and Difference*. London: Routledge, 1988.

Provine, Robert R. *Curious Behavior: Yawning, Laughing, Hiccupping, and Beyond*. Cambridge, MA: Belknap Press, 2012.

Ravid, Barak. "Arab justice's refusal to sing Israel's national anthem sparks furor among right-wing MKs." *Haaretz* online, February 29, 2012 (accessed July 2012).

Rée, Jonathan. *I See a Voice: Deafness, Language and the Senses—A Philosophical Inquiry*. New York: Metropolitan Books, 1999.

Rhode, Eric. "The boy who had dreams in his mouth." Found on the author's website (accessed July 2013).

Rhode, Maria. "Developmental and autistic aspects of vocalization." In *Signs of Autism in Infants. Recognition of Early Intervention*, edited by Stella Acquarone, 227–235. London: Karnac, 2007.

Riley, Denise. "'A voice without a mouth': Inner speech." *Qui Parle*, 14(2) (Spring/Summer 2004): 57–104.

Rodenburg, Patsy. *The Right to Speak: Working with the Voice*. London: Methuem, 1992.

Rose, Jacqueline. *Sexuality in the Field of Vision*. London: Verso, 2005.

Rose, Tricia. *Black Noise: Rap Music and Black Culture in Contemporary America*. Hanover, NH: Wesleyan University Press, 1994.

Rothenberg, David. *Why Birds Sing: A Journey into the Mystery of Bird Song*. New York: Basic Books, 2005.

Ruebsaat, Norbert. "When there is no sound." *Soundscape Newsletter*, No. 7 (January 1994): 17–18.

Sapir, Edward. *Culture, Language and Personality*. Berkeley, CA: University of California Press, 1964.

—. *Language*. London: Granada Publishing, 1971.

Schechner, Richard. *Performance Theory*. London: Routledge, 2003.

Segal, Naomi. *Consensuality: Didier Anzieu, Gender and the Sense of Touch*. Amsterdam: Rodopi, 2009.

Serres, Michel. *Genesis*. Ann Arbor, MI: University of Michigan Press, 1997.

Shell, Marc. *Stutter*. Cambridge, MA: Harvard University Press, 2005.

Silverman, Kaja. *World Spectators*. Stanford, CA: Stanford University Press, 2000.

Spero, Moshe Halevi. "The joke envelope: A neglected precursor of the psychic envelope concept in Freud's writing." *The Psychoanalytic Study of the Child*, 64 (2009): 193–226.

Spitz, René. "The primal cavity—A contribution to the genesis of perception and its role for psychoanalytic theory." *The Psychoanalytic Study of the Child*, 10 (1955): 215–240.

Stahmer, Annette, ed. *Parole #1: The Body of the Voice*. Cologne: Salon Verlag, 2009.

—. *Parole #2: Phonetic Skin*. Cologne: Salon Verlag, 2012.

Stanley, Faye. "Vygotsky—From public to private: Learning from personal speech." In *Making Sense of Theory and Practice in Early Childhood*, edited by Tim Waller, Judy Whitmarsh, and Karen Clarke, 11–25. Berkshire, UK: Open University Press, 2011.

Stidworthy, Imogen. "Topography of the voice." In *Parole #2: Phonetic Skin*, edited by Annette Stahmer, 18–30. Cologne: Salon Verlag, 2012.

Stoop, David. *You Are What You Think*. Grand Rapids, MI: Revell, 1996.

Stott, Andrew. *Comedy*. London: Routledge, 2005.

Taussig, Michael. *Mimesis and Alterity: A Particular History of the Senses*. New York: Routledge, 1993.

Trudgill, Peter. *Sociolinguistics: An Introduction to Language and Society*. London: Penguin Books, 2000.

Underhill, Ruth Murray. *Singing for Power: The Song Magic of the Papago Indians of Southern Arizona*. Tucson, AZ: University of Arizona Press, 1993.

Undo. *Vito Acconci—Waterways: Four Saliva Studies* CD. Montréal, Canada: Squint Fucker Press, 2001.

Vattimo, Gianni. "Bottles, nets, revolution, and the tasks of philosophy." *Cultural Studies*, 2(2) (May 1988): 143–151.

—. *The End of Modernity: Nihilism and Hermeneutics in Postmodern Culture*. Baltimore, MD: John Hopkins University Press, 1991.

Voice: Vocal Aesthetics in Digital Arts and Media, edited by Norie Neumark, Ross Gibson, and Theo van Leeuwen. Cambridge, MA: MIT Press, 2010.

Vrbančič, Mario. *The Lacanian Thing: Psychoanalysis, Postmodern Culture, and Cinema*. Amherst: Cambria Press, 2011.

Vygotsky, Lev. *Thought and Language*. Cambridge, MA: MIT Press, 1986.

Weiss, Allen S. *Feast and Folly: Cuisine, Intoxication, and the Poetics of the Sublime*. Albany, NY: State University of New York Press, 2002.

—. *Perverse Desire and the Ambiguous Icon*. Albany, NY: State University of New York Press, 1994.

—. *Shattered Forms: Art Brut, Phantasms, Modernism*. Albany, NY: SUNY Press, 1992.

—. *Varieties of Audio Mimesis: Musical Evocations of Landscape*. Berlin: Errant Bodies Press, 2007.

Westerkamp, Hildegard. "Whisper study." Composition appears on the audio compilation, *20 Jahre Interventionen II*. Berlin: Edition RZ, 2011.

Wittig, Monique. *The Lesbian Body*. Boston, MA: Beacon Press, 1975.

Wolf, Fred Alan. *The Eagle's Quest: A Physicist Finds Scientific Truth at the Heart of the Shamanic World*. New York: Touchstone, 1991.

Wolfson, Louis. *Le Schizo et les langues*. Paris: Éditions Gallimard, 1970.

Woodward, Ashley. "The Verwindung of capital: On the philosophy and politics of Gianni Vattimo." In *Symposium* (*Canadian Journal of Continental Philosophy/ Revue canadienne de philosophie continentale*), 13(1), Article 5 (2009): 73–99.

Zupančič, Alenka. *The Odd One In: On Comedy*. Cambridge, MA: MIT Press, 2008.

INDEX

Page numbers in **bold** refer to figures.